changing
the way we Teach

changing
the Way We Teach

Writing and Resistance in the Training of Teaching Assistants

SALLY BARR EBEST

SOUTHERN ILLINOIS UNIVERSITY PRESS • CARBONDALE

Library of Congress Cataloging-in-Publication Data
Ebest, Sally Barr.
   Changing the way we teach : writing and resistance in
the training of teaching assistants / Sally Barr Ebest.
      p. cm.
   Includes bibliographical references and index.
   1. Graduate teaching assistants—Training of—United
States—Case studies. 2. English language—Rhetoric—
Study and teaching (Graduate)—United States—Case
studies. I. Title.
   LB2335.4.E24 2005
   378.1'25—dc22
   ISBN 0-8093-2614-0 (cloth : alk. paper)
   ISBN 0-8093-2615-9 (pbk. : alk. paper)   2004020531

Printed on recycled paper. ♻

The paper used in this publication meets the minimum
requirements of American National Standard for Information Sciences—Permanence of Paper for Printed Library
Materials, ANSI Z39.48-1992. ∞

For Ron

contents

Acknowledgments

I want to thank my students for agreeing to participate in this study. Not all of them made it into the final version, but I learned from every one of them. Specifically, I'd like to thank the graduate students whose stories constitute the heart of the book: Mary Jo, Melva, Barbara, and Bob; Gail and Paul, Susan and Jeff, Pattie and Ken; Melissa, Jenny, Jimmy, Missy, and Auggie; Kim, Shannon, and Carolyn. Some of the names have been changed, but they know who they are. Obviously, I could not have completed this project without their cooperation.

Through the many revisions, I've been blessed with sound advice and constructive criticism from my friends and colleagues. I'm greatly indebted to Marilyn Sternglass. I wish I'd told her so more often; I wish she was still around to see this work come to fruition. During graduate school, she made it possible for me to gain valuable administrative experience, introduced me to composition studies, and strongly encouraged me to work with David Bleich. Bleich deserves a great deal of thanks, for he guided and advised me every step of the way. I didn't always appreciate his advice, but he was almost always right. Thanks to my colleague Jane Zeni, who read parts of various drafts and provided valuable suggestions. Thanks, too, to my friend and former graduate student Carolyn Brown, who read every page and knew from the beginning what needed to be done. Thanks especially to the readers at Southern Illinois University Press. The first reader recognized a spark of intelligence, was steadfast in her support through the subsequent revisions, and provided invaluable advice; the final reader, Cinthia Gannett, offered important and substantive suggestions for revision. All of these people played a significant role in shaping this book. They underscore the value of peer response.

I could not have gotten to this point without the support of Terry Jones, former dean of Arts and Sciences at the University of Missouri–St. Louis, who gave me a semester off to write. Thanks also to the University of Missouri–St. Louis Research Board, which granted a later semester's leave. Needless to say, neither of these leaves would have been possible without the support of my department chairs during this period: Jane Williamson, Deborah Aldrich-Watson, and Barbara Kachur.

The editors directly and indirectly involved in this project deserve a big round of applause. Thanks especially to Karl Kageff at Southern Illinois University Press. He believed in this project and never gave up on it or me.

Portions of "Going Against Nature? Women's Resistance to Collaborative Learning" are reprinted by permission from *Common Ground: Feminist Collaboration in the Academy* edited by Elizabeth G. Peck and JoAnna Stephens Mink, the State University of New York Press © 1997 State University of New York, all rights reserved. Portions of "Collaborative Learning in the Graduate Classroom" are reprinted by permission from *Writing With: New Directions in Collaborative Teaching, Learning, and Research* edited by Sally Barr Reagan, Thomas Fox, and David Bleich, the State University of New York Press, © 1994 State University of New York, all rights reserved. Portions of "When Graduate Students Resist" are reprinted by permission from the *Journal of Writing Program Administration* (Fall/Winter 2002) edited by Marguerite Helmers and Jeffrey Lynch © 2002, Purdue University Press.

Finally, I would like to thank my husband, colleague, and best friend, Ron Ebest. He listened to my ideas, read my drafts, dried my tears, and cheered me on. I could not have done this without him.

Part One

CONTEXT AND THEORY

1. Researching Teaching

This book unites research in composition, higher education, and psychology, three seemingly disparate arenas that actually share a number of commonalities. It is based on longitudinal case studies that explore how graduate students respond to the process movement in composition, examining how they accept this pedagogy as students and how their acceptance affects their performance as instructors and future professors. The study is framed by discussions of the scholarship on composition pedagogy; conceptions of postsecondary teaching; theories of cognitive, social cognitive, and educational psychology; and issues surrounding gender, voice, and writing. My audience is professors of composition, their graduate students, and other academics. My purpose is to persuade these readers that postsecondary teaching must be improved, that composition pedagogy answers the calls for change in university teaching, and that by adopting this pedagogy and changing the way they teach graduate students, faculty will better prepare the next generation of professors.

Research in composition studies has only recently begun to explore the ways in which graduate students are prepared to teach. Some composition scholars have experimented with mentoring by faculty and experienced teaching assistants to model good pedagogy and to support new TAs during their initial forays into the classroom. Other researchers have interviewed and observed TAs throughout their first year to trace their gradual conceptualization of teaching and their role in the undergraduate classroom. Composition professors have brought TAs into their own classrooms as team teachers, studied graduate students' responses to practices such as active learning, and reported on these students' attempts to deal with cultural issues such as racism, sexism, or homophobia. Still others have analyzed the curricula used in the preparation of new TAs. But surprisingly few studies have focused on the role of writing in TAs' professional development while even fewer have acknowledged graduate students' resistance to our attempts to prepare them—or the role writing can play in overcoming that resistance.

Considering the field they are about to enter as well as the pedagogical strides composition studies has made since the early 1970s, it is amazing that the role of writing in graduate students' professional development has not been thoroughly researched. In undergraduate classrooms, we engage students in freewriting, explaining that they must learn to write reflectively, to explore ideas without fear of censure, to discover what they want to say. In undergraduate classrooms, we ask students to write drafts and share them with their peers. Writing is a social process, we tell them; language development is a matter of social construction, we say. In undergraduate classrooms, we ask students to take their drafts and their peers' responses and rethink, revise, redraft. Writing is a process, we remind them. The more you write, the better you get. In undergraduate classrooms, we assign response journals to ensure that our students will better comprehend their reading and assimilate the conventions of texts. We do so because writing about reading gives students a voice; it promotes interaction with the text; it helps them take new and difficult material and make it their own. In undergraduate classrooms where these strategies are practiced, we maintain that students emerge better thinkers, readers, and writers. Yet, in graduate seminars, too often we assume these strategies are unnecessary.

Most of us who teach writing came to it late, embracing composition pedagogy after years of teaching—and being taught—differently. We believe in these strategies because they work. We know this because we have prior teaching experiences on which to base our understanding. But, somehow, perhaps because of ingrained beliefs about postsecondary teaching, perhaps because graduate students are more mature than undergraduates, perhaps because many of us do not consciously freewrite, draft, journal, or reflect (or have the time to do so), we have overlooked a few things. We forget that our graduate students may have tested out of freshman composition, so they have not practiced what we preach to their undergraduate counterparts. We forget the tension and paranoia of graduate school. Anxious to succeed, many graduate students aim for perfection. Such feelings can lead them to avoid freewriting in the belief that they must labor over every sentence. Because of this process, they often lack the time to reflect and revise. In competition with their peers, they may be unlikely to indulge in any form of peer response. Overburdened with teaching and preparing and grading and reading and writing and attending class, they seldom have time to reflect on their reading, even though the texts they encounter in their pedagogy seminars may be unlike anything they've ever read before.

The end result? Too many TAs exit their pedagogy seminar without fully developing an understanding of their writing or their teaching. For many of these students, composition studies remains a boring, blurry subdiscipline. Such results are not only a disservice to these future professors and their future students but also to composition studies, for our pedagogical theory and practice answer the calls for change in higher education.

Recent research in a variety of disciplines has begun to focus on the need for better teaching at the postsecondary level, on the changing demographics resulting in this need, on resistance to change by the present faculty, and on the logical solution to this resistance, better preparation of graduate students. This research has in turn led to discussions of gender differences in the classroom and, to a considerably lesser extent, the role of writing in developing research skills. The case studies described in this book build on the foregoing by exploring the role played by composition pedagogy in graduate students' conceptualization and actualization of teaching.

Scholars and critics alike have called for improved postsecondary instruction without necessarily describing what that would entail. This study answers those calls and investigates the process. It focuses on the work of a cross section of graduate students in English over a five-year period during (at least) one pedagogy seminar requiring their engagement in the strategies defined by composition pedagogy—reflective writing, journaling, drafting, and active learning—the very strategies described as meeting the needs of the new breed of undergraduate student. The graduate students in this study came from varying demographic backgrounds and exhibited types and degrees of resistance, which differed by gender. In practically every case, writing was the catalyst for resistance; paradoxically, writing was also the "cure."

Despite its ubiquity, the role of writing is rarely discussed in relation to the professional development of graduate students. More often, the focus is political, revolving around the ethical and financial inequities of using these students to teach. These are, of course, important issues. Books and articles have been devoted to the subject, and I have no desire to replicate or improve upon them. My goals are more pragmatic: to investigate how teaching writing as a process in graduate seminars enhances students' understanding of composition theory and pedagogy, to illustrate how this understanding is internalized through writing and applied in the students' teaching, and to explore the reasons for and manifestations of students' resistance. This focus is important, I argue, if we are to adequately prepare these students for a profession which demands the ability both to teach and to produce writing.

Obviously, writing plays a significant role in our graduate students' lives. Their strong writing skills probably helped them to test out of freshman composition as undergraduates and may well have led them to major in English and to excel. The writing sample was their entree into graduate school. In every graduate course, their writing determines their grade. Writing permeates graduate students' lives, for it is the primary determinant of their career trajectory. Thus, it should come as no surprise that graduate students might resist attempts to engage them in what they consider nontraditional modes of writing called for by composition pedagogy, viewing them as interference with their composing processes.

I had always required such writing in my graduate seminars; however, I did not realize the extent of my students' skepticism until I began this research. Although I had previously explained my research methodology, the first time I prepared to tape-record conversations during peer response, one female graduate student protested so vehemently that I had to honor her feelings and limit that element of my research to observations. This young woman's resistance so confounded me that I felt I must continue collecting data. The following semester, a male student's resistance to keeping a response journal took the form of angry outbursts and obscene comments. In that same course, one of his peers argued with me throughout the term about the value of freewriting and small-group work. The following semester, I fought similar epistemological battles with another male TA, and one of the female students displayed resistance in the form of writer's block. Prior to the onset of my research, I had assumed my students accepted and understood these teaching strategies, but clearly, I was mistaken. And so my research continued.

Initially, my intent was to illustrate how small-group work benefited female graduate students. However, as I discovered repeated patterns of resistance in both male and female students, my focus evolved from an examination of the effects of collaborative learning to a larger view: A certain percentage of graduate students were reacting not just to group work but to their engagement in every aspect of composition pedagogy. Consequently, my research expanded to include the reactions of male and female graduate students alike. Because not everyone resisted, and most of those who initially resisted eventually overcame their objections, I began to explore the various causes of resistance, to trace the rise and fall of resistance, and to identify factors that would enable or, alternatively, prevent students from resolving their fears.

One of the more important findings emerging from this focus was the discovery that resistance is not uncommon. Among college students, an average of 21 percent of students will resist in any given class (Kearney and Plax 89); this figure held true for my graduate students as well. Similarly, my graduate students' resistance paralleled that of undergraduates. Kearney and Plax list nineteen "student resistance techniques." At one time or another, the students in this study displayed the following:

- blaming the teacher
- avoiding class-teacher interactions
- reluctantly complying
- actively resisting (e.g., failing to complete assignments)
- deceiving the teacher (e.g., playing dumb or pretending to be prepared)
- disrupting the class
- making excuses
- passively resisting (e.g., refusing to complete assignments appropriately)
- challenging the teacher's authority
- verbally defying or confronting the teacher
- rejecting the teacher's advice (91–92)

Anyone who has experienced these behaviors tends to view them negatively, for they often disrupt the class, but resistance need not have negative results. Indeed, Kearney and Plax suggest that the definition include both constructive and destructive behavior.

Constructive resistance might encompass

> asking substantive or procedural questions, providing spontaneous assistance to other students, working on projects together without teacher sanction, correcting or clarifying lecture or textual material, and challenging the teacher's credentials or opinions. (Kearney and Plax 86)

In this study, questioning, correcting, and challenging most often characterized constructive resistance. These behaviors are common among new TAs, whose conceptions of teaching may be questioned or refuted upon entering their first pedagogy course. Doug Hesse reminds us that many TAs are not in graduate school because they want to learn to teach—at least not to teach writing. Such students may regard the writing program's curriculum as "'repressive' or 'hegemonic,' or 'workmanlike,' or 'dull'" (qtd. in Payne and Enos 55). Their resistance may thus lead them to develop what Hesse terms a "stereotypical teacherly identity, becoming the very dogmatic teachers against which they complain" because they perceive teaching freshman composition as unimportant (55). Whatever form their resistance takes, this action brings with it the opportunity for discussions between TA and writing program administrator or between TA and pedagogy instructor, which can lead in turn to "reflection and change in both individual and program praxis" (Farris, "Too Cool" 100). In other words, resistance can be "generative" (Rickly and Harrington 113).

These feelings are neither linear nor static. Regardless of the perceived ideology, individuals repeatedly move between and negotiate feelings of resistance, "often being in contradictory locations simultaneously" (Lather 127). If resistance is to be generative, instructors must not only recognize resistance and discuss it with their graduate students, they must also reflect upon how their attitudes, instruction, or writing curriculum might be improved. In this way, resistance can become generative for all parties involved. "Such a movement," writes Pattie Lather, "both creates complicating fragmentations and provides a richer understanding of the situations in which we do our oppositional work" (146).[1]

Of course, resolution requires that individuals recognize the source of their feelings. During my research, I began to realize that resistance stemmed not only from graduate students but also (perhaps more so) from their professors. For change to occur, both cohorts would have to recognize its necessity. To grasp the importance of teaching and writing at the postsecondary level, both faculty and graduate students need to understand its context: the original importance of university teaching, its displacement by research, the resulting critiques, the effects of open admissions, the consequent need for change, current efforts toward that end, and the role composition studies plays in meeting those needs. To respect the pedagogy they are expected to practice requires familiarity with the theories underlying it—not just composition theory but also cognitive psychology, social psychology, and educational psychology—so they will recognize the applicability to learners at any level. To reinforce this lesson and gain the background knowledge and flexibility necessary to apply these theories in the classroom, seminars need to be constructed so that graduate students can practice teaching. To see how these theories work, TAs should be engaged in journaling, drafting, and collaborative learning in a risk-free environment. Equally important, to trace their efficacy, both sides could benefit from engaging in action research. Such engagement would, in turn, introduce graduate students and their professors to one of the most important, yet undervalued aspects of teaching at the university level—empathy. These tenets represent this book's conceptual framework.

METHODS AND METHODOLOGY

The study described in this book investigates how using composition pedagogy in graduate seminars influences TAs' teaching and writing. More specifically, the study examines the attitudes and behaviors evinced when graduate students are engaged in every aspect of the composing process, from reflective writing to drafting to participating in peer response. I used observations and tape-recorded discussions as my primary sources of data and the students' writing samples—that is, freewrites, drafts, journal entries, and peer response sheets—as secondary sources. The study's design is informed by principles drawn from composition, feminist, and ethnographic research, each of which addresses traditional concepts such as objectivity, validity, and reliability.

As Gesa Kirsch explains, these approaches encompass

> an open discussion of (1) the researcher's *relation* to the subject (the researcher's presence and authority are never neutral); (2) the *purpose* of the researcher's questions (they must be *grounded* in the subject's experience and be relevant to the subject); and (3) the researcher's *agenda* (it is never disinterested). ("Methodological" 256, Kirsch's emphasis)

Within composition studies, "this kind of research means opening up the research agenda to subjects, listening to their stories, and allowing them to actively participate, as much as possible, in the design, development, and reporting of research" (257). Similarly, ethnographic research always includes a discussion of researchers' roles as participant-observers because they affect the cultures they study. . . . Most important of all, by implementing [feminist principles,] composition researchers will aim to combine roles of observer and participant, teacher and researcher, student and ethnographer. In other words, researchers will make a conscious effort to break down the rigid hierarchy that now exists between observer and the observed. To do so, researchers will need to confront their own agendas and interpretive stances. (257–58)

These principles were particularly appropriate for this project. My *relation* to the student-participants was clear-cut yet multifaceted: I was their professor in at least one composition pedagogy seminar, but I was simultaneously researching the effects of my pedagogy, observing the students' interactions, and participating in our discussions and classroom activities. These roles thus relegated me at times to student while I recorded my findings as ethnographer. My *purpose* and *agenda*, however, were less easily defined, for they evolved as the study developed.

In the summer of 1990, I began what I thought would be a one-semester study of the effects of collaborative learning on my graduate students' teaching, learning, and writing.[2] My goal was modest: I wanted to illustrate how small-group work benefited female graduate students. However, when one of the women actively resisted collaborative learning, I felt I must continue the project, for social constructivism was one of the theoretical bases of our writing program. If female graduate students were resisting it, what were the males doing? If all the TAs were resisting, how did these feelings affect their teaching? As I continued collecting data, my focus evolved from an examination of the effects of collaborative learning to a larger view. Collaboration, I realized, was not the only teaching strategy differentiating my graduate seminars from others in the English department. In addition to small-group work, I was asking my students to reflect upon their teaching, the readings, their research, and their writing process; to write and revise multiple drafts of personal, analytical, and researched essays; and to design and teach lessons based on the class readings. In sum, I was integrating theory with practice by modeling for my graduate students what I considered good teaching strategies. In doing so, I was teaching writing as a process, a movement that had begun thirty years before at the undergraduate level but had not yet reached most graduate students.

My reasons for this approach were threefold. Despite the findings of my first study, my reading of feminist research had led me to believe that such pedagogy was empowering. The variety of informal writing and small-group work offered my female students opportunities to develop their voices within the graduate classroom, a context described by Aisenberg and Harrington as "chilly" for women. Because the majority of my graduate students had tested out of first-year composition, I assumed that such teaching strategies would be foreign to them. This pedagogy might be equally empowering for my male students, for it could help them reconceptualize teaching. These perennial overachievers had reached the level of graduate school regardless of and most likely unconscious of their teachers' efforts. For the most part, they learned individually and independently. Because this worked for them, I feared they would assume this model should work for everyone. As a graduate student, I had held similar beliefs, so I knew that unless my students actually participated in small-group work, consciously revised multiple drafts of papers, and experimented with reflective writing in their journal assignments, they would neither appreciate the pedagogical value of these strategies nor understand how to use them. Without this engagement, most of them would leave my seminar and teach as they had been taught throughout their previous sixteen years of school.

Because I was responsible for their teaching, I wanted to make sure the students were prepared; because I believed strongly in this pedagogy, I wanted to trace its effects. Consequently, my research questions evolved: How did reflective writing strengthen women's voices? How did participating in peer-response groups contribute to an understanding of collaborative learning? How did peer response impact the students' composing processes and attitudes toward writing? How did reflection enhance students' understanding of nontraditional pedagogy? How did action research help them reconceptualize teaching? What type of students were likely to resist these activities, and how could I address their concerns? In sum, my research reflected Peter Elbow's argument that "our success in pursuing and increasing theoretical knowledge usually depends on respecting and trusting practice for a while and afterward interrogating it as a rich source for new theory" (*What* 87).

To answer these questions, I continued to collect all of my students' writing during the semester they took Teaching College Writing and in any subsequent courses they took with me. I triangulated these data by observing the interactions during in-class, small-group work, recording my thoughts and observations after each class meeting and (with the students' permission) taperecording the discussions occurring during peer response. At the end of each semester, I asked the students to submit their work in portfolios; at the end of each school year, I organized, analyzed, and reflected on the new data. When I had completed drafts of individual case studies, I followed Lather's guidelines regarding feminist empirical research: I shared drafts with my student-participants to ensure "dialectical theory-building" and to avoid "theoretical imposition." This process not only helped to establish validity but also enabled those involved to "change by encouraging self-reflection and a deeper understanding of their particular situations" (56).

Through ongoing analysis and reflection, I discovered fairly quickly that the resistance I observed in the first round of research was neither anomalous nor gender-specific. I was not surprised by the male students' resistance. After all, male students have a tendency to expect and relate to the traditional, hierarchical classroom.[3] Because of their socialization, they are accustomed to what Robert Connors has termed the "agonistic" method of instruction based on individual competition: They tend to dominate discussions whether or not they are called on, to volunteer information, or to interrupt others' comments. Most of them have also mastered the objective, impersonal voice expected in academic writing. Given these predispositions, it followed that men might resist participating in small-group work—especially when it involved getting feedback on their drafts—and use their response journals as another way of taking notes or as a means of attacking the new theories they encountered rather than as a site for reflection.

But I had not expected resistance from my female students. Studies by feminist researchers led me to believe that because women had been socialized to prefer negotiation to confrontation and relationships to competition, because they had been silenced in the classroom and made to feel unwelcome, that they would appreciate the opportunity to participate in small-group work in a nonhierarchical setting and accept feedback from a variety of readers.[4] Similarly, because I assumed my female students would eagerly embrace the philosophy of the de-centered classroom, I was surprised when I visited their classrooms and observed some fairly traditional teaching strategies. Yet, resistance to change could not be attributed to gender. Although the type and duration of resistance varied with the students' gender, I found that despite initial resistance, after engaging in, writing about, and reflecting upon these pedagogies, most students eventually lessened their resistance as they came to understand why I taught in this way and observed how it impacted their teaching and their writing.

Nevertheless, my students' reactions led me to reflect upon my teaching and gradually reconceptualize the project. Instead of focusing on the effects of my teaching, I began to examine the process of learning. Because of this focus, I found that I was studying not only my students' learning but my own as well. Thus, rather than dismissing my students' resistance as unenlightened, I began to explore their feelings in order to honor and understand what Lather has described as "the complexity of the interplay between the empowering and the impositional at work in the liberatory classroom" (76).

J. W. Creswell's *Qualitative Research* describes this method of inquiry as comprising five strands: biography, phenomenology, grounded theory, ethnography, and case study. As I began to analyze and develop the data, I found that these strands ran throughout. My own biography was certainly a component for without it, the background and rationale for the study might not be clearly understood. Like my own graduate students, I had been skeptical of the pedagogical theories I read for my doctoral seminars in composition theory. Because these seminars rarely included group work, I felt uneasy with this strategy until I began collecting data for my dissertation in a linked reading-writing course for basic writers. As a participant-observer, I regularly worked in small groups with the students and thus came to understand how and why collaborative learning could be effective.[5] This experience convinced me to engage my graduate students in small-group work and the various results led, in turn, to this research.

Because my students' attitudes, behaviors, and resistance initially confounded me, it was necessary to study elements of their biographies to understand their actions and motivations. Because I was studying my own experiences as professor and writing program administrator and those of my students as developing teachers, sharing these findings with them, and incorporating their voices within the narrative, we were mutually involved in the production of knowledge. As Ruth Ray explains, "When teacher-researchers collaborate with students, rather than merely assigning them a place in the final write-up, they are constructing classroom 'reality' as the co-creation of events by all participants" (Afterword 294). To understand my students' actions and motivations, this study incorporated what Ray terms the "lived experiences" of me and them, inside and outside the classroom, before and after they took my seminar. The theory that emerged from this approach—grounded or active theory— "is both an intellectual and a practical engagement done for the sake of self-understanding and promoting change in schools and classrooms" (Ray, *Practice* 18).

Ray argues that this latter purpose further places this approach within action research (also known as *classroom research* or *teacher research*), which emphasizes "change from the inside out—from the classroom to the administration" and whose methodology includes "journal keeping, participant observation, interviews, surveys, questionnaires, and discourse analyses of student texts" ("Composition" 172). Action research "grows out of a classroom problem," uses narratives "to re-create the classroom context," and "emphasizes the collaborative nature of learning and teaching" (176). Most importantly, action research requires ongoing reflection, for data analysis occurs throughout the process. According to ethnographer Beverly Moss,

> Early analysis can help the ethnographer become more focused and may contribute to refined research questions. The ethnographer who waits until all the data have been collected . . . runs the risk of being totally overwhelmed by the amount of data collected as well as finding out too late that she has focused on one aspect of the community while patterns in the data indicate she should have focused on another. (160)

In *Writing Ethnographic Fieldnotes*, Robert M. Emerson, Rachel I. Fretz, and Linda L. Shaw differentiate between traditional research methodologies, which begin by trying to prove or disprove a hypothesis, and action research, which is more open-ended. This does not mean that the action researcher ignores theory. Rather, her

> assumptions, interests, and theoretical commitments enter into every phase of writing. . . . The process is one of reflexive or dialectical interplay between theory and data whereby theory enters in at every point, shaping not only analysis but how social events come to be perceived and written up as data in the first place. (167)

Lather's explanation of feminist research methodologies adds a final gloss on the importance of reflexivity:

> Research which encourages self and social understanding and change-enhanc-ing action . . . requires research designs that allow us as researchers to reflect on how our value commitments insert themselves into our empirical work. Our own frameworks of understanding need to be critically examined as we look for the tensions and contradictions they might entail. (80)

DEVELOPING CASE STUDIES

Over a five-year period, forty students participated in this study—that is, they agreed to submit portfolios containing all of their in-class writ-ing; their reading, teaching, and research logs; the drafts, peer-response sheets, and final versions of their seminar papers; and they agreed to allow me to tape-record the interactions of their peer-response groups. Al-though their majors varied, all of these students were pursuing their master's degrees in English. Some were specializing in composition, and some were pursuing an MFA; the majority were majoring in literature. Regardless of major, ninety percent of the students took Teaching Col-lege Writing with me. Many of them also enrolled in one or more of my other seminars—such as Reading-Writing Theory, Reader Response Theory, Contemporary American Women Writers, Radical Pedagogy, or Teaching as a Feminist—explained in more detail within the case-study chapters. At the beginning of each semester, I announced my research interests; at the end of the semester, I distributed permission slips that allowed me to use their work, promised that refusal would not impact their final grades (because I would not review the permissions until grades had been turned in), and asked what, if any, pseudonym they wanted to use. All but three students wanted me to use their own name.

The forty students varied in age, gender, and background. Some had entered graduate school at age twenty-two, immediately after earning their bachelor's degrees, but most were nontraditional students ranging in age from twenty-five to fifty, returning to school either to retool or to earn the credentials that would allow them to progress in their cho-sen fields. Fourteen were male, twenty-six female. The majority of these students were white; during this period, I had only one black student and one of Asian descent. Given their various ages and backgrounds, these students' prior teaching and writing experiences were far from uniform. They ranged from brand-new TAs to experienced teachers, from English majors who had succeeded by figuring out what the professor wanted and giving it to him to a former journalist who had published literally thousands of articles.

Because this was an action-research study, all of the participants were graduate students in my seminars at the University of Missouri–St. Louis, an urban university with a population of approximately thirteen thousand. It is primarily a commuter campus; indeed, all of the graduate students in this study lived off-campus, many of them with their families. This context might appear to distinguish these students from those at more traditional, residential campuses, but increasingly, graduate students (as well as undergraduates) are nontraditional ages, live off-campus, and attend school part-time (Gardiner). Consequently, I believe these student-participants are representative of first-year students in graduate English programs across the country.

Action research is often presented in the form of case studies. But even though action research is gaining increased acceptance in the field of composition, the analysis and presentation of data remain somewhat controversial. According to Linda Brodkey, questions tend to arise concerning "whether data are presented or analyzed, or, put another way, whether the researcher or the research methodology is telling the story" (26). To quell these arguments, Brodkey reminds us that individuals' experiences cannot be "reproduced"; they must be narrated. Because researchers bear the responsibility of analyzing and organizing the data within a narrative format, they must be especially aware of what Thomas Newkirk terms the "narrative lens." Researchers need to consider how their role, race, gender, and experiences affect their perceptions (and those of their students); how they select which information to include and omit, when to interpret, when to quote, and when to seek input from the student-participants. All of this impacts the narrative slant. Newkirk notes that case studies are usually "transformative narratives, ones in which the individual experiences some sort of conflict and undergoes a qualitative change in the resolution of that conflict" (134). Yet stories in which the characters fail to change are equally instructive, for they require that researchers ponder the various reasons for stasis without assigning blame or imposing their own value systems. It is impossible to be objective, but it is necessary to be fair. "Ethnographers need to reflect upon and write about how their situatedness . . . influence[s] an understanding of their data," writes Elizabeth Chiseri-Strater. Researchers must disclose how their "stance-position-location affects the entire ethnographic process" from their relationships to their reactions (117–18).

The case studies described in this book reflect my attention to these caveats. Although forty students consented to participate, I was able to locate trends and behaviors sufficiently consistent to develop eighteen representative studies by annually analyzing, categorizing, compiling, and comparing their case studies during the research process. These do not wholly follow the traditional narrative format, however. To maintain the reader's interest while developing each chapter's argument, I divided each case study into three mininarratives, addressing the relationships between personal construct, self-efficacy, and use of composition pedagogy, respectively. Writing about resistance was the most difficult. Initially, I was looking for conversion narratives, so my first impulse was to dismiss those students who simply didn't get it. However, when the data revealed that both males and females were resisting, I had to dig deeper, review previous material, and rethink my conclusions. I had to acknowledge that some of these students periodically infuriated me; to analyze the roles my teaching, age, and gender played in their resistance; and then to balance these so that the writing samples described rather than demeaned the students' behaviors. Resisting students were not my only source of frustration. Writing about women with strong voices required a good deal of soul-searching because initially, I disliked every one of them. This was a gender issue. According to Roxanne D. Mountford, such feelings can influence how a researcher interacts with students, how researchers view their findings, and how researchers ultimately write their case studies (211). Happily for me, these realizations, prompted by reciprocal sharing of information and facilitated by ongoing reflection, helped me to move beyond my biases and recognize these young women's strengths. The passage of time aided this process, for the more distance I gained, the easier it was to overcome my own annoyance or antipathy and consider their sources. Perhaps the easiest chapter to write was the one representing significant social problems—development of women's voices, misperceptions of feminism, socialization of males, and marginalization of homosexuals—each of which could be attributed, to some extent, to the academy. The students described in this chapter became good friends of mine; therefore, developing their case studies meant going beyond the obvious straw men and considering other possible exigencies. This led me to consider the influence of factors beyond the classroom on students' behaviors.

Clearly, these case studies do not correspond with traditional conceptions of research. They are neither detached nor disinterested; they are certainly not objective. The absence of these qualities thus situates the findings firmly within the parameters of feminist ethnographic research in composition studies. This is, as Patricia A. Sullivan says, "a type of research that is not only *about* the other but *for* the other, a research practice that is concerned at the level of methodology—and not simply in its implications—with the good that it might do" ("Ethnography" 111, Sullivan's emphasis).

ORGANIZATION

I begin by presenting the historical and theoretical background for my argument. In chapter 2, "Establishing Context," I bring together two opposing schools of thought: traditional attitudes toward teaching in the university (which ignore the changing demographics of the student body) and recent research that describes the cultural and intellectual differences among today's undergraduates (who require—and deserve—more than the traditional teacher-centered classroom). These findings are then contrasted with current attempts to prepare graduate students—ranging from presemester orientations and workshops to centers for teaching excellence to the Preparing Future Faculty (PFF) movement—to suggest that despite good intentions, the attempts' designs (often shaped by university rules) may preclude their efforts for change. In chapter 3, "Teaching Theory," I present theories from cognitive psychology, social cognitive psychology, and educational psychology to explain why traditional teaching methods are ineffective, to demonstrate those that are, and to underscore their parallels with composition theory and pedagogy. Whereas chapter 2 helps readers to see that composition pedagogy is neither trendy, exclusive, nor inappropriate, chapter 3 enables readers to analyze current efforts for change, recognize their shortcomings, and realize the validity of composition pedagogy.

These chapters set the stage for the heart of the book, the case study analyses. Chapter 4, "Resisting Change," characterizes the relatively small cohort of graduate students who will resist pedagogical change. Through these case studies, I suggest that such students will be unable to over-come their resistance if these changes contradict their personal constructs and undermine their feelings of self-efficacy. Chapter 5, "Overcoming Resistance," focuses on a much larger group. These case studies suggest that although composition pedagogy may incite resistance because it threatens some students' perceptions of self-efficacy, two factors deter-mine the students' ability to overcome resistance: their already-developed personal constructs coupled with engagement in and reflection on the very strategies they resist. Chapter 6, "Building Confidence," discusses the ways in which socialization and traditional pedagogy inhibit the development of voice and self-confidence in marginalized groups and circumscribe the voices of those in dominant groups. This chapter also argues that composition pedagogy can help most students develop self-confidence and a voice that reflects it. The final chapter in part two ex-tends this argument. Chapter 7, "Strengthening Voice," focuses on a group of women whose strong, unified voices and well-developed per-ceptions of self-efficacy were atypical among female graduate students their age. This chapter argues that nurturing, mentoring, and modeling professional behavior should be essential elements of the graduate cur-riculum, for they benefit faculty and students alike. Finally, chapter 8, "Changing Our Teaching, Our Students, Our Profession," traces the ripple effect from individual to institution to reiterate the calls for change, to suggest directions for future research and teaching, and to remind readers of the possibility of change.

The portraits of these students, their attempts to learn, and our grow-ing relationships are rich in detail, for I have drawn upon their back-grounds and their writing, their classroom behaviors as students and as teachers, and our mutual interactions as teachers, students, and writers. I learned that for some graduate students, change represents too great a risk, whereas others simply need time and opportunity to react and reflect. Regardless of gender, myriads of external factors ranging from teaching load to course load to workload and home life may impact graduate students' openness to new modes of teaching and writing. Internal factors incul-cated by family, society, or education similarly determine a student's willingness to change. Despite these potential roadblocks, the majority of these graduate students ultimately found reflective writing, drafting, and collaborative learning not only freeing but empowering. Women attributed their ability to fight sexual harassment and to find an authoritative voice in the classroom and in their writing to supportive peers in their permanent small groups. Men acknowledged that participating in peer response helped them understand how collaborative learning could work in an undergraduate classroom, that reflective writing helped them (and their students) express feelings and develop ideas, and that portfolio evaluation provided the opportunity to reflect on the lessons learned. Both genders discovered something I, too, learned: that action research opened their eyes, challenged their prejudices, and improved their teaching.

ACTION RESEARCH AND CHANGE

Just as research has become the primary function of the professoriate, action research may hold the key to increasing respect for teaching and learning.[6] Yet, to date, there has been a paucity of research on TA training, especially qualitative research using case studies and action research. Precedents for this methodology can be found in studies of teachers at all levels of education. In *The Dreamkeepers*, Gloria Ladson-Billings studied the teaching of elementary school teachers and developed case studies to describe how best to meet the needs of children of color. To gather data for *Writinglands,* Jane Zeni was a participant-observer in a sixth-grade classroom to study the effectiveness of using computers to teach writing. Kathleen Weiler's *Women Teaching for Change* and Frances A. Maher and Mary Kay Tetreault's *Feminist Classroom* used case studies of feminist teaching in high schools and universities, respectively, to underscore "the value of students' own voices, subjective experiences of power and oppression, and the worth of their class and ethnic cultures" (Weiler 149).

At the graduate level, Marilyn Sternglass's *Presence of Thought* argues that reflective, introspective writing is essential to the development of certain cognitive skills. To illustrate this relationship, Sternglass relied on case-study methodology to follow the progression of her graduate students' thinking and writing skills as exemplified in their introspective journal entries. Similarly, Wendy Bishop's *Something Old, Something New* used case-study methodology to examine the influence of composition theory and pedagogy on experienced high school teachers during and after a semester of graduate study. More recently, Elizabeth Rankin's *Seeing Yourself as a Teacher* and Christine Farris's *Subject to Change: New Com-*

position Instructors' Theory and Practice relied on case studies to describe the attitudes and practices of TAs during their first year of teaching.

It is no accident that these latter studies focused on TAs in departments of English, for composition specialists have led the way in establishing TA-training programs and emphasizing the importance of teaching. In their theoretical orientation; their focus on writing, race, and gender; their feminist methodology and qualitative research; and their arguments for change, these studies establish clear precedents. But, to date, no research has examined the integral role played by active learning, research, writing, and reflection *within* the graduate teaching seminar on the development of TAs' attitudes and abilities in the classroom. Such research represents the heart of this book.

In chapters 4 through 7, I present the results of a five-year study of graduate students' teaching and learning that illustrate the possibility of change. This is not a story full of quick answers, for enacting change is no easy task. Merely calling for change or even outlining what is needed ignores the human element—the feelings engendered by teacher and student alike as they try to adapt their conceptual frameworks, buck the traditional system, experiment with processes that always worked, and deal with the resulting frustrations. The effect, said one student, was "like sending an earthquake through a place that was always home." Yet, she, like the majority of her peers, eventually overcame such feelings after engaging in these very strategies and finding they helped both her teaching and her writing.

Perhaps for the first time, this study presents a picture of what can take place in the graduate classroom, how the instructor can initiate change, how and why students resist, and how to recognize and address these issues. The findings suggest two keys to change. The first is *faculty*: They must be willing to commit and involve themselves, modeling good teaching and research practices (Lambert and Tice 17). The second key is *writing*. By providing graduate students with pedagogical sites for research and reflection, faculty enable them to express their anger or fear, study their sources, and quite often write their way to a new understanding. In sum, I illustrate the potential for change when composition pedagogy is applied to graduate education.

2. Establishing Context

Across the country, teaching-assistant training is still in its infancy. Although many universities recommend that TAs participate in presemester workshops or orientations, faculty and administrators often hesitate to require attendance. Even in departments of English, where TA training is superior to that of other disciplines, requirements vary. Although the majority of writing program administrators (WPAs) observe their TAs' teaching, provide mentors, hold summer workshops, and offer pedagogy seminars, these methods of professional development are required only half the time. When TA training is not required, less than a third of first-year TAs elect to take it; worse, only 6.4 percent of doctoral students do so. The necessity of preparing TAs to teach has yet to be accepted, even though 95 percent have no prior teaching experience.[1]

TA training remains a matter of choice because teaching is still considered secondary to research within academia. This mind-set represents a conundrum to new TAs, for they have seldom encountered the strategies they are supposed to teach, and they have excelled without them, so they see no need to adopt them. In this, they are not unlike the majority of their professors. To help graduate students—and their professors—understand this need, teaching must first be put into context. Across the disciplines, researchers have taken various approaches to the subject. Historians have demonstrated that teaching was once a respected and important element of the university and pinpointed its various stages of decline. Scholars in education have analyzed the critiques of higher education to detail the difficulty, and necessity, of preparing TAs to teach. In educational psychology, studies have explored issues ranging from socialization and diversity to program design and active learning. In English, research has run the gamut from TAs' changing conceptions of teaching to the role of reflection, the variation in TA-training programs, and teacher affect and efficacy, to the importance of teaching to the future of the profession. Nonetheless, academics' feelings regarding professional development remain ambiguous. In *The Rise and Fall of English*, Robert Scholes zeroes in on the problem:

I grew up in this system, I benefited from it, but I am deeply troubled by its inadequacies for our present situation. And when I speak of inadequacies, I am not just talking about some methodological problems that we can rectify by tinkering with our curriculum. I am talking about a set of assumptions about teaching that are so out of touch with our real situation as to be both ludicrous and dangerous. (76)

In this chapter, I address both parts of Scholes's indictment: the assumptions about teaching and the changes in higher education that make those assumptions ludicrous. I begin by discussing the influence of the Germanic model of education on the American colonial college system and trace its subsequent effects. To demonstrate the need for change, I describe the demographic shift in student population, which has resulted in a generation of college students increasingly unprepared for and unresponsive to traditional modes of teaching. Finally, to underscore the need to redefine teaching, I describe the present efforts, which have thus far failed to meet the approval of many faculty and therefore have not been wholly accepted by the graduate students needing to change their attitudes.

A BRIEF HISTORY

In his preface to the 1996 reconsideration of John Henry Newman's *Idea of a University*, editor Frank M. Turner maintains that the battle for the minds and souls of the professoriate has raged since the nineteenth century. During the late 1800s, competing models of university education were being established in England, Europe, and the United States. In England, the question was whether to continue the tradition of educating young men to be gentlemen or to begin preparing students for a professional career, an argument Newman characterized as the difference between a liberal and a utilitarian education. In his lectures promoting the establishment of a Catholic university in Ireland, Cardinal Newman argued in favor of a liberal education, for although it might disseminate a great deal of "useless" information and would not prepare students for a profession, such an education would expand their "outlook, turn of mind, habit of thought, and capacity for social and civic interaction" (Turner xv). This expansion would occur not because of good teaching but as a result of the students' own independent learning.

> To discover and to teach are distinct functions. They are also distinct gifts, and are not commonly found united in the same person. He, too, who spends

23

his day in dispensing his existing knowledge to all comers is unlikely to have either leisure or energy to acquire new. The common sense of mankind has associated the search after truth with seclusion and quiet. The greatest thinkers have been too intent on their subject to admit of interruption; they have been men of absent minds and idosyncratic [*sic*] habits, and have, more or less, shunned the lecture room and the public school. (Newman qtd. in Turner 5–6)

Since its first printing, Newman's treatise has "exerted extraordinary influence over the discussion and conceptualization of higher education" (Turner ix). When *The Idea of a University* was first published, Scotland, France, and Germany were developing their own research institutions (Garland 269) while America vacillated between the German model and the colonial college model emphasizing teaching and students (Boyer 4–5). But in the late 1800s, following the establishment of land-grant colleges and the rise of professionalization, the German model took precedence.

The result, as David R. Russell details in his curricular history of *Writing in the Academic Disciplines, 1870–1990,* was that American colleges changed from unified discourse communities where teaching was "active, personal, [and] language-dependent" into a conglomeration of specialized, research-oriented departments in which teaching became passive and impersonal, relying on lectures and testing (21). Although faculty initially believed that undergraduates would be sufficiently motivated to engage in independent research, it soon became clear that the faculty and students held different interests. Russell sums up the situation by quoting Laurence Veysey, an early chronicler of the American university system: "If investigation was the principle aim of the university, then giving one's energy to immature and frequently mediocre students could easily seem an irritating experience" (71). Thus, faculty members not only grew more distant from their undergraduate students but also began to focus their teaching more narrowly to reflect their own research interests (72). As a result, "Today the researcher's neglect of undergraduate teaching has become an educational cliche" (71).

The irony of this dichotomy, as Martha McMackin Garland points out, is that Cardinal Newman's goal in establishing the Irish university was not to foreground research but to foster teaching (274). Indeed, Turner believes that academics who cite Newman's work must have read only the first few lines, for the emphasis on teaching has been for the most part overlooked. Instead, Cardinal Newman's legacy has been perpetuated in the liberal arts, where those who might be said to promote "useless learning," such as literature or history, tend to look down upon those who foster "utilitarian" knowledge, like writing and pedagogy, as well as other less-controversial subjects such as engineering, journalism, or foreign languages (Turner 291).

Part of this attitude stems from the research model in which university professors have been trained; another part stems from the increasing pressure brought upon tenure-line faculty to bring in grants and sponsored research from business, industry, and the government (Turner 291–92). Since the late 1970s, this focus on research rather than learning has led some faculty members to view teaching and interacting with students as impediments rather than responsibilities (292). As a result, too many professors consider publications, grants, research, and visibility at national conferences—all of which help develop a national reputation—as their primary concern, whereas teaching is viewed as "only" a local concern (Von Blum 27). This outlook has contributed to the belief that "almost anyone can teach, but only first-rate professors can achieve national and international reputations" (28). It is reinforced by the fact that faculty who excel in teaching are generally paid much less than their counterparts who research and publish (Gebhardt 10).

In his comparison of Cardinal Newman's idea of a university to the present reality, Turner notes that most arguments against teaching "conceal the refusal or, more disturbingly, the inability of specialized professional scholars to provide general education" (299). Yet, behind this seemingly amorphous understanding of teaching, there are certain unspoken rules:

> [T]he contemporary academic world, in general, retains the notion of an authorized body of knowledge; relies primarily on classroom-based or laboratory learning; does not stress subjective experience as a legitimate source of knowledge; has a hierarchical structure that stresses individual achievement; and maintains a fairly standardized and accessible set of rules governing classroom behavior and interaction . . . which dictate in part that all things flow to and from the teacher. (Treichler 85)

This positivist view of learning and education exemplifies the attitudes of many faculty and the majority of administrators, scholarly journals, and grant-funding agencies. George Hillocks, who has been fighting these attitudes for at least two decades, maintains that teaching at the postsecondary level proceeds from the assumption that "knowledge is objective and may be acquired directly through words and the senses." In other words, teaching is equated with transmitting information (*Ways* 19). Following his study of college teachers' attitudes and approaches, Hillocks concluded that the vast majority take an objectivist approach wherein "teaching is tantamount to telling. If one tells or gives students appropriate information, their learning will indicate that they have received the information and made use of it" (19). In such classrooms, the teacher holds center stage while the students sit passively, presumably absorbing information—an approach Hillocks and others have found ineffective.[2] A more successful stance is what he terms "constructivist," which assumes that "students must themselves be active agents in their learning, transforming what is to be learned through the screen of their own experiences and existing understandings." Teachers holding this view "believe that to be successful, learners must construct or reconstruct, for themselves, what is to be learned" (93). Unfortunately, this approach is rarely found outside undergraduate composition classrooms. Ernest Boyer, former chairman of the Carnegie Foundation's Commission on Teaching, agrees: "The truth is that on most campuses the German university tradition is the model that shapes normative behavior. Teaching is not highly prized" (5).

These problems have not gone unnoticed. The need for change was recognized as early as the late 1930s and has been raised practically every decade thereafter.[3] But in recent years, the public's perception of university faculty has worsened. In their introduction to *Preparing Graduate Students to Teach,* Leo M. Lambert and Stacey L. Tice maintain that the rising cost of postsecondary education coupled with falling resources has led increasingly to questions about the faculty's "workload, productivity, commitment to teaching, and competence as teachers" (v). In 1997, Peter Drucker, the Nostradamus of the twentieth century, concurred, predicting:

> Thirty years from now the big university campuses will be relics. Universities won't survive. It's as large a change as when we first got the printed book. Do you realize that the cost of higher education has risen as fast as the cost of health care? . . . Such totally uncontrollable expenditures, without any

visible improvement in either the content or quality of education, means that the system is rapidly becoming untenable. Higher education is in deep crisis.[4] (qtd. in Lenzner and Johnson 122)

These concerns have been fostered by critiques such as Harold Bloom's *Closing of the American Mind,* Donald Sykes's *Profscam,* Page Smith's *Killing the Spirit,* Dinesh D'Souza's *Illiberal Education,* Geoffrey Douglas's *Education Without Impact,* Martin Anderson's *Impostors in the Temple,* and other jeremiads indicting the professoriate as lazy incompetents who take advantage of the taxpayers' money while they ignore teaching and whine about their salaries. Such works exemplify the Carnegie-commissioned Holmes Group's report that "America's dissatisfaction with its schools has become chronic and endemic" (3). Although the Holmes Group focused on problems in the public schools, it concluded that the solution rested with postsecondary faculty, for they prepare the nation's teachers. The group recommended that university faculty move away from "weak pedagogy, the preoccupation with 'covering the material,' the proliferation of multiple-choice tests, and accept primary responsibility for graduate and undergraduate education" (4–5). Clearly, such a move would require the reconceptualization of teaching, for "few of these specialists know how to teach well, and many seem not to care" (16).

The professoriate's lack of teaching skills became even more evident with the advent of open admissions. Once the college doors swung open, the demographics of the student body changed significantly. In the past three decades, this population has become increasingly diverse as students enter with a wide range of interests, abilities, and preparation. After serving for five years as dean of humanities, Annette Kolodny detailed the challenges presented by the new student body. In the nation's public schools, more than one-third of the students are minorities, and among that cohort, three million (an increase of 20 percent) are predicted to enter the nation's colleges and universities between 1997 and 2015 (34). Across the nation, more than 3.5 million students live in families for whom English is their second language; over 150 different languages are heard in the public schools; at least five million "children of immigrants" entered the public schools during the 1990s; and demographers predict that by 2025, "almost half the students in our colleges and universities will be the children of parents who have only recently arrived on our shores" (175).

This is not the homogeneous student body of the past. These students will bring with them not only cultural diversity but also what Kolodny refers to as *cognitive diversity*:

> [D]ifferent cultural groups can privilege certain cognitive styles over others. For example, a culture or cultural subgroup may purposefully (or even unintentionally) emphasize assimilating new knowledge by various means: listening to instruction about a skill rather than watching it performed by those already adept; reasoning by analogy instead of a strict linear logic; taking an inductive approach to problem-solving instead of a deductive; favoring empathetic identification with human agency as a means of understanding a situation over analysis by abstract principles. (163)

In *Lives on the Boundary,* Mike Rose personifies these cultural and cognitive differences. Discussing his own feelings of alienation as an undergraduate at Loyola University, he writes, "I felt like a janitor at a gallery opening, silent, intimidated, little flecks of knowledge . . . sticking to the fiber of my broom" (181). A generation later, he describes Marita, a minority student from the inner city accused of plagiarism because she "was adrift in a set of conventions she didn't fully understand; she offended without knowing why." Her assignment assumed she could comprehend a complex argument, that she could draw on personal experience to create her own stylistically complex rebuttal, and that her culture and gender would not inhibit her from taking on such a task. In sum, "Marita was being asked to write in a cognitive and social vacuum" (181). Another student, Denise, came from a Hispanic family that had worked hard to move into the middle class and assimilate themselves within the dominant culture. Although Denise found it difficult to compare Henry Roth's *Call It Sleep* to problems faced by contemporary immigrants, she rejected Rose's suggestion that she compare it to Hispanic assimilation:

> She looked at me as though I'd whispered something obscene in her ear. 'No!' she said emphatically, pulling back her head, 'that's rude. . . . You don't want to put that in a paper. That doesn't belong.'" In Denise's community, decent people put those things behind them; they moved on. (179)

Consider the cognitive dissonance academia presents to returning students. Rose describes Lucia, a twenty-eight-year-old, single parent majoring in psychology because she wanted to understand her brother's psychotic breakdown. Lucia's roadblock occurred when she was assigned

Thomas Szasz's *Myth of Mental Illness*, for her personal experience had demonstrated the disease's reality. In addition to rejecting the author's premise, Lucia stumbled over his vocabulary and use of analogies. "Students like Lucia," Rose writes, "are often thought to be poor readers or to have impoverished vocabularies (though Lucia speaks two languages); I've even heard students like her referred to as culturally illiterate (though she has absorbed two cultural heritages)" (184). But Lucia's real problem dealt with "her belief system and with her lack of familiarity with certain ongoing discussions in humanities and social sciences—with frames of mind, predispositions, and background knowledge" (184). Rose taught Lucia and students like her how to work through their misunderstandings by drawing on their personal experiences to establish connections with their academic texts (150). This teaching strategy eventually gave these students the confidence to take risks with their writing, which led to yet another problem: "Saying complex things forces you away from the protected syntax of simple sentences. But error that crops up because a student is trying new things is a valuable kind of error, a sign of growth" (151). How many faculty have been taught to recognize these problems, address them, and respect the resulting signs of growth? And if faculty are not prepared, how can they possibly prepare their TAs?

To meet these demands, faculty and TAs need to be familiar with a variety of teaching strategies and cognizant of different learning styles—two elements notably absent from most graduate curricula. Indeed, Kolodny suggests that if faculty and graduate students were to analyze their own learning styles, they would find that they generally favor pedagogical approaches that replicate the ways *they* learn best. And because most of the present and future professoriate are white, middle- to upper-middle-class Americans, their learning styles will very likely differ from those of their students. To broaden their pedagogical skills, both faculty and graduate students must become aware of their strengths and experiment with alternative modes of teaching so as to meet the needs of a variety of student learners (166).

Taking her own advice, when Kolodny returned to the classroom, she began by trying to assess the needs and learning styles of her undergraduate students through a series of questions. The first set helped her determine the students' background knowledge. In a course on literature of the American frontiers, she asked students to list words and phrases they associated with the term *frontier* and the sources of this information. Such an exercise helped initiate discussion while establishing the course's context. Kolodny's second set of questions asked students to describe their most positive learning experience, tell what made it unique, and what types of classes fostered this type of experience. Through these answers, she was able to assess their cognitive styles. This is the type of attention the new generation of learners needs. Unfortunately, Kolodny found, "What is lacking is any systematic attentiveness, *across the disciplines and across the nation's campuses*, to the very fact of cognitive diversity. That lack of attentiveness makes progress slow and piecemeal" (168, Kolodny's emphasis).

Kolodny's approach exemplifies the keys to meeting the needs of this diverse population—what Lion F. Gardiner and others refer to as *active learning* (vii). In *Redesigning Higher Education,* Gardiner analyzed "hundreds of studies on various aspects of higher education" to determine how best to meet the needs of the new student body (4). Gardiner lists eight areas of "critical competencies" considered essential for success during school and throughout students' careers:

> Conscientiousness, personal responsibility, and dependability; the ability to act in a principled, ethical fashion; skill in oral and written communication; interpersonal and team skills; skill in critical thinking and in solving complex problems; respect for people different from oneself; [and] the ability and desire for life-long learning. (7)

The most effective way to develop and mature these competencies is through active learning. To substantiate this claim, Gardiner cites a 1993 study of 24,847 students from 192 colleges that concluded that student interactions with peers influenced both learning and retention. Students need to be challenged, supported, and engaged in active learning, which provides "clearly defined outcomes, frequent assessment, and prompt feedback" (23–24). Although no single approach works for every student, providing "mastery experiences" within a small-group setting dramatically influenced the students' learning across the board, a finding that led researchers to conclude that "the higher the quality of instruction, the less relevant to achievement are the entering student's abilities" (97). Such findings in turn led Gardiner to conclude, "If we would do what works and stop doing what does not, virtually all of our students could learn" (103).

ANSWERING THE CALLS FOR CHANGE

Composition pedagogy answers these calls for change. In the 1970s, writing-as-a-process emerged from research on cognitive processes, social constructivism, psycholinguistics, and numerous other areas. This research has not remained in the professional journals. Rather, because of compositionists' interest in teaching, the results have been applied in the writing classroom. In *Composition in the University,* Sharon Crowley explains:

> Composition scholarship typically focuses on the processes of learning rather than on the acquisition of knowledge, and composition pedagogy focuses on change and development in students rather than on transmission of a heritage. Composition studies encourages collaboration. It emphasizes the historical, political, and social contexts and practices associated with composing rather than concentrating on texts as isolated artifacts. (3)

These beliefs have been translated into classroom practice. Writing instructors routinely de-center the classroom and allow students to work in small groups, generating and critiquing ideas, sharing and presenting information, reading and responding to each other's writing. Instead of serving as benign dictators, many composition instructors have become coaches and facilitators:

- They develop literacy problems for students to solve by pooling their knowledge
- They link reading with writing assignments so that students begin to assimilate the conventions of language
- They assign response journals so the students can explore ideas, reflect on what they have read, and develop their voice and fluency
- They design essay assignments which draw on the students' prior knowledge
- They sequence the assignments so that they gradually build on acquired skills
- They require multiple drafts and/or have the students submit their best writing in portfolios at the end of the semester so that students learn that writing, like learning, is a recursive, ongoing process

All of these strategies reflect the shift in composition theory and pedagogy from teaching writing as a product to teaching writing as a process. In classrooms where these strategies are practiced, students cannot be passive learners; they are actively involved in each aspect of the process through brainstorming, mapping, journaling, freewriting, drafting, and revising. In these classes, students are less likely to feel alienated because they are allowed to select their own topics, express their feelings, and explore ideas in their journals; discuss the readings and share their drafts with their peers in small groups; and decide which papers their instructor should evaluate in a final portfolio. Because of these strategies, students cannot slide through class unprepared—they must bring their reading journals or drafts in order to participate in their group work. Because of these assignments, students must actually stop to reflect on what they know and what they have learned. This is not spoon-feeding or coddling as some have deemed it. In these composition courses, the students are actively constructing knowledge; they are aided in this endeavor by their instructors, who design the class so that learning is active, engaged, student-centered, and integrated.

Writing across the curriculum (WAC) extends this approach beyond departments of English. In his curricular history of *Writing in the Academic Disciplines,* David R. Russell traces the original WAC movement to the early decades of the twentieth century. Between 1910–1920, John Dewey and his followers proposed

> a new integrated curriculum, with communication at its center . . . which would produce a generation of articulate citizens who, through improved communication, would heal the divisions in industrial democracy and transcend its dehumanizing specialization and alienation. (200)

Unfortunately, this early movement did not succeed because Dewey and his followers were housed in departments of Education, failed to offer a politically and pedagogically attractive approach, and ultimately split into divisive schisms. It didn't resurface until the 1970s, coinciding with the advent of open admissions and the reconceptualization and professionalization of composition. Proceeding from the work of James Britton, WAC emphasizes "informal classroom talk, especially in small groups; expressive writing; and teacher-student collaboration," all of which facilitate students' language acquisition (277).

Conceived by composition faculty, WAC and writing-intensive courses reflect the same premises on which the current composition classroom operates. In his examination of the political ramifications of the WAC movement, Toby Fulwiler, one of its early proponents, lists the following features:

1. Learners construct knowledge for themselves
2. Learners learn best when they pose and solve meaningful problems for themselves
3. Language is an instrument for learning
4. Language is an avenue to personal growth, social success, political power
5. The faculty are the primary determiners of the way language is presented and used within academic institutions (180–81)

When these programs are widely adopted, they can make a significant difference in how both teaching and learning are conceptualized. Among faculty, it can instill a pride in teaching, a feeling of collegiality, and a sense of agency in instituting curricular change as well as an understanding that language is an essential element of learning (Russell 287). Among informed administrators, WAC is viewed as a means of improving student retention by establishing discourse communities that engage students in learning (290). Among students, Fulwiler claims that WAC programs "change the nature of the classroom learning from individual, passive, and competitive to communal, active, and collaborative" (182). On an individual basis, such teaching changes the quality of instruction; on a larger scale, WAC carries political impact:

> The more students educate themselves through the active use of their own language, the more ownership they exert over what they learn, and the more they trust (own) their own perceptions. Students so educated are more likely to speak with their own authority within the academic community. When students learn (are allowed to learn? encouraged to learn?) that knowledge is not something received whole and memorized . . . but rather a construct that they themselves participate in making, the nature of so-called higher education changes. (182)

When writing and writing pedagogy are incorporated into the curriculum, the relationships between faculty and students, faculty and their colleagues, and faculty and their institution, all undergo change because the fundamental nature of higher education, which Fulwiler posits is inertia, is challenged (187). But herein lies the problem:

> In articulating these premises to reasonable people who care about student learning, they sound pretty much like God, mother, and apple pie. However, if and when they are used as the basis for reformulating or restructuring academic programs, they begin to threaten business as usual. (181)

Fulwiler argues that professors often resist WAC because it represents a form of faculty development. Meeting in a workshop environment, faculty write about and discuss the role of writing, activities that ideally "address real deficiencies in college curricula with workable solutions" (181). To some faculty, instituting writing means increasing their work load while to others assigning writing to aid learning challenges their beliefs regarding their role in the college classroom. Thus, despite the benefits in student learning, WAC has not been widely accepted.

In a 1987 survey of 2,735 universities, Susan H. McLeod found that 38 percent had WAC programs (*Strengthening* 103). According to Fulwiler, WAC is most often found at teaching colleges and least often at research universities, where research and publication take precedence over teaching (182). Even when teaching is valued, and ranked faculty participate in the teaching of undergraduates, WAC is still difficult to maintain. In their analysis of successful WAC programs, Eric Miraglia and McLeod concluded that administrative support, faculty support, and strong, consistent program leadership were the keys to the growth and development of WAC programs (48). If the administration only rewards research and publication, faculty will not focus on teaching. If the administration does not provide funding or release time for course development or in-service workshops, the faculty will not participate. And if faculty do not believe that WAC is important, it will not succeed. Changing the way they teach requires "a willingness or desire on the part of faculty to accept some responsibility for their students' academic literacy— an acceptance . . . that many faculty are unwilling to make" (51–52).

Ten years after McLeod's study, Barbara E. Walvoord et al. determined that WAC programs existed in only 33 percent of postsecondary institutions. WAC may be dwindling for many of the same reasons Dewey's initial movement failed. Emanating from departments of English where writing is often marginalized, WAC may be perceived as unimportant or detracting from the teaching of literature. Outside English departments, traditional faculty reject WAC's pedagogical approach because it de-centers the classroom and supposedly interferes with coverage and because they doubt the correlation of writing with learning. Even within WAC's own ranks, various compositionists have disputed WAC's claims that expressive writing aids learning (Russell 294). All of these problems are, of course, exacerbated by ever-decreasing funding for higher education in general. Russell summarizes the problem quite succinctly as resistance to "reforming American pedagogy" (302).

These difficulties suggest that change may be virtually impossible to achieve among the majority of the current faculty. Rather than continue an exercise in futility among a cohort rapidly approaching retirement, why not focus on the teaching of graduate students so they will possess these abilities when they become faculty? That is the emphasis of centers for teaching excellence.

The last ten years have seen a tremendous growth in faculty development. Centers for teaching excellence offer a variety of instruction and supervision for interested faculty and graduate students. In their nationwide survey of graduate school deans and department chairs employing significant numbers of TAs, Nancy L. Buerkel-Rothfuss and Pamela L. Gray report that the majority of graduate student orientations average one day or less (32). These sessions usually include a combination of workshops, lectures, and plenary sessions; they may also provide videotaping of micro-teaching and a teaching handbook. However, the survey also revealed that just 13 percent of the respondents required attendance, and 95 percent estimated that, at best, only half their TAs attended. Considering that only 26 percent of the responding institutions offered campuswide training, these numbers suggest that very few TAs are receiving adequate preparation (32).

Whether or not teaching centers are being established, leading institutions are beginning to offer more TA training (Lambert and Tice viii). According to the National Survey of Teaching Assistant Training Programs and Practices, TA programs exist in 71 percent of the members of the Council of Graduate Schools. Forty-six percent of these schools require TA training, and the rest recommend it. Thirty-seven percent hold a presemester orientation, 34 percent have year-round programs, and 23 percent have developed special programs for international students (Lambert and Tice 5–7). Departmental training programs exist across all disciplines, with the humanities predominating (10). The primary techniques used within these programs are micro-teaching, which is videotaped and critiqued, and viewing of model teaching tapes made by experienced professors.

But what are the TAs learning in these seminars? According to recent research, not enough. One impetus for the development of the University of California–Berkeley Classroom Research Project was the finding that TA training programs are too often brief and insufficient, one-shot affairs in which the TAs are passive recipients (Angelo and Cross 105). Generally, these sessions do not focus on teaching; instead, they cover the "basics," such as writing examinations, building rapport, creating interest, managing the classroom, grading, and developing course policies. Other activities include critiquing each other's assignments, team-building, and grading—but not teaching per se (Lambert and Tice 32). Thus, despite their intent, the seminars appear to be perpetuating traditional pedagogy rather than helping graduate students reconceptualize teaching.

Only 25 percent of these programs critique the TAs' teaching, despite the fact that across the disciplines, at least 70 percent of all TAs have never taught before (Gray and Buerkel-Rothfuss 41). Often, these critiques are based on videotapes of a micro-teaching exercise, the value of which has not been clearly demonstrated. Some studies show that teaching improves with such feedback while others reveal only short-term change. As a rule, teaching does improve with training; however, considering that the majority of TAs have neither prior training nor experience, some improvement is bound to occur (Abbott, Wulff, and Szego 111). Nevertheless, given the limited exposure in these orientations, the effects of training workshops tend to be only temporary (121).

Even when a variety of topics or strategies is introduced in the workshops, time is still a determinant factor. In general, a disproportionate number of topics is covered; alternatively, the topics are addressed in concurrent, nonrepeated sessions so not all can be attended (Bort and Buerkel-Rothfuss 250). In their research on TA training, Mary Bort and Buerkel-Rothfuss analyzed the TA training materials used at twenty-nine different universities, then compiled a list of thirty-one topics typically covered in a TA workshop or orientation. These ran the gamut from the TA's role, student profile, and philosophy of education through lecturing, using visual aids, selecting textbooks, and writing a syllabus to departmental and university policies. Those teaching strategies considered most important for undergraduates—that is, engagement, active learning, and establishing a student-centered classroom—were not among the thirty-one topics (although they might have been alluded to under the rubric "other teaching strategies") (246–47).

When TA training is offered by the university, most workshops consist of a one-day session prior to fall semester (Buerkel-Rothfuss and Gray 32). Considering the amount of time and the number of areas to be covered, this one-day session is far from sufficient, especially if it is not followed by a discipline-specific seminar. This need becomes even clearer when TA workshops are compared to traditional teacher training. Undergraduates preparing to become teachers generally take sixty hours within Education, whereas most graduate students preparing to be TAs and eventually university professors take one day. Not surprisingly, national surveys have found that much of this training has little effect on TAs' knowledge, abilities, attitudes, or understanding of their future professions.[5] Such findings led Bort and Buerkel-Rothfuss to conclude that overall, there is a need for university TA-training sessions followed by a clear link to a seminar in the TAs' content areas.

But even when the training is integrated within the disciplines, TAs often receive instruction only in the basics of classroom management, while teaching strategies are ignored. Such evidence suggests that research-based, constructivist pedagogy cannot and will not be introduced unless teaching is reconceptualized. Instituting change will require clear-cut goals, results, and curricula; an understanding of learning styles and cognitive development; and effective and innovative instruction (Gardiner 113–17). Only when this happens will TA training in departments and centers for teaching excellence take the first step in faculty development.

One of the most recent trends in faculty and graduate student development, the Preparing Future Faculty (PFF) initiative, attempts to do so. Sponsored by the Association of Colleges and Universities and the Council of Graduate Schools, the purpose of this initiative is to better teach undergraduates by better preparing those who will teach them— our graduate students. The program's first phase began in 1993 with the development of model PFF programs at eighty-eight postsecondary institutions divided into seventeen clusters, defined as "an anchor, doctoral degree-granting institution or department collaborating with various partner institutions or departments." Each cluster designs a program that introduces its graduate students to the various responsibilities—that is, teaching, research, and service—that they will encounter in their future careers. Among these, the most pertinent to the present study are "arranging for a teaching experience [and] working with a teaching mentor," but overall, participating graduate students are expected to work with "multiple mentors and receive reflective feedback" on each of the three areas of faculty life ("Preparing Future Faculty Web: Contents" 1).

PFF's second phase, running from 1997–2001, was designed to "institutionalize and spread" the program. With the third and fourth phases, the program developed specializations in science and mathematics and in the humanities and social sciences, respectively. At this writing, PFF had developed seventy-six clusters incorporating three hundred institutions covering all four phases with the potential to impact 208,222 doctoral students ("Preparing Future Faculty: History" 1). With the advent of phase 4, faculty in history, political science, psychology, sociology, communication, and English became specifically involved (4–5). The National Council of Teachers of English sponsored the latter and initiated calls for proposals from interested colleges and universities.

PFF offers a variety of resources and support for developing teaching strategies. Recognizing the need for broad-based and up-to-date pedagogy, its clusters "include preparation for using technology to do academic work and instruction for developing expertise in newer, active, collaborative, experiential, or interdisciplinary approaches to teaching and learning" ("Preparing Future Faculty: Useful" 2). Recognizing the concurrent need to interact with and learn from other professionals, PFF encourages mentoring for teaching, research, and service and provides a variety of resources, print and electronic, to inform faculty and students how to access them (3–4). In addition, information regarding teaching skills is provided via case studies and Web sites covering resources, developing teaching portfolios and philosophies, and links explaining learning styles, learning theory, and the pros and cons of distance learning (6).

What do these programs look like? At Michigan State University, a certificate in college teaching program within the Department of Kinesiology entails "course work, workshops, and seminars to provide basic information on teaching and learning, . . . a mentored teaching experience, and the development of a teaching portfolio" ("Certificate" 1). To receive certification, graduate students must exhibit knowledge and competency in "adult students as learners," "teaching strategies," "assessment of learning," "use of technology in the classroom," and "understanding the academy" (2). This is not a required program; interested doctoral students must apply and have the support of their academic advisor. These requirements typify those Catherine Latterell found in practica for graduate TAs. In her national survey of TA preparation among doctoral programs in composition-rhetoric, Latterell concluded that TA training moved along a continuum from practical to theoretical, with the practicum the most prevalent (18). The problem with the latter approach is threefold: by focusing primarily on a skills-based approach, the practicum ignores the epistemological bases of teaching and in turn perpetuates the perception that teaching is not a valued, complex, intellectual activity (19–20).

At the University of Missouri–Columbia, interested graduate students apply to be accepted in a seminar in higher education that meets two hours twice a month throughout the academic year (twenty times altogether) and includes participation in two weekend retreats. Teaching methods practiced and discussed include experiential learning, lecturing, and group and collaborative activities. Students are required to choose a mentor and enroll concurrently in a discipline-specific seminar about problems in teaching and learning. Course requirements include reading and responding to three texts (*College Teaching, The Teaching Portfolio*, and *Using Active Learning in the College Classroom*), micro-teaching, presenting reports, participating in listserv dialogue, compiling a teaching portfolio, observing the classes of two peers, and maintaining an ongoing reflective journal (collected and responded to twice during the year). Although the course is graded pass/fail, each of these requirements is allotted points, and the overall total is one hundred points. Because of the various writing assignments—a philosophy of teaching, lesson plans, the reflective journal, and class observations—the seminar is deemed writing intensive ("Preparing Future Faculty: Similar Versions 3). Like Michigan State's offerings, the effects of this skill-based focus seem limited.

To bring about change, PFF needs to be institutionalized. In addition to the above, the University of Missouri has added a minor in college teaching, entailing twelve credit hours beyond doctoral students' major programs. Although the minor is available to all doctoral students, they must apply, submit letters of recommendation and a philosophy of teaching, and be approved for admission. Core courses, equaling six hours, include the above-mentioned seminar and either a course in college teaching or completion of the graduate teaching scholars seminar. A teaching practicum of three to six hours may be taken within the students' major field—for example, agriculture, communication, education, nursing, or philosophy. The final three hours may be drawn from a range of electives already on the books, such as foundations of educational psychology or human learning and memory (*Graduate Minor*).

A more intensive (and nationally known) PFF program is offered at the University of New Hampshire. Graduate students who have completed their first year of doctoral work and are recommended by their graduate advisors may take a twelve-credit cognate in college teaching or earn a thirty-two–credit master of science for teachers while pursuing course work for the Ph.D. The cognate requires four core courses, four courses within the student's field, and four "praxis" courses. The master's degree has a similar emphasis, requiring sixteen hours of core courses, eight within the discipline, and eight praxis. An often-heard objection to PFF course work is that it interferes with students' progress toward their degrees; UNH addresses this by offering the core courses during summer session. These requirements include issues in college teaching; teaching with writing; cognition, teaching, and learning; and classroom research and assessment methods. Course work within the disciplines is available throughout the school year and includes topics such as teaching and learning in science, teaching sociology, or college teaching in the life sciences and agriculture. The praxis element requires development of a teaching portfolio, which is reviewed by faculty from the student's field and from the UNH Teaching Excellence Program (*Academic*).

By expanding PFF through cognates, minors, and master's degrees, universities such as Missouri and New Hampshire answer the calls for reconceptualizing teaching, linking theory with practice, and institution-alizing change. However, unless and until doctoral programs across the country follow suit, large-scale change cannot occur. Lee Seidel, director of the Teaching Excellence Program at New Hampshire, and Jerry Gaff, national director of PFF, argue that PFF should be more than an option for graduate students (6). Although every assessment of PFF has been positive (5), as long as the movement remains voluntary and essentially peripheral to doctoral programs, its overall effects will be limited to those students wise enough to recognize the value and need for teaching skills.

MOVING BEYOND THE LEGACY OF CARDINAL NEWMAN

Graduate students represent the future of the profession. We can help them reconceptualize teaching, but to do so, we will have to change the way we teach them. *As If Learning Mattered*, Richard E. Miller's analysis of the (il)logic of educational bureaucracy, argues that change is possible if those who want it consider their own sense of agency and its potential. Faculty may not be able to change the university system, but we can make a difference if "agency is understood as learning how to work within extant constraints" (211). Focusing on changing the attitudes and practices of graduate students represents the opportunity and the context for personal agency.

This will not be easy. Jody D. Nyquist and Robert W. Wulff, who between them share forty years of work with TAs, found that graduate students tend to teach one of two ways: They either try to model their supervising teacher's approach, or they try to do the opposite (*Working* 2). In other words, TAs will either lecture or flounder, for Pamela D. Scherer's survey of eighty-five teaching assistants suggests that new TAs are familiar only with nonparticipatory classrooms. Most have had little or no experience with active learning, group work, presenting information, or leading discussions; in fact, the majority are uncomfortable speaking in class, leading group discussions, or designing learning activities (257). This discomfort and the intransigence of these beliefs are illustrated by Gray and Buerkel-Rothfuss, who surveyed TAs in 126 institutions. In a postworkshop evaluation regarding the importance of teaching skills, TAs rated "giving effective, interesting lectures" fifth, while "leading small-group discussions," "processing group activities," and "assigning group projects" ranked thirteenth, eighteenth, and nineteenth out of twenty-four. Even more disturbing is the finding that "whether trained or not . . . TAs felt that their teaching ability was close to excellent" (47). In sum, without changing our attitudes and practices, TAs will teach as they were taught: they will lecture and probably find it difficult to stimulate students intellectually. These people have the potential to enact change, but because they do not know how, they are unable to do so. Such conditions represent only a few of the extant constraints under which faculty must prepare graduate students.

Analyzing the difficulty of change in higher education, Miller points out that graduate students need to realize that a good portion of their careers will be spent teaching undergraduates (208). Kolodny has stated that if she were still in the dean's office, she would ask faculty and students to "rethink the training of graduate students" to better prepare them for a career that will largely consist of teaching (192). Bemoaning the fifty-percent attrition rate among doctoral students in the humanities, Elaine Showalter argues:

> All graduate students should receive formal training in teaching and communications and . . . those who make the commitment to go on for the Ph.D. should have a variety of teaching experiences that constitute a true, and not a rhetorical, apprenticeship. Graduate students are called apprentices and assistants in teaching, but they are not trained to teach. (324)

Finally, Richard Fulkerson reminds us that such training should be considered an essential if not an ethical obligation to our graduate students:

> To certify a candidate who then cannot do the job is just as unethical as it would be to certify a surgeon or lawyer who had put in the years in a program but could not in fact remove an appendix or draw up a will. Both the candidates and those they might later work for have been ill-served. (122)

Fulkerson's analogies touch on a key component of professional development. TA training must move beyond skills-based approaches, for these alone will provide neither impetus nor sufficient understanding to graduate students who survived their undergraduate careers among professors lacking pedagogical skills. To reconceptualize and respect teaching, graduate students must recognize it as an intellectually challenging, complex endeavor. To do so requires that they—and their professors—be introduced to the theories behind the practice.

3. Teaching Theory

The past three decades have shown some progress in the recon-ceptualization of teaching. Writing-across-the-curriculum, centers for teaching excellence, TA workshops, and the Preparing Future Faculty movement all represent incremental steps toward a better understand-ing of the value and necessity of good teaching. But they don't go far enough. Each of these initiatives is voluntary, which means they reach only a minority of their intended audience. More troublesome is that too often, their primary focus is on teaching strategies rather than on the theories underlying them. To reverse Richard Fulkerson's analogy, we would not want a surgeon who knew how to cut but did not know anatomy, nor would we want a lawyer who knew how to argue but did not know the law. Effective teaching entails more than methods or sub-ject knowledge. To understand how and why to engage the new genera-tion of undergraduates in learning, graduate students and their profes-sors should know the theories underlying their practice.

The goal of this chapter is to introduce faculty and graduate students to the theories basic to an understanding of teaching: cognitive psychol-ogy, social-cognitive psychology, and educational psychology. This dis-cussion focuses first on the needs of undergraduate students, because that's who our TAs will teach, but these same theories also apply to gradu-ate students, for they, too, are learners. Although graduate students are cognitively more sophisticated, they share commonalities with their un-dergraduate students. When graduate students are introduced to peda-gogical theory, the vast majority find themselves on unfamiliar ground. Paradoxically, graduate students may flounder in pedagogy workshops not because they are poor students, but because they have always excelled. Because they succeeded in every academic context, graduate students are generally unaware of how they were taught. As a result, they lack sufficient background knowledge to easily comprehend pedagogical theory, and they find the teaching strategies they are expected to prac-tice alien. This mind-set is complicated by the fact that graduate students generally represent the majority population and have assimilated the objectivist pedagogy aimed at them. Because they are familiar with passive learning, the prospect of using active learning will most likely be resisted, if not dismissed. Therefore, once postsecondary teaching has been contextualized, the next step in overcoming resistance is to introduce the theories behind the pedagogy.

COGNITIVE PSYCHOLOGY

If faculty truly want to change the way teaching is perceived, they would do well to draw on research in psychology. Indeed, Lion F. Gardiner's review of the literature on effective teaching concludes, "If the preeminent outcome we value is students' cognitive development, the curriculum should at all points focus on producing this result" (111). Such a knowledge base is invaluable for faculty and TAs alike, for it explains how people learn and how to facilitate the process. In this section, I begin by describing the research that informs composition pedagogy: Frederick Bartlett's schema theory, Howard Gardner's theory of multiple intelligences, Robert Sternberg's triarchic theory, and Albert Bandura's theory of self-efficacy. In the next section, I describe how these theories are exemplified in active learning, linked reading-writing assignments, and reflective writing—activities alien to undergraduates and graduate students alike—for these activities are seldom practiced outside the composition classroom and are virtually nonexistent in most graduate seminars. As chapter 2 detailed, the lack of such teaching strategies is detrimental to undergraduates' learning. This lack is equally harmful to graduate students, for unless they are engaged in learning the strategies they are expected to teach, they are unlikely to understand them and are likely to blame their students when they fail to learn. This is a no-win situation.

Schema theory lays the groundwork. First introduced by Bartlett in 1932, schema theory posits that individuals learn from experience. When new information is encountered, learners compare it with prior knowledge already stored; if they have had previous, related experiences, the new information updates the old. If the information is completely foreign, it will be difficult to retain unless a conscious connection can be made between the new and the older, slightly related, or parallel experiences. As psycholinguist Frank Smith explains in *Understanding Reading*, synonymous terms for schema theory are prior knowledge, nonvisual information, or long-term memory, all of which are incorporated within the concept of cognitive structure (8–9). This structure, or "theory of the world," as Smith terms it, organizes information and memory so that learners can comprehend new information. In this regard, the brain could be said to be an information system akin to a computer (10).

Everyone has developed schemata to understand the world. For example, because they have a restaurant schema, most people know how to behave at McDonald's. They did not read about it; they learned from experience. Similarly, from reading a wide variety of books, readers develop "book" schemata that include knowledge of text conventions ranging from grammar, syntax, and punctuation to recognition of paragraph and organizational structures, all of which aid the comprehension and production of language (Smith, *Understanding*). Knowledge of schema theory provides the rationale for gradually increasing complexity in course work, providing students with relevant examples, helping them to make conscious connections between new and old material, and linking reading with writing to help them assimilate the conventions of texts.

Building on an understanding of schema theory are Gardner's theory of multiple intelligences and Sternberg's triarchic theory. Gardner maintains that there are seven different types of intelligences: linguistic, musical, logical-mathematical, spatial, bodily-kinesthetic, intrapersonal, and interpersonal (Ormrod 154). Although some faculty have been known to dispute this theory, its logic is obvious by examining the range of university departments—English, music, mathematics, art, physical education, psychology, and sociology, respectively—correlating with each type of intelligence. Simply stated, the theory governing multiple intelligences is that individuals learn differently. An English major may not excel in math, while a student might know everything about computer programming but possess little or no social skills. Understanding this theory might help faculty accept the fact that more than one approach is necessary in the classroom.

Gardner's theory was followed closely by Sternberg's triarchic theory positing that intelligence is not only multidimensional but also context-dependent. According to Sternberg, intelligence relies on three interdependent factors: (1) the environmental context in which the behavior occurs; (2) the way in which one's prior experiences are brought to bear on a particular task, and (3) the cognitive processes required by each task (Ormrod 151).

Each factor can be broken down into specific cognitive abilities. Environmental context influences an individual's problem-solving ability, verbal ability, and social competence. For example, an otherwise fluent and intelligent student who has been bored or frustrated in an English class may find that her verbal ability deteriorates in the context of subsequent English courses. The degree to which her verbal skills develop will depend on her ability to adapt to the learning context. The second factor determining intelligence, prior experience, is an application of Bartlett's schema theory: Individuals learn how to deal with new situations by drawing on past experiences. If a student has extensive literacy experiences, he may excel in composition courses because he can draw on his knowledge of language conventions. This same student can apply his reading and writing experiences to comprehend a biology text. In other words, he is able to excel in other course work because his cognitive processes—which encompass ways of thinking such as interpreting, classifying, identifying, finding relationships, and using feedback effectively—have been well developed (Ormrod 152).

THEORIES OF SELF-EFFICACY

Bandura's theory of self-efficacy ties all of this together. According to Bandura, "Among the different aspects of self-knowledge, perhaps none is more influential in people's everyday lives than conceptions of their personal efficacy. Self-efficacy is central to human agency" (390). Knowledge and ability are not sufficient to ensure that individuals can apply what they have learned. Even if students diligently study, memorize, and understand their course work, they may not perform capably or demonstrate their knowledge if they do not perceive themselves as capable. Self-perception affects both motivation and behavior (391). Although this theory applies to all learners, it is especially pertinent to the new generation of nontraditional students.

In their explanation of these students' needs, Nancy Chism, Jamie Cano, and Anne S. Pruitt point out that as a rule,

> Students from nontraditional groups have simply been expected to adjust to the prevailing environment and culture of the classroom. The curriculum is heavily based on the Western intellectual tradition, and expectations for students are based on years of experience with young white males from college-preparatory programs. (23)

Despite the influx of women, ethnic minorities, returning adults, gays and lesbians, and students with disabilities,

> Most universities have not yet found ways to integrate appreciation and respect for students' diversity into regular curriculum offerings, instructional strategies, and expectations or to benefit from the insights, perspectives, and cultural knowledge that these new student populations possess. (24)

The unfortunate result of such disregard for these students ranges from fear to alienation, hostility, anxiety, and withdrawal (25). An examination of most universities' retention rates underscores the need for change as well as the negative effects of traditional pedagogy on these students' perceptions of self-efficacy.

Perceptions of self-efficacy help to determine how students behave, think, and react in stressful situations. For example, students with a poor sense of self-efficacy will avoid tasks and situations they believe exceed their capabilities and attempt only activities they believe they can handle. Obviously, these beliefs impact opportunities for growth. Depending on the individual, self-perception can affect effort and persistence as well as reactions to setbacks. Individuals with low perceptions of self-efficacy dwell on what they consider deficiencies and create distress that in turn undermines their ability to function and cope. These people will attribute failure to their own lack of ability, whereas individuals with higher self-perceptions will attribute failure merely to insufficient effort and try harder.

How does this relate to undergraduates' learning? Context and incentive can help or hinder students' execution of skills and thus affect their feelings of self-efficacy. Within the classroom or learning context, students need task information and performance feedback for incentive. Students learn best through what Bandura calls "enactive attainment," or direct mastery experience—in other words, they learn best by doing, by being engaged with a task, and by receiving immediate feedback on their performance. Among learners with lower levels of self-efficacy, modeling the tasks or skills they are expected to learn increases their feelings of capability. Once students receive feedback, they can begin to apply this knowledge and the resulting feelings of success or mastery to other, related activities. In sum, modeling, participation, and positive feedback appear to be the keys to individuals' cognitive and psychological development, whereas passive uninvolvement may contribute to a failure to learn (Bandura 399–400).

At first glance, Bandura's theories might seem primarily related to the needs of undergraduates; however, the theory of self-efficacy also provides a sound rationale for changing the way we teach graduate students. For most students, learning is reflected in their grades. Graduate students are accustomed to earning good grades, for that was one criterion for admission to graduate school. Their sense of self-efficacy varies by gender and context, but in general, they believe that if they study hard enough, they will continue to earn good grades. However, when graduate students find themselves in a pedagogy seminar, their context and incentive for learning may change. Instead of reading and memorizing to participate in discussion and write the traditional term paper, they may be expected to apply what they have learned by teaching, writing about teaching, or reflecting on their philosophy of education. This context brings into question their perceived self-efficacy, for very few graduate students have taught before, and most are unaccustomed to writing reflectively. They can study, they can write the objective academic paper, but they have little experience literally enacting their knowledge. Moreover, most graduate students have rarely paid attention to teaching or been aware of its effects; they have merely achieved. Consequently, when asked to contemplate the subject or engage in teaching, their sense of self-efficacy will most likely be called into question.

Those students whose general perception of their efficacy is strong will try to master these concepts, but this holds true only if they perceive the concepts as worth mastering, if they perceive the instructor as knowledgeable, or if they can relate in some way to their instructor (Bandura 405–6). In other words, graduate students will try to master teaching strategies if they—and their professor—believe teaching is important. Even if these factors are present, and students believe themselves capable of mastering these new concepts, they will not learn to teach if "necessary subskills for the exercise of personal agency are completely lacking. . . . Nor will perceived self-efficacy be expressed in corresponding action if people lack the necessary equipment or resources to perform the behavior adequately" (Bandura 95). Nevertheless, in such situations, graduate students' perceptions of their efficacy often exceed the reality (Bandura 396). This is not the students' fault but their professors'. By failing to model good teaching, to engage students in mastery activities, or to provide opportunities for reflection and feedback, faculty may be hindering their graduate students' development as future teachers.

The importance of these elements is explained by Bandura when he notes that if no feedback is received, if it is received only occasionally, or if there are no consequences for failing to learn (as evidenced in a pass/fail grade or no-credit practicum), graduate students—like their undergraduate counterparts—have little or no incentive to learn (396). The value of feedback is affected by "temporal disparities." Immediate feedback carries much more weight and influences self-efficacy more accurately than delayed or dated responses. In sum, occasional feedback, or as is more often the case in the graduate classroom, end-of-semester feedback, will have little effect on a TA's learning or sense of self-efficacy.

Feedback is also influenced by the "potency of intervening experiences." Graduate students need ongoing engagement to instill in them both the concepts and the importance of what they are learning about teaching (396). Engagement is essential to learning, especially learning to teach, because without close examination, teaching might appear fairly easy. For many graduate students, teaching connotes lecturing or asking discussion questions. Because their primary experiences occur as participants in graduate seminars where their peers are similarly motivated and prepared, teaching may not seem very complex. So, unless they read about pedagogy and practice it, the various components will remain undefined, resulting in students "underestimating the task demands [which] produces errors in the direction of overassurance" (Bandura 397).

Anyone who has ever tried to generate discussion in an undergraduate classroom is well aware of the complexity of engaging students; however, graduate students who have eagerly participated in discussion or actively taken notes during lecture rarely consider what teaching entails. For these reasons, pedagogy seminars that engage graduate students in subskills such as forming small groups, designing group activities, or determining how to make each group accountable are essential to the development of a judicious sense of self-efficacy. To generate these feelings about teaching, TAs need to be consistently engaged in mastery activities and receive feedback on their performance (Bandura 425). Without engagement and feedback, graduate students lacking strong self-efficacy, like students of any age, may perceive themselves as ineffective teachers and avoid trying new strategies or even avoid teaching altogether. But participation in a variety of activities—ranging from the vicarious (wherein they observe their professor model teaching strategies) through cognitive (in which they read pedagogical theory, generate teaching assignments, and share them with their peers) to enactive (when they actually engage in micro-teaching)—provides the types of experiences that can lead to a positive sense of self-efficacy. Of these three activities, "enactive mastery produces the highest, strongest, and most generalized increases" in efficacy—if students believe they can do it. If not, then "self-perceived learning efficacy will determine how much effort they put forth" (Bandura 427).

Without such experiences, TAs may begin to perceive composition pedagogy as too difficult and revert to lecture to retain control. Bandura notes that "to the extent people believe they can prevent, terminate, or lessen the severity of aversive events, they have little reason to be perturbed by them" (440). Perceived control is the key to retaining feelings of self-efficacy. Like the seasoned professor who shudders at the thought of teaching composition, such feelings help to explain why inexperienced graduate students might not feel compelled to master new teaching techniques that threaten their feelings of authority, self-control, and self-efficacy. These feelings can in turn affect the learning environment they create in the classroom.

As a rule, TAs will be teaching undergraduates who are unlike themselves. Although TAs without a knowledge of pedagogy will be able to identify with and support their motivated students, new TAs may inadvertently undermine the self-efficacy of those undergraduates who are unmotivated or unprepared (Bandura 416). If TAs believe they can help their students learn, they will spend more time with learning activities, help students who fall behind, and praise them when they succeed. Conversely, those teachers lacking a sense of efficacy will "spend more time on nonacademic pastimes, readily give up on students if they do not get results, and [be] prone to criticize" (431). Traditional teaching practices, such as lecture and testing, negatively affect undergraduates' perceptions of their self-efficacy. However, classes using group work and individualized instruction—what Bandura refers to as a "personalized classroom structure"—have been shown to develop a stronger sense of self-efficacy among at-risk students (417).

Students develop the ability to determine their self-efficacy through active engagement, introspection, and comparison with their peers. In most graduate seminars, opportunities for engagement and introspection are generally absent; therefore, comparison with others (usually via grades) remains the primary source of graduate students' self-knowledge regarding their ability to learn. When these comparisons are the only source, graduate students may develop a faulty sense of their abilities as well as misperceptions about themselves and their knowledge, for such appraisals require self-knowledge as well as a fairly complex knowledge of those being compared (Bandura 420). As a result, poorly prepared TAs may not only unwittingly produce a classroom of underachieving students; they may also blame the students for their failure to learn. Faculty can reverse this problem if they are willing to take the time to change the way they teach. Ultimately, good teaching requires more than a knowledge of the subject, the theory underlying it, or effective pedagogy. Good teachers also need a strong sense of self-efficacy to put forth the effort necessary for success in the classroom.

Although the foregoing discussion represents a simplified overview, research in social-cognitive psychology provides theory-based explanations as to why students at any level need more than one passive approach in the classroom to promote and facilitate learning. In *Writing and the Writer*, Smith reiterates the universality of this approach. Smith maintains that three constituents "determine what is learned, when it is learned, and whether indeed learning will take place at all" (190). The first is *demonstration*: Learners must be shown how to do it. The second condition is *engagement*: Learners must be engaged in an activity to understand how it works. Finally, there must be *sensitivity,* which Smith defines as "the absence of any expectation that learning will not take place, or that it will be difficult" (193). Given these definitions, it follows that a fourth element is *context*. Learning does not easily occur individually or in isolation. Smith, like other social constructivists, argues that learning is "a social event." We learn from others whether they are demonstrating a skill, engaging us in a relevant learning activity, or establishing an environment in which learning seems natural and easy. Conversely, learning can be incredibly difficult if students are not shown how something works, if they are not expected and encouraged to try it, or if they believe they will not be able to do it. In sum, Smith's constituents closely parallel the elements Bandura argues are necessary for the development of self-efficacy.

EDUCATIONAL PSYCHOLOGY AND COMPOSITION THEORY

Educational psychologists have developed pedagogical strategies that enact these theories: active learning and engagement in student-centered classrooms. Deborah Hatch and Christine Farris define active learning as including "writing tasks, speaking activities, small-group activities, case study method of instruction, simulations, role plays, and field studies" (89). Students might use writing, for example, to take notes, jot down ideas on paper, reflect on the day's reading or lecture, or define concepts. Armed with their ideas and interpretations, the students would bring with them a focus for discussion within small groups (95). Following these discussions, the small groups could synthesize and present their ideas to the class, where they would in turn hear ideas generated by the other groups. These activities engage students in learning. These approaches are now considered integral to the definition of a good teacher, described by Ernest Boyer as including integrity, subject knowledge, and the ability to relate knowledge to students' lives through active learning (8).

Unfortunately, these strategies are also those ridiculed by traditional faculty who maintain that the strategies are inappropriate for students at the university level because they "dumb down" education. Nothing could be further from the truth. Certainly active learning is diametrically opposed to the traditional passive form of instruction. In the student-centered classroom, instructors do not lecture; they design in-class activities that encourage cooperation, collaboration, and creativity (Boyer 11). In this environment, students can no longer sit passively or get by without reading, comprehending the material, or attending class. They must come to class prepared to engage in learning, to consciously link prior knowledge with new ideas in order to solve problems posed to them by their professors.

John Bean's *Engaging Ideas* exemplifies the value of active learning. In the book's preface, Bean reminds the reader that these philosophies proceed from the work of John Dewey, who argued that "critical thinking—and indeed all significant learning—originates in the learner's engagement with problems" (xi). Such engagement occurs when reading is linked with appropriate writing assignments. Bean summarizes this approach:

Exploratory writing, focusing on the process rather than the product of thinking, deepens most students' engagement with course material while enhancing learning and developing critical thinking. Most teachers who try exploratory writing in their courses testify that they would never go back to their
old way of teaching. The payoff . . . is students' enhanced preparation for
class, richer class discussions, and better final-product writing, [which in turn
helps] students become more active and engaged learners. (118)

Bean acknowledges that the use of exploratory, reflective, or expressive
writing has been criticized by academics as inappropriate at the postsecondary level. However, recent research supports the value and necessity
of these types of writing. In *Readings and Feelings*, David Bleich illustrates
the application of reader response theory and social constructivism to the
composition classroom. According to Bleich, an individual's natural response to reading is affective, yet emotional responses are generally considered inappropriate in the classroom. In keeping with the emphasis on
the teaching of literature as the transmission of knowledge from teacher
to student, responses are expected to be critical (or New Critical) rather
than personal. Bleich maintains that by writing about their personal
response to literature, students not only better comprehend the material but also better relate to it. This understanding as well as the reasons
for it is further enhanced by allowing students to read each other's responses and analyze the language features contained therein.[1] By working together in permanent groups, reading each other's responses, and
receiving feedback from their peers, over the course of the semester students develop an understanding of their own language as well as an appreciation of the literature to which they respond. Through case-study
analyses of his students' work, Bleich demonstrates the effects of reflective writing and its applicability, if not transference, to the students'
ability to write and reason analytically.

Whereas *Readings and Feelings* explained the pedagogical application
of Bleich's theory, *Subjective Criticism* detailed the theoretical rationale.
In his subsequent books, *The Double Perspective* and *Know and Tell*, Bleich
expands this discussion to analyze the effects of reflective writing and peer
response on students' constructions of race, gender, and class. He illustrates the efficacy of his approach by drawing again on the writings of
the students who participated in this type of writing and group work
during his seminars. Bleich's work lends credence to the arguments of

social constructivists such as Kenneth Bruffee and John Trimbur regarding the value and necessity of group work, also known as active or collaborative learning, in the classroom. Equally important, in *Know and Tell*, Bleich argues persuasively for the use of these pedagogical approaches for undergraduates and graduate students alike. Although his research is persuasive theoretically, his use of case studies illustrates how group work can be organized and demonstrates how it benefits students regardless of gender, race, class, or age.

These approaches echo those advocated by Paulo Freire and his disciple Ira Shor, who refers to such teaching as *Empowering Education*. Shor explains that the purpose of active learning is not to disseminate knowledge but to empower students by encouraging dialogue between teacher and student and between the students themselves (14–15). This way of teaching does not condone anarchy; on the contrary, "Students in empowering classes should be expected to develop skills and knowledge as well as high expectations for themselves, their education, and their futures" (16). This context is established by instructors who use their knowledge of constructivist pedagogy to shape the classroom environment via activities promoting engagement.

If TAs are going to meet the needs of their nontraditional and multicultural students, they will need to know how and why to develop active learning activities. Teaching involving such interaction "dramatically reduced the impact of students' abilities upon entry and enabled all students to learn at a high level" (Gardiner 97). Again, because the majority of the professoriate lack the theoretical grounding supporting this pedagogy, they tend to avoid it. Some might agree it's appropriate for undergraduates, but most faculty dismiss it out of hand at the graduate level. However, it is equally effective—and important—for graduate students.

One of the few studies illustrating these effects is Jennifer G. Haworth and Clifton F. Conrad's *Emblems of Quality in Higher Education*. Analyzing characteristics gleaned from an examination of forty-seven exemplary master's programs across the United States, these researchers concluded that interactive teaching and learning constituted the most successful approach for graduate students. This approach consists of five elements:

- critical dialogue: Students are encouraged to share ideas, opinions, and experiences. Teachers use large and small groups, role-playing, and student-led seminars; dialogue and reflection; thinking instead of regurgitation. As a result, "students become more holistic, critical, and discriminatory thinkers . . . [and] more self-assured and creative problem-solvers" (84–89).
- integrative learning: Teachers integrate theory with practice and self with subject by introducing real-world situations, simulations, and hands-on activities in the classroom. They reinforce the value of this approach by modeling how they integrated theory with practice and by sharing professional experiences. Such an approach results in students taking classroom learning and applying it in their lives and their practices (90–98).
- mentoring: Faculty are aware of their students' career choices and focus courses and course work accordingly. They periodically work one-to-one with students and provide feedback on the development of their professional skills (99). Mentoring also includes student advising, open office hours, and visiting students' classes and labs. The effects are evident in students' high levels of self-confidence and strong feelings of competence, both of which helped them advance in their chosen careers (104).
- cooperative peer learning: Students participate in study groups, research teams, group projects, and group presentations. The faculty models such behaviors by team-teaching and collaborating on research to illustrate its value. As a result, students learn how to work with others, delegate and negotiate responsibility, deal with conflict, communicate, and listen—all of which further develop confidence and competence (110).
- out-of-class activities: Brown-bag colloquia seminars and raise students' awareness and appreciation for collaborative learning (36).

Overall, graduate students in programs using these approaches appreciated and respected a "collaborative approach to inquiry, problem-solving and leadership," which in turn improved communication and teamwork abilities (75). Such approaches moved students out of the mind-set of the solitary learner and encouraged them to take risks. Risk-taking was promoted by the faculty, who gave students the opportunity to discuss, challenge, explore, and experiment in environments free from competition, ridicule, or penalty (76). They further promoted risk-taking by modeling such behavior themselves and sharing their experiences with their students (78). Consequently, graduates of these programs were not only more "competent and self assured" but also "more imaginative and resourceful professionals," thus making them more marketable and eventually successful in their careers (81). Key to this development was treating students as colleagues and enabling them to participate in the construction of knowledge (Haworth and Conrad 70).

ACTIVE LEARNING IN THE GRADUATE SEMINAR

As Wendy Bishop has detailed in *Something Old, Something New*, there are a variety of opinions within departments of English about how best to prepare TAs (xiv–xv). Some believe in a specific approach while others advocate eclecticism so that graduate students can determine for themselves which philosophy best suits their personalities and beliefs. Perhaps more important than what is taught is *how* TAs are taught, for modeling these approaches provides concrete illustrations of how they work while dispelling any misconceptions TAs may have developed. Indeed, in her contribution to *The Future of Doctoral Studies in English*, Nancy Comley argues that modeling by experienced professors is absolutely essential to "impart their respect for teaching as an art" (45).

In their research on teaching and learning, Jo Sprague and Jody Nyquist argue for a developmental model of TA training that moves from "direct instruction in basic skills followed by opportunities to practice the skills in increasingly challenging and diverse settings" (298). Their goal in TA training is to develop professionals who "draw on knowledge-in-action rather than simple mechanical rules. They operate holistically, seek patterns, and tolerate considerable ambiguity while discovering novel solutions to novel problems" (300). Such behavior requires the development of self-reflection as well as relationships with role models and mentors. Sprague and Nyquist maintain that the result of this process is "an extremely complex and dynamic phenomenon. . . . People who have acquired competence or become master professionals are changed in the ways they think and even in who they are" (304). Like their undergraduate counterparts, TAs develop not through "traditional instructional methods" but through "unconscious and holistic performance"

(304–5). In sum, developing TAs into professionals requires a movement from orientation to an emphasis on teaching skills to a "reflective practicum" (309–10).

To put these theories into practice, Bishop suggests that participatory TA seminars be developed that include, among other things, response journals, peer groups, and examination of writing processes (*Something* 134). This approach has been supported by numerous researchers who have suggested that for TAs to develop an awareness of themselves as professionals, they need to practice self-reflection. Donald Schon, author of *The Reflective Practitioner*, maintains that teachers who reflect on their actions are better able to adapt and adjust. Similarly, Bishop believes that reflective teaching logs provide the "major focus points of learning for most teachers" as well as safe sites for questioning, responding to teaching, and expressing fears (17–18). This is not to suggest that teaching logs become the academic version of a personal diary. Because TAs are usually inexperienced teachers, guided reflection can help to focus their entries. Teaching-log entries might include reflections on readings, peer visits and consultations, one's successes and failures as a teacher, or observations by one's supervisor or mentor. These reflections should not exist in a vacuum. Because TAs are novice teachers (and to model optimal use of journals), faculty should respond to them weekly so TAs can learn from and apply their professors' feedback.

Of course, TAs cannot rely on reflection alone to guide their teaching. They also need information about teaching, guided practice, and teaching experience. Schon suggests that those responsible for the professional development of graduate students should help them to "practice reflective teaching in the context of the doing" (qtd. in Allen 314). To engage TAs in these types of activities requires the development of what Kathleen M. Galvin terms an "interactive learning community" that proceeds from the following assumptions: that students learn about themselves and the course content by exchanging ideas with their peers, that students have knowledge to contribute to discussions, that teacher and students learn best in a de-centered classroom, and that teachers need to learn these skills, for they are not inborn (263). In other words, TAs need the same pedagogical context as undergraduates.

Galvin argues that this context should be established from the first day of the TA seminar (266). Once a general level of comfort is attained, TAs can be engaged in active learning such as brainstorming sessions or problem-solving within small groups—activities necessary to help them reconceptualize teaching, especially the teaching of writing, and discover how to help their students become "mutually responsible for learning" (McKeachie 230). TAs will not learn how to design small groups, to make group members accountable, or to anticipate and address group members' concerns by listening to a lecture about collaborative learning; they must be involved both within group work and in the design of collaborative activities. Such engagement will lead to higher "involvement and affiliation," which in turn lead to a willingness to take risks, better communication skills, and "internalization of content" (Galvin 266).

When graduate students are asked to work together in small groups—an activity they are unaccustomed to and/or skeptical of (Galvin 264)—they will need clear-cut reasons and concrete results for doing so. Bishop reports that often group work is omitted by professors because it is too time-consuming; consequently, it is dismissed by graduate students as "fake or nonproductive" because they have no way to judge its effectiveness (*Something* 17). But if these students are being asked to write during their theory and pedagogy seminars, then the logical activity for group work is to read and respond to each other's drafts. Because TAs need to learn how to establish small groups and design substantive activities, it follows that after the instructor has modeled the process one or two times, TAs should take on the responsibility—in consultation and with feedback from the instructor—in subsequent class sessions. Unless they are engaged in these activities, most graduate students will not become aware of what they think about teaching and will continue to teach as they were taught.[2]

Just as opinions are mixed as to how TAs should be trained, so, too, are the opinions as to what they should write. There is one point of agreement. Researchers agree that unless TAs write, write often, and write in modes replicating what they ask their students to do, they will be unable to empathize with them (Bishop, *Teaching* 107). Many faculty resist this focus. In her study of graduate students' writing, Patricia A. Sullivan found that most professors of literature assume that their students already know how to write. Consequently, only a minority of faculty discusses or assigns specific paper topics or provides instruction on how to conduct research or develop an argument, and even fewer ask for drafts or provide students with the opportunity to share their writing with their peers ("Writing" 286). When asked about their attitudes, these professors "explicitly stated that such processes cannot or ought not be taught because discussion of the writing task would mean intervening in the writing process either in superfluous or counter-productive ways [such as] inhibit[ing] students' creativity" (294).

Despite their beliefs that graduate students already know how to write and hence need no instruction, Sullivan learned that the writing the students produced "was not valued for what it contributed to the course and to other students' understanding of the issues. Rather, it was valued primarily for its evaluative properties as an academic exercise, as a basis for a grade" (287). Similarly, Ruth Ray reports in *The Practice of Theory* that graduate students are usually expected to demonstrate an understanding of their subject by "showing in their writing that they can frame ideas in terms of established theory and can say how their own thinking supports, refutes, or extends this theory. *How* students learn to write papers of this type is not of particular interest" (146, emphasis added).

The problem with this attitude is twofold: It continues the traditional emphasis on receiving rather than constructing knowledge, and it relieves faculty of the responsibility of teaching the requisite skills (Ray 147). Such attitudes lead to a number of self-perpetuating problems. First, if graduate students' writing is found deficient, they are blamed rather than the institution (or faculty) that failed to prepare them (Sullivan, "Writing" 288). Second, as Ray found, these students tend to leave their graduate seminars without an understanding of the intrinsic value of research to themselves as writers or as future professionals. This mind-set leads to a third problem: Graduate students may devalue writing not only for themselves but also for their present or future students. As a result, TAs will either teach as they were taught and blame students for their writing problems (attributing to them a similar personal deficiency), or they will continue to pass on the misperception that composing is a private, individual process not to be interfered with for fear of quashing creativity. Either way, they will be unable to help their students learn to write or to view writing as a mode of learning.

Within graduate composition practica and seminars, writing assignments vary greatly. In her survey of doctoral programs in composition-rhetoric, Catherine Latterell found that in TA practica, evaluations are based primarily on the students' written reflections in a teaching note-book; in teaching-methods courses, the most common type of writing appears to be assignments that mimic those done in freshman composi-tion; and in theory seminars, short-response papers and a research pa-per are usually the bases for evaluation, although "a statement of teach-ing philosophy" is the most-often assigned paper (17). In short, the modes and frequency of writing differ according to what is deemed the course's level of difficulty. Thus, the range of TAs' writing experiences depends on the types of preparatory courses they elect or (less often) are required to take. Some professors, such as Bishop, appear to advocate that TAs write the same assignments their students do, although she seems to assume the TAs will write *with* their students rather than in a graduate seminar. But if TAs are writing to learn about their teaching and their writing (and in the process, about themselves) and if they are to respect these assignments enough to engage in them, they need to be at a sig-nificantly higher level than what is expected of freshmen.

In *Bitter Milk*, Madeleine R. Grumet describes one such assignment. First, the students are asked to write "three narratives of events or mo-ments in their lives that they associated with the phrase 'educational experience.'" To conclude the essay, they are to move beyond "what hap-pened" to "what it means to me" (66). This type of narrative allows the use of the personal voice and autobiographical knowledge but then asks the students to make a cognitive leap to trace the threads running throughout and analyze their import, a task more equal to the talents of graduate students. This assignment and the metacognitive process it entails help to broaden the students' conceptions of teaching, learning, and education while it encourages them to reflect about how to foster a positive learning environment.

Graduate students gain even more insight into teaching and learning by conducting action research, an approach that clearly differentiates the graduate composition seminar from other means of TA training—and is exemplified in this study. Thomas A. Angelo and K. Patricia Cross, cofounders of the University of California–Berkeley Classroom Research Project, define action research as "a learner-centered, teacher-directed approach to improving the effectiveness of higher education where it matters—in the college classroom" (101). This approach is particularly useful for new TAs, for it provides them with the opportunity to investigate a pedagogy they have seldom experienced. For example, skeptical TAs who want to disprove the value of group work, journal writing, or drafting are given the opportunity—and taught the methodology—to follow their students' progress across the semester to determine the influence of a pedagogical approach.

This methodology, which Ruth Ray terms *teacher research* in *The Practice of Theory*, helps develop a sense of professionalism as graduate students begin to learn a new research methodology while gaining a deeper understanding of what occurs in the classroom and why it succeeds or fails (72, 80). Action research employs many of the methodologies of ethnographic research: It is relatively long-term, in-depth, and naturalistic; it is qualitative rather than quantitative; and it constructs knowledge rather than reporting it. As such, it is recursive rather than linear, moving from initial hypotheses to examination and reconceptualization of the problem as the research proceeds. These examinations involve reflection fostered through analyses of the researcher's descriptive field notes and followed by analytical or descriptive writing. To facilitate reflection, faculty can require their graduate students to keep research logs in which they describe, speculate, reflect, and trace the development of hypotheses and conclusions.[3] In sum, a research log provides the scholarly rationale for the reflective writing called for by Schon and others to aid in professional development.

By including action research in TA training, faculty bring naturalistic assessment into the classroom, integrate teaching and research, and encourage innovation and assessment of its effects (Angelo and Cross 102). Action research focuses on the students' learning, thus determining teacher effectiveness and requiring personal initiative (106). It simultaneously engages graduate students in teaching, reflecting, researching, and writing—all the skills they will need as professionals—while also demonstrating the intellectual complexity of teaching and the integral relationship between teaching and research. Indeed, as the following case-study chapters demonstrate, engaging graduate students in action research may be the most effective means of addressing and overcoming their resistance to pedagogy.

LINKING THEORY TO PEDAGOGY

This overview describes the theories underlying the pedagogy called for in critiques of higher education and enacted in undergraduate writing classrooms where the process movement has been adopted. These same theories underlie the pedagogy found to best prepare graduate students for their professional careers, because learning theory is applicable at any level. When instructors link reading with writing assignments, they are applying psycholinguistics and schema theory when they establish a classroom atmosphere in which students feel comfortable offering their opinions and taking risks, when they design assignments drawing on students' interests and prior knowledge, when they engage students in activities requiring them to interpret or classify information, find relationships, or use feedback, the instructors are drawing on Sternberg's triarchic theory of intelligence. When they assign response journals or experiential essays, they are developing three of Gardner's seven areas of multiple intelligence—linguistic, intrapersonal, and interpersonal. And when they ask students to work together solving problems in small groups, they are developing Gardner's category of interpersonal development while applying social-constructivist theory.

These teaching methods most affect intellectual development among undergraduates, but they are equally effective among graduate students. This pedagogy incorporates at least four of the five elements Haworth and Conrad maintain are key to successful learning among graduate students: critical dialogue, integrative learning, mentoring, and cooperative peer learning. Moreover, these approaches promote feelings of self-efficacy which, as Bandura has noted, affect both motivation and behavior (91). In sum, theories drawn from cognitive, social-cognitive, and educational psychology underscore the parallels between undergraduate and graduate learners. Thus, it follows that if the process movement was adopted in the graduate seminar, graduate students could reap the benefits we know their undergraduate counterparts have experienced from the same approach.

Part Two

CASE STUDIES OF RESISTANCE AND CHANGE

4. Resisting Change

I have taught Teaching College Writing since 1988. Throughout, I've made a conscious effort to teach in such a way that my TAs would be able to apply what they were reading and understand the rationale for this approach. My teaching strategy is best defined by George Hillocks. In *Ways of Thinking, Ways of Teaching*, Hillocks argues that to fully engage students in learning, teachers should practice constructivist teaching:

> Teachers cannot simply tell their students what is to be learned and expect them to learn it. They suggest that students must themselves be active agents in their own learning, transforming what is to be learned through the screen of their own experience and existing understandings. They believe that to be successful, learners must construct or reconstruct, for themselves, what is to be learned. They adopt a constructivist stance toward teaching and learning. (93)

Because I believed constructivist teaching parallels composition pedagogy, I assumed my graduate students would accept it, but that was not the case. Over the course of this five-year study, 80 percent of my male students and 20 percent of the females initially resisted this pedagogy. Although the majority eventually overcame these feelings, a certain percentage could not. After studying these students' backgrounds and behaviors, I determined that the resistant few were unable to overcome their resistance because constructivist pedagogy contradicted their personal constructs and threatened their sense of self-efficacy. In this chapter, I explore the reasons behind and manifestations of their resistance. My purpose in doing so is fourfold: to help educators recognize this behavior, to understand what motivates it, to learn from my mistakes and also to suggest that some beliefs and behaviors are too deeply ingrained to change.

I begin by defining the terms and establishing the context in which the students' resistance occurred. In subsequent sections, I define and discuss the elements that must be satisfied if resistance is to be overcome: personal construct and self-efficacy. These concepts are illustrated by describing the graduate students' attitudes and behaviors and by allowing them, through their writing, to reveal the reasons behind their actions.

DEFINING RESISTANCE

In his study of *Theory and Resistance in Education*, Henry Giroux argues that students' responses to learning fall into one of three categories: accommodation, resistance, or opposition. Students who *accommodate* accept what they are taught. Students who *resist* refuse to learn because they see the classroom ideology as infringing upon their personal beliefs. In contrast, students who are *oppositional* fail to learn because they refuse to "engage in behavior that would enable them to learn" (Chase 15). Giroux views these concepts as political; consequently, he seems to dismiss those students who accommodate as submitting to the "dominant ideology" whereas those who resist have a "revealing function, one that contains a critique of domination and provides theoretical opportunities for self-reflection and for struggle in the interest of self-emancipation and social emancipation" (108–9). This view of resistance depends upon how the dominant ideology is defined. Giroux equates it with objectivist pedagogy, one-way teaching that does not take into account the students' ideas, interests, or beliefs. However, when the so-called dominant ideology is constructivist, resistance takes on a different meaning.

Although Ira Shor is usually associated with the political ideology espoused by Giroux and Paulo Freire, his definition and examples of resistance are less narrowly political. For Shor, resistance can take a variety of forms and behaviors. Two of the most common are "playing dumb" and "getting by." Students pretend to be dumb when they "ask the same questions again and again; they ask for instructions to be repeated; they miss assignments and deadlines; they do the second thing first and the first thing second, like reading next week's chapter this week." Students will play dumb to waste time, subvert the focus of the class, or undermine the teacher's authority. Their behavior may be conscious or merely "a reflexive resistance to authority." As a result of playing dumb, students "get by" by doing as little of the assigned work as possible. Sometimes, they drift through the semester and then work hard at the end in the hopes that their teacher will grade on improvement. But when they begin to work, their writing may take on the words and values of the teacher, a strategy much easier than trying to understand concepts (138). According to Shor, "Many students who copy teacher-talk and mimic teacherly values appear to do what's expected of them while actually memorizing the least necessary information, using it in the least demanding way, and forgetting it soon" (139).

Such behavior is generally learned as a way to resist authority and express contempt for an educational system whose traditional approaches ignore the students' needs and interests. Because they have internalized this behavior, however, students may display it in both objectivist and constructivist classrooms. Theoretically, a constructivist classroom would defuse these behaviors by focusing instruction around the students' interests and experiences, yet this pedagogical approach might also raise the resistance level of students used to "getting by." They would find it difficult to succeed if their performance was evaluated on the basis of their ability to engage in and work at student-centered activities such as participation in group activities and preparation of end-of-term portfolios (Shor 144). A de-centered classroom might also incite resistance if students perceived it as imposing what Shor terms an "alien culture" (139). And to a certain percentage of graduate students, reflective practice, writing-as-a-process, and collaborative learning were indeed alien.

These students were a paradox. Sometimes, they appeared to accept what and how I was teaching, but at other times, they resisted. Recognizing and understanding the reasons for their resistance was a challenge, for their stance contradicted my own beliefs about teaching and learning. On a professional level, I tried to address their concerns and clarify what I perceived as their misunderstandings, but on a personal level, my feelings ranged from empathy to annoyance. These feelings helped to formulate my initial research questions. What differentiated resisting students from their peers? What factors influenced their feelings? Why did some students resist and others accommodate what was being taught? Were the other students really learning, or were they merely getting by? As I began to analyze the data, I took into account researchers' admonitions to consider the students' race, gender, personality, and reasons for refusal. I also remained cognizant of how these factors influenced the way I conducted fieldwork and interpreted the results. Most importantly, throughout this process, I engaged in ongoing reflection, which helped me to discern how my own attitudes and behaviors may have contributed to the students' feelings and behavior.

THE CONTEXT

Like 90 percent of the students in this study, those discussed in this chapter took Teaching College Writing with me. Required of all new TAs and open to others interested in teaching, this three-hour graduate seminar meets once a week during Fall semester. Although the readings have varied and been updated over the years, I have consistently intermixed theory and pedagogy. Because the readings are generally unfamiliar (and sometimes unsettling) to the students, I assign a weekly response journal to provide a site where they can reflect on both the theory and the pedagogical applications. Similarly, because the majority of the class is teaching and/or applying these new principles for the first time, I also assign a weekly teaching log.

Although I originally conceived of this approach as a way to provide consistent feedback and support to my novice TAs, this practice is supported by research on the role of reflection in learning.[1] Among these researchers, Donald Schon is perhaps the most familiar. Schon argues that experienced professionals "often reveal a capacity for reflection on their intuitive knowing in the midst of action and sometimes use this capacity to cope with the unique, uncertain, and conflicted situations of practice" (viii–ix). This ability is no less intellectually rigorous than that entailed in scholarly research; thus, it follows that the ability to reflect on one's professional actions does not occur naturally. Indeed, the objectivist epistemological stance upon which the university is based tends to dismiss if not ignore the existence and potential of reflection.

By enrolling in a pedagogy course concurrently with their first semester of teaching, new TAs have the opportunity to reflect in their logs after each day of teaching. These logs provide new teachers with the opportunity to function also as students. Instead of berating themselves or coasting along blithely unaware, instead of rigidly adhering to a single approach or rejecting one that initially failed, TAs can use this log to describe their daily teaching, compare it to what they are reading, and raise questions along the way. Each week, I ask my students to turn in their logs; the following week (or sooner), I return them with my feedback and response to establish an ongoing dialogue about their classroom practices.

Because I want the students to reflect on their reading and teaching, I ask them to freewrite. Many graduate students are not easily persuaded that freewriting is acceptable, let alone possible. Most of them are more comfortable writing academic prose, and among those who are not, many still believe that is what's expected. To put their minds at ease, I distribute an entry written by a former student, and we discuss its form and style; then I hand out a freewrite I have written in which I introduce myself to the class. After reading this, the students can see that freewriting is informal, sometimes stream-of-consciousness writing bearing the author's distinctive voice (Elbow and Belanoff 12–13). At the same time, they see that I am willing to share my writing, imperfections and all, and that I expect them to do so with me. Then I have the students freewrite on the topic of their first essay—learning experiences—and we compare responses to gain a larger sense of what the topic might include. Through this process, I try to establish an atmosphere of openness and trust while modeling constructivist—and composition—pedagogy. By engaging my graduate students in freewriting, I hope they will come to understand how it works and apply it in their own classrooms.

In addition to requiring weekly logs, I ask my students to design and teach assignments. Throughout the semester, each student is responsible for teaching thirty to forty-five minutes of class and for developing reading-writing assignments and collaborative learning exercises that they exchange with their peers and practice in class. Again, I model these processes and collaborate with the students when they ask for suggestions on how or what to teach. Because the students also have to compose three essays ranging from extended narrative to analysis to research, I use these assignments as occasions to model the pedagogy they might use to teach similar papers in their own classes. For each essay, I ask the students to bring first and second drafts and to workshop them in small groups; therefore, most of the students' practice teaching revolves around these assignments. For example, they might design group activities that help their peers generate ideas, conceptualize an essay's structure or develop a questionnaire to guide peer response. At the end of the semester, I ask the students to turn in a final portfolio—everything they have written—which becomes the basis for the seminar grade. This approach simultaneously models how to use portfolios, frees students from the pressure of writing for a grade, and reinforces the value and necessity of revision.

Two of the four students discussed in this chapter (as well as some in subsequent chapters) also took my seminar in reader-response theory. My purpose in this second seminar paralleled that of the first—to introduce theory and relevant pedagogy and to engage the graduate students in teaching and writing activities so they could apply what they were learning in their own classrooms. In addition to journals, writing assignments included midterm and final essays in which the students analyzed their use of language to develop an understanding of how it reveals their attitudes, beliefs, and personalities. To aid in these analyses, students worked in permanent groups of three, which met each week to read, respond to, and analyze their peers' journals and freewrites using David Bleich's categories of language features introduced in *Readings and Feelings*—such as, preferred topics, expressions of feeling, essay structure, or syntax—an approach that demonstrates how language is developed within discourse communities.

The graduate students discussed in this chapter—Mary Jo, Barbara, Melva, and Bob—were approximately forty years old and married with children. Mary Jo and Barbara were TAs, Bob was a high school English teacher, and Melva was an administrator in the university's College of Education. Mary Jo and Barbara had decided to earn their master's degrees so they could teach at the postsecondary level. Bob and Melva were established in their careers and working full time, yet neither seemed particularly happy in their work, leading me to believe that entering graduate school represented a readiness for change. But change is risky, especially as one grows older. Perhaps none of these students had considered that the knowledge and experience they gained in graduate school might disrupt their professional lives and upset their self-images. As educational theorist C. T. P. Diamond found, "Seeking change is itself an event of great significance. . . . If teachers do not come to believe that change is possible, their classroom renewal may be postponed. What we do not look for we may not find" (59).

THE RELATION OF RESISTANCE TO PERSONAL CONSTRUCT

According to educational psychologist Jeanne Ellis Ormrod, one's personal construct comprises prejudices, beliefs, and practices developed from the confluence of home environment, parental influence, interactions with peers, and educational history. This system of beliefs is a result of experiences, which in turn are colored by perceptions of those experiences. By the time students reach their college years, their personal construct is pretty well established. This system of beliefs can affect what and how students learn; in fact, it is so internalized that college students may ignore certain theories or pedagogies inconsistent with their personal construct. When this happens, it can disrupt classroom interaction and affect the students' subsequent learning (285). Teachers can sometimes facilitate conceptual change by discussing misconceptions at the beginning of the semester, convincing students that their conceptions are erroneous or motivating them to accept a new way of thinking (295). Research in educational psychology suggests this can be done most effectively by moving from traditional ways of teaching that impact individual construction of knowledge toward social-constructivist pedagogy.

When working with graduate students, faculty may help them reconceptualize their ideas about teaching and learning by de-centering the classroom, using collaborative learning activities, and providing opportunities for collaboration and reflection. Yet, as the case studies in this chapter reveal, even these efforts may fail if the students' personal constructs are exceptionally strong or if change represents too great a challenge to their beliefs.

Mary Jo: Daddy's Girl

When Mary Jo began Teaching College Writing, she seemed resistant to the theories she was encountering, for in her first response journal, she noted that after reading about de-centered classrooms and collaborative learning, her gut reaction was "No, I totally disagree!" Nevertheless, she ended that entry on a contemplative rather than a rebellious note, signing off with "Interesting."[2]

Mary Jo had grown up in the South, the eldest daughter in a traditionally patriarchal family. Her father made the rules while her mother alternated between apparent compliance and bouts of weeping to subvert his orders. Mary Jo adored her father, and he reciprocated those feelings. Because his sons had not lived up to his expectations, he raised Mary Jo like a boy, encouraging her academic successes and teaching her to stand up for herself. This affiliation was so strong that Mary Jo identified more with her father than her mother; consequently, Mary Jo found her mother's behavior demeaning and vowed to avoid such "feminine" excesses.[3] She tried to fulfill this vow and her father's plans for her by earning a bachelor's degree in political science, where she adopted the academic stance that reified individualism and learned the conventions of detached academic writing.

Raised by her father to be independent and outspoken, Mary Jo considered herself a feminist.[4] After graduating from college, she married and taught high school, but eschewing the role she had watched her mother fulfill, her marriage became a partnership between equals. She and her husband shared responsibilities for raising their son and maintaining their household; when she began graduate school, her husband took over all the household duties so Mary Jo would have time to complete her studies.[5] Taken altogether, these traits suggest that Mary Jo had developed a fairly liberal self-construct.

Barbara: The Antifeminist

Barbara seemed like Mary Jo's polar opposite. Married after high school, she stayed home to raise her children and postponed her college education until they were grown. Barbara completed her first two years of undergraduate work at a local community college. As an older, motivated, and well-read student, she consistently outperformed her younger, often less motivated classmates.[6] After receiving her associate's degree, Barbara finished her bachelor's degree, applied for a graduate teaching assistantship, and began working toward her master's. But graduate school was worlds away from the community college. In addition to teaching two sections of freshman composition and taking Teaching College Writing, Barbara also enrolled in feminist drama. This seemed an odd choice, because she announced on the first night of class that she was "a little bit antifeminist" because she believed the feminist movement disapproved of women who stayed home to care for their children.[7] This stance, which she repeated in various forms throughout the semester, suggests that Barbara's personal construct was fairly traditional.

Unlike Mary Jo, Barbara had majored in English as an undergraduate. "At last count," she bragged,

> I wrote over seventy essays as a college undergraduate, receiving A's on all of them and even winning an essay contest on one. Add to that the countless essay tests, journals, poems, and miscellaneous writing projects I've produced in school—well, let's just say I've done my share of writing.[8]

She was similarly explicit when reflecting on her first paper in Teaching College Writing, claiming, "I think I wrote a damned fine essay."[9] This veneer of confidence, however, quickly faded in the classroom. Like Mary

Jo, Barbara was quite outspoken, but whereas Mary Jo's comments were generally insightful and to the point, Barbara's were usually irrelevant or tangential. Although I attributed her constant interruptions to a desire for perfection, her questions became so frequent and unnecessary that by the end of our presemester TA workshop, I was ready to scream.

Barbara's behavior annoyed me and antagonized some of her classmates, yet she remained oblivious to their rolled eyes, and she ignored my requests to stay on the subject. I thought this behavior might cease when classes began, but it didn't. In practically every meeting of Teaching College Writing, I had to steer Barbara back to the topic, ask her to quit talking, and ignore or postpone answering an irrelevant question. I didn't realize it at the time, but Barbara's behavior paralleled that described by Shor as resisting authority by "playing dumb" to waste time, subvert authority, or change the focus of the class.

I found similar resistance when I observed Barbara's teaching. Although her constant questions in our graduate seminar suggested a desire to grasp every nuance of pedagogy, she was quite traditional in her own classroom. When her students failed to participate in discussions because they had not read the assignment, she began giving daily quizzes. This punitive strategy, which reinforces memorization rather than comprehension,[10] directly contradicted the composition pedagogy we read and discussed. When I discovered this strategy while observing her teaching, I advised Barbara to assign reading journals and to have the students discuss their work in groups so that class time would be spent in a manner more conducive to learning. When I raised this issue during our postobservation discussion, Barbara agreed to try it, but in her teaching log the following week, she said she'd decided I was wrong. She intended to continue the quizzes.[11]

Melva: The Activist

Melva's case had parallels with both Mary Jo's and Barbara's. Like Mary Jo, Melva believed in the epistemological and pedagogical soundness of composition pedagogy as well as its rhetorical appropriateness in the classroom. Melva's written voice also resembled Mary Jo's: Formal and detached, it contained few if any expressions of feeling. An education graduate, professional administrator, and grant writer, Melva had mastered the objective academic voice: "Student collaboration, coached by reflective practitioners in the absence of formalists' value judgments, may be exactly that to which this student of writing and English can commit." As a black educator, Melva was concerned with the need to reach out to alienated, marginalized students, a theme raised in her first journal entry and reiterated throughout the semester:

> This country can ill afford the hostility and alienation manifested currently by the violence of inner-city African-American and Hispanic youth. Largely turned off by the education establishment . . . these young people reject traditional values primarily because curriculum and pedagogy fail to be relevant to their lives.[12]

After teaching high school English, working as a curriculum coordinator, and directing programs in higher education over the course of twenty years,[13] Melva enrolled in Teaching College Writing to prepare herself to return to the classroom. She had decided to resume teaching in the secondary schools because she wanted to make a difference in students' lives, to empower them through the gift of language: "The reading for this course is helping me to confirm the rightness of my feeling that my answer lies somehow in the return to studying/teaching English. The process of discovering self/voice in writing is indeed a way to understand."[14]

Although Melva believed in the readings and their pedagogical application, she had difficulty applying them to her own writing. She reflected on her first essay, which lacked a consistent voice: "I knew that the personal, more emotionally connected narrative was very powerful, but I think I hesitated to give that much of myself to what I previously considered an objective, academic activity."[15] After spending twenty years mastering the formal voice, Melva, like many graduate students, was unaccustomed to using a personal voice and had difficulty seeing its relevance to her or in the graduate classroom. These conflicting beliefs—in the value of personal voice for high school students but of its irrelevance to graduate students—were issues she wrestled with throughout the semester.

Bob: Mr. Negative

In my field notes describing Bob's first night in Teaching College Writing, I wrote, "I'll bet he won't come back." I based these feelings on Bob's verbal and nonverbal behaviors, for he said little and looked bored. But to my surprise, he did return. Bob was my student for two semesters, following Teaching College Writing in the fall with Reader Response Theory in the winter.

A former pastor, Bob had been teaching high school English for eight years and seemingly hated every minute of it: "My typical student often can't begin to articulate what he wants to do in an assignment. . . . I don't think he's ready to explore yet because he doesn't have the skills necessary." High school students, he claimed, "simply aren't that introspective or interested." Although Bob admitted that his students appreciated class discussions of literature, he attributed their engagement to the fact that they felt good "even to be expected to have ideas in the first place," yet he believed they preferred to work on grammar because it was "easier in that it requires no creativity or self-exploration." Little of the theory and pedagogy we were reading would be applicable to his students, he said, because his classes were too large, and his students too slow.[16]

Bob's teaching style reflected his conservatism. To illustrate the theme of "Sinners in the Hands of an Angry God," he burned a spider in front of his high school English students. He said he taught writing as a process, but then admitted he "dumbed it down" by teaching the students to write five-paragraph themes. He disagreed with the idea of freewriting to discover one's focus, insisting that "a sixteen-year-old can't function within these parameters. He needs the security of some direction." He focused his grading wholly on error, then wondered why students spent so much time on the mechanical and ignored the "subjective." He said he could see the value of using journal writing, but his primary reason was disciplinary: It kept the students quiet while he took roll.[17]

As these comments suggest, Bob was a very traditional man. He always addressed me as "Mrs. Reagan" (my name at the time), even though I hold a doctorate, yet referred to his male professors as "Doctor." When citing examples of student behavior, he used the male pronoun. In his responses to the initial readings, which introduced constructivist pedagogy, Bob said he disliked the notion of students being free, even provoked, to question authority. Throughout that first semester, Bob and I carried on a running dialogue about the value of freedom and creativity in the classroom. I defended it while he steadfastly maintained that "there is nothing inherently good about questioning society's values . . . there is nothing inherently valuable about questioning and being creative."[18]

THE RELATIONSHIP BETWEEN RESISTANCE AND SELF-EFFICACY

An individual's personal construct is closely related to feelings of self-efficacy; the former leads to the latter. Feelings of self-efficacy are influenced by three factors: how individuals have behaved or performed in the past, how others behave toward them, and what others expect of them (Ormrod 100). In other words, both internal and external factors influence one's sense of competence. In her research on the relationship between teachers' motivation and feelings of self-efficacy, Patricia Ashton separates these factors into four contexts: the classroom; the relationships among the teacher's major settings—home, classroom, and school; the outside forces influencing these settings; and the teacher's cultural beliefs (145). Each factor can have positive or negative effects. Unlike personal constructs, which are internal and fairly stable, feelings of self-efficacy are context-specific. Student ability, class size, teachers' feelings of expertise, and definitions of their role all may impact their feeling about teaching (McLeod, "Pygmalion" 378). Among older students, the achievement and performance of peers are especially influential. Even though professors tend to hold the highest expectations for their graduate students, unless those expectations are clearly communicated, the achievements of peers may create even more pressure to excel. Conversely, if students do not possess a strong sense of self-efficacy, the achievements of others will reinforce their negative feelings (Bandura 420).

By the time they enter graduate school, students' perceptions of their self-efficacy are fairly stable and therefore "increasingly resistant to change" (Ormrod 103). Because of this stability, these students' performances will be consistent with what they believe they can achieve. Students with strong feelings of self-efficacy will look for positive feedback, whereas those with weaker feelings tend to look for affirmation of their negative beliefs. To improve these students' performances, instructors need to address their learning difficulties but in a manner that simultaneously conveys respect (Ormrod 102). To quote Albert Bandura, in order to achieve change, students need "modeling, guided performance, and self-directed mastery experiences" (qtd. in Ashton 164).

These concepts are seldom taught outside the educational psychology classroom; consequently, professors sometimes seem unaware of the influence of positive interactions with their students, regardless of their performance. However, as the following examples suggest, the relationships between students—even graduate students—and their peers and their professors can affect what and how they learn.

Mary Jo: In Control

Although Mary Jo had majored in political science as an undergraduate, teaching high school led her to focus on English in graduate school. Yet, because of her background, she felt at a disadvantage. These feelings were a recurring theme in her journal responses and appeared to color her view of herself and her abilities. She believed she was an overly slow writer, an "inadequate" reader, and an inexperienced teacher; she felt "somewhat intimidated" when collaborating with one of her classmates who was a TA and "humbled" after working with a secondary teacher who seemed "much more confident in her writing."[19]

These feelings appeared to affect Mary Jo's composing processes, for everything had to be done carefully and perfectly. While some students were filling their response journals with statements like "I hated this book," Mary Jo wrote: "This text is cursed for me. . . . I found the reading to be laborious. . . I am in basic disagreement with a major feature of [the author's] position."[20] Even though the journal responses were supposed to be informal freewrites, Mary Jo's were always formal with a clear introduction and conclusion, well-developed body paragraphs, strong transitions, consistent use of academic words and phrases, and few if any expressions of feeling. While her peers scrawled their responses in longhand, Mary Jo submitted perfect, laser-printed essays. "A big part of writing for me," she wrote, "is having a particularly strong handle on where I'm going."[21]

This need for control was also evident in her teaching. Although Mary Jo claimed to believe in composition pedagogy, when I visited her classes, I found that they were never wholly de-centered. Rather than allowing her students to work on problems in groups, Mary Jo told them what to do and how to do it. When she used small groups to read and respond to each other's drafts, she undercut their authority by taking up the drafts and marking them herself, a habit that led students to disregard their peers' advice. In sum, despite her former teaching experience, Mary Jo's training in political science coupled with her perfectionism and inexperience in English studies led her to retain control in the classroom and in her writing so she could keep a "strong handle" on both.

Barbara: Out of Control

Barbara tried to maintain a similarly "strong handle." During our seminar's peer-response sessions, she told her partners what to do and how to do it; when it was her turn to receive feedback, she paid little or no attention and heeded none of her peers' suggestions. I gained some insight into Barbara's behavior when I read her description of her composing process and once again found similarities between her and Mary Jo. Whereas Mary Jo described her writing process as "manic obsessiveness,"[22] Barbara epitomized this behavior. Every page had to be perfect: "I spend anywhere from two to five hours per page on an essay. Each page is basically done at the end of that time period; then I print it and move on to the next page." This was not a gradual process; it was grueling and intense. Because of this process, Barbara postponed writing until the last minute, when all conditions had to be perfect. Usually, she waited until after her husband had gone to bed and then wrote for ten to twelve hours at a time.[23]

Although both Barbara and Mary Jo were perfectionists, their attitudes about the finished products differed considerably. No matter how much time she spent composing, Mary Jo never felt her writing was quite good enough. Conversely, because she had spent so much time composing each page, Barbara could not view her papers critically. She proudly claimed never to write drafts—she came to her computer with ideas clearly formed and began to write. This process, she maintained, was just as effective and labor-intensive as writing multiple drafts.[24] However, by narrowing her focus to a single, cosmetically perfect page, Barbara was also limiting her horizons. Psycholinguist Frank Smith explains the reasons for this difficulty when he discusses the cognitive competition between transcription and composition, maintaining that writers have one-track minds (*Writing* 19–20). Although experienced writers can and do write mechanically correct, well-developed drafts, an exclusive focus on mechanics closes the mind to an exploration of new ideas. The results of this focus could be seen in Barbara's writing, for she tended to write around the subject rather than delve into it. However, when I pointed out the need to revise and develop her ideas, she rejected the advice. Because she had put the time into her writing, any negative comments occurred because the teacher "had either missed altogether or chosen not to recognize" her good points.[25] Barbara did not consider that the problem might lie with her.

Melva: Out of Her Element

Melva did not appear resistant initially; she seemed to relish new pedagogical approaches. After the first peer-response session in Teaching
College Writing, she complained that her group had "spent no time on
establishing community. We just paired off, read, and waltzed around
what we were asked to do," and provided little or no substantive feedback. Although she and her peers had participated in activities designed
to introduce them to collaborative learning, Melva said she felt ill at ease
when her group began to respond to each other's drafts of essay 1, a three-
part, personal narrative describing learning experiences.[26] Such feelings
are not uncommon during these first sessions; as Patricia A. Sullivan
found in her survey of graduate student writers, this group is particularly unaccustomed to sharing their writing ("Writing"). Melva also may
have felt uncomfortable because she was not used to writing personal
essays and because she had been grouped with three people possessing
considerable experience: Pattie had been writing (and publishing) since
she was ten, and Chris and Dale were both aspiring creative writers.
Because Melva was an experienced grant writer, I assumed she would be
comfortable working with other writers of similar age and levels of experience, but this belief led me to overlook yet another factor—Melva
may have felt uncomfortable because her group members were white.

The interactions during peer response to the second draft of essay 1
suggest that all three may have contributed to Melva's discomfort. I base
this conclusion on Melva's failure to revise much beyond the addition
of a rather stilted and formal introduction, on her control of the group
during the second peer-response session, and on Lisa Delpit's contention that black students often resist and fail to benefit from the process approach and the collaborative learning characteristic of the process-
oriented classroom because they view such pedagogy as weak and irre-
sponsible on the teacher's part. When the second meeting of her peer
group began, Melva focused the discussion immediately, saying, "I have
two issues I want addressed. Does [my paper] flow, and do I have three
vignettes?" Then she read her draft to the group. When she finished, there
was silence, so she asked her peers to complete the first question on the
peer-response sheet. After a brief discussion of her paper, Melva retained
control, determining that Dale would read next, allowing Pattie to delay
reading because her draft was too personal, and directing the discussion

of Chris's paper. When questions were addressed to Chris, Melva answered them; when Chris asked the others for advice, Melva either interrupted or contradicted their responses. By the end of the session, Melva was the only one talking. As they concluded their work, she said, "Thank you, guys. This was good."[27] But it was not good. Melva not only interrupted and directed the conversation; she also failed to listen to her peers' papers and to their suggestions for revising her own. As a result, she consistently contradicted the feedback they tried to give each other, and she ignored the suggestions directed to her, which led to unrevised and undeveloped essays. This latter behavior seemed to contradict Melva's understanding and acceptance of the theories we were reading in class. On the one hand, her commitment to political reform through pedagogical change remained constant, for she had stated in an early journal that

> reading/language learning for young readers and readers with limited dominant culture social experience is best accomplished when social learning is embedded in the reading/language learning experience, i.e., class discussion, role play, collaborative/group writing.[28]

She also supported the use of journals and expressive writing:

> Changing my practice reflects my growing concern about the urgency to empower students to learn. I believe that most students will become more effective writers if they are freed to explore the process, without inhibitions, anxieties and other constraints posed by grades awarded on the basis of transactional . . . writing assignments and/or tests.[29]

Despite this political stance, Melva could not or would not address these issues in her own written work. Although her attitude about nontraditional pedagogy was positive, she found it difficult to change her behavior perhaps because, as Ashton explains, for change to occur individuals must have "a combination of attitude and behavior change" (165).

Bob: Regaining Control

Bob's writing and attitudes were similarly contradictory. When I asked the students in Teaching College Writing why they wanted to teach, Bob wrote, "I like to be in an environment where learning/exploring ideas is the central focus. I like to be around discovery. I like to be around kids (most of the time). . . . I am a teacher because I like to help students see new things about themselves." Even though Bob's descriptions of his students and his classroom activities seldom conformed to this vision, he maintained that he found "fulfillment" in teaching.[30] Yet, after a semester of Teaching College Writing, he began to admit his frustrations with teaching and to seek solutions. In his final essay, he announced his decision to change jobs and move to a smaller school so he could regain these positive feelings within a supportive community. In response to his peer group's comments that they would like to know what happens in a small school and how he related a sense of community to learning, Bob added two pages of anecdotes and examples. These reflections led him to provide specific examples of the source of his frustrations:

> It is no joy to be constantly cast in the role of adversary by many students. Since we don't know each other, it becomes easier to dehumanize each other. This means that I become the teacher who must constantly be prepared to deal with students who seemingly are only in class to be impediments to learning. I become the "prison warden." . . . The impersonal approach to education affects the classroom too. We must follow the curriculum guide religiously even when it would make better sense to consider the needs of students. We faithfully give objective final exams each semester, reinforcing the idea that what really counts in the classroom is rote memorization of meaningless facts and not the ability to think. Undoubtedly the classroom . . . suffers because of community's absence.[31]

This paper was light years away from the stilted, impersonal prose with which Bob had begun the semester. It was so improved that I read it aloud to the class. This degree of revision also suggested Bob's changing attitude regarding collaborative learning. Although Bob's group members had changed weekly at the beginning of the semester, when he began working with an all-male group at midterm, his resistance began to diminish. He closed the semester declaring, "Peer revision is an exhilarating experience. For me, anyway, in this class. I wish it could be for my students."[32]

Although Bob began the semester with an extremely low sense of teaching efficacy—that is, he doubted that his students would work or could learn—these feelings gradually began to change as the semester progressed. Due to what Bandura describes as the "modeling, guided performance, and self-directed mastery experiences" in the graduate classroom via involvement in small-group work, reflective reading and teaching logs, and practice teaching, Bob gained a sense of how these strategies might work. Gradually, he began to assign freewriting and allow his students a voice in topic selection; he started really teaching writing as a process, assigning multiple drafts and having students peer edit them in groups; and he expanded his grading criteria from an emphasis on mechanics to content as well.[33] As a result, his teaching became more enjoyable, and his students appeared to be learning, and so his sense of teaching efficacy also improved. According to Ashton, this sense of efficacy is critical in explaining why teachers are willing to change their instructional strategies and continue to experiment even when faced with student resistance (144). However, Bob's subsequent experiences in my Reader Response Theory seminar reveal how feelings of efficacy can be undermined when the context lacks collegial support (157).

APPLYING THEORY

In their longitudinal study of young children's writing, Gerald Harste, Virginia Woodward, and Caroline Burke found that three-year-olds never hesitated to try new writing tasks and four-year-olds "were initially more reluctant," while five- and six-year-olds "would give an acceptable but safe surface text" (138–39). If there is this degree of difference between the ages of three and six, imagine how deeply ingrained the need for caution is by the time students reach graduate school. Indeed, Harste et al. conclude that "with increasing experience comes an increased awareness of risk and a concomitant reluctance to engage in risk-taking" (138).

Those students willing to take risks generally possess a strong personal construct and high levels of self-efficacy. Recall that students' personal constructs are influenced by how they have performed in the past, how others behave toward them, and what others expect of them. Self-efficacy proceeds out of these experiences: "The stronger the perceived self-efficacy, the more likely persons are to select challenging tasks, the longer they persist at them, and the more likely they are to perform them successfully" (Bandura 397). The difference between the two is that personal construct is a general attribute, whereas self-efficacy is affected by context. In the classroom, these feelings would be influenced by past writing experiences and by the attitude and behaviors of the students' teacher and peers as well as by a classroom atmosphere that encourages risk-taking. If a discourse community has been established in which peers are trusted and supportive, if the instructor promotes and encourages experimentation, and if she provides a safe environment in which to do so—through collaborative learning, reflective writing, peer response to drafts, and portfolio grading—then even graduate students might be willing to take risks. All of these elements are important indicators of how and why students might overcome their resistance.

Mary Jo: Collaborative Learning and Self-Efficacy

When Mary Jo enrolled in my Reader-Response seminar, I grouped her with Karen and Sister Gisela because of their similar ages and backgrounds as high school teachers. Despite these similarities, the group did not initially function to Mary Jo's satisfaction, for she wanted more in-depth feedback.[34] Eventually, the three women coalesced into a strong discourse community that did not hesitate to provide the kind of feedback Mary Jo desired, if not more so. Fairly quickly, Karen and Sister Gisela's analyses of Mary Jo's writing led them to point out that her recurring topics were a need for organization and control, both in her life and in her writing, and a tendency to set forth her opinions in detached academic language.[35] Throughout the early weeks of the semester, Mary Jo's prose style remained fairly detached even when the topics were personal. For example, when describing her argumentative style, she wrote: "It is indeed unfortunate that I must now move on to the second part of this assignment because I realize the person I currently argue the most with is S, my fifteen-year-old son."[36]

Mary Jo also retained control over her writing by ignoring her group's suggestions for revision. But as the semester progressed, she grew more comfortable with her group; her writing became slightly less formal and complaints about her group members tapered off. Consequently, I was taken aback when she came to my office in tears when the class began drafting their final essay, an analysis of their language use. Crying seemed completely out of character, for I had assumed that Mary Jo was strong-willed and stoic, yet here she was in my office trying to hold back her tears and saying tremulously, "I can't write this paper. I've tried and tried, but nothing will come out. I've never had writer's block before, but I just cannot write this paper." Knowing Mary Jo's penchant for perfection, I assured her she didn't need all the answers; she need only attempt an analysis. But nothing I said was of help. Finally I told her that if she could not finish the paper by the end of the semester, she could take a delayed grade.

The following summer, I read Mary F. Belenky et al.'s *Women's Ways of Knowing*, which posits that women move through five different epistemological positions, progressing from silent knower to received, separate, and connected, to constructive. As I read, I began to find some explanations for Mary Jo's previous writing style and her present writer's block. Mary Jo could be described as a "separate knower." She had learned to write the "correct" paper—that is, she could express her ideas—but she could not express her feelings and personal opinions. Even though their papers may earn high grades, separate knowers are not comfortable with their writing. They feel they have fooled the professor for they know this is not their own voice (110). These women may have gone through a great deal of their lives unaware of this disparity or at least discounting it because, as Belenky et al. point out, in most colleges and universities, "the subjective voice was largely ignored. . . . It was the public, rational, analytical voice that received the institutions' tutelage, respect, and rewards" (124). When these women realize their voice is unnatural or untrue to themselves, they panic.

This certainly sounded like Mary Jo. It also reminded me of her response to Patrocinio P. Schweikert's feminist theory of reading. In her discussion of women's voice, Schweikert maintains:

> The cultural reality is not the emasculation of men by women, but the *immasculation* of women by men. As readers and teachers and scholars, women are taught to think as men, to identify with a male point of view, and to accept as normal and legitimate a male system of values, one of whose central principles is misogyny. (41–42, Schweikert's emphasis)

Mary Jo said that this passage completely upset her view of herself. She had always believed herself a feminist, but after reading this, she felt like a fraud. Rather than writing like a feminist, she felt she had been writing like a woman trying to write like a man.[37] This realization, coupled with her group's findings, paralyzed her. Uncertain of who she was or what she believed, Mary Jo could not put pen to paper without breaking into tears.

Because I had come to know Mary Jo fairly well during her two years as a TA, I felt comfortable sending her the Belenky chapters, which seemed to shed light on her feelings, along with a note asking her to let me know if they helped. Within a few weeks, she wrote back acknowledging their usefulness, and at the end of the summer, she handed me her final paper wryly entitled "How I Spent My Summer Vacation." In this paper, Mary Jo explained why she had resisted her group's feedback and how she overcame her resistance. She began by admitting, "I did not realize how difficult and painful the process of growing up and believing in myself would be. I did not realize how much I would resist." Part of this resistance was manifested in Mary Jo's response to her group's feedback, which ultimately took the form of writer's block.[38]

Mary Jo's resistance seemed to stem from the dysjunction of her personal construct of herself as a feminist with her peer group's description of her as a writer displaying the traditionally "masculine" traits of detachment and objectivity—disparate images that undermined her feelings of self-efficacy. When she finally began to compose her final paper, Mary Jo was able to cite numerous instances where her group had pointed out these language features, only to be ignored. In her conclusion, she admitted:

> Karen really forced my hand . . . when she pointed out that for her the main difference between my writing the first half and the second half [of the semester] is that of "a cool, somewhat argumentative, scholarly writer and a writer who reveals herself to be more of a 'traditional' woman caught between her traditional roles and her raised consciousness. . . . " She is right, of course. What I have learned from this writer's block that grew out of looking closely at the language features of my writing, through the responses of my peers, and under your enabling tutelage is that life, success, intelligence, whatever, do not have to be defined as elements of control. What is important is the realization that the journey, the process of knowing and learning, are unpredictable and not easily controlled. . . . Out of all this chaos, though, I have grown and changed—matured. Even the anger and frustration of not being able to write because it hurt too much to acknowledge my inability to manage my life perfectly and the anger I felt . . . has [sic] been worth the pain.[39]

Barbara: Lack of Community and Self-Efficacy

Whereas Mary Jo's resistance surfaced as writer's block, Barbara's was manifested in her teaching, in her classroom behavior, and in her refusal (or inability) to fulfill the requirements of her graduate pedagogy course. The most obvious of these was evident in her final portfolio. At the end of Teaching College Writing, Barbara had a week in which to revise essay 1 (an extended personal narrative) in need of an analytical conclusion and essay 2 (an analysis of her composing process), which basically lacked any analysis at all. Instead, she revised nothing more than syntax. Although I had grown accustomed to Barbara's resistance in her teaching and during group work, I had expected that she (like the student who plays dumb) would fulfill the seminar requirements for the portfolio. In many ways, she reminded me of Mary Jo, yet Mary Jo had overcome her resistance while Barbara had not. What made the difference?

After some reflection, I realized that experience was a major factor. Although Reader Response Theory was Mary Jo's first graduate seminar, she brought to it a considerable amount of teaching experience and a matured composing process. Moreover, she had the summer to compose her final paper. This combination of teacher knowledge, the opportunity to reflect, and the time to do so contributed to her ability to complete the course. In contrast, Barbara had been introduced to new ways of teaching and writing at the beginning of the semester just fifteen weeks previously. Moreover, in her first semester of teaching freshman composition and taking graduate course work, Barbara felt she had no time to do anything. Overwhelmed and frustrated by the workload, she felt out of control, and indeed she was. In order to maintain perfection, Barbara claimed that she was working twenty hours a day.[40] When she wasn't preparing to teach or grading, she was reading and writing for her graduate seminars. Worse, because she hated to write, she delayed composing until the deadline loomed, and the timing was "perfect." Unfortunately, this occurred only after midnight, at which point she might write until dawn.

Barbara had insufficient time to reflect on what she was reading about teaching and writing. In *Teaching Writing as Reflective Practice*, Hillocks explains that reflection is limited by the "very components that make it possible. To some extent or other, the frames that teachers set necessarily depend upon the knowledge they bring to them. Thus, reflection is necessarily limited by the nature of teacher knowledge" (129). This factor becomes even more important when the readings contradict a new teacher's personal construct, and the modes of writing challenge her feelings of self-efficacy.

Could these problems have been alleviated if Barbara had been willing to experiment with drafting, if she had given herself permission to be less than perfect? If Mary Jo could accept her "imperfections," why couldn't Barbara? One answer may lie in the role and structure of the two women's peer-response groups. As Bleich has explained in *The Double Perspective*, when students are members of permanent groups, the stability and intimacy of these discourse communities contribute to a growing trust and eventual willingness to heed their group members' advice (284ff). Week after week in the Reader-Response seminar, Mary Jo's group members pointed out her recurring language features; week after week, I echoed these comments in my responses to her papers. If I had been the only person pointing out these language features, Mary Jo might have dismissed my responses; however, her group members' input lent credence to these findings, and eventually she attended to them.

Barbara, however, was not in a permanent group. During the semester she enrolled in Teaching College Writing, the seminar consisted of five students whose attendance fluctuated; therefore, they seldom worked with the same partner for more than one draft. As a result, Barbara did not receive consistent feedback from people she trusted, nor did she have the opportunity to establish a feeling of trust. The only consistent responses came from me, and Barbara's behavior suggested she did not value my responses too highly. I had quickly tired of her obstinance and interruptions, so I was not inclined to seek her out and offer my help as I had with Mary Jo. Perhaps I should have. In her discussion of the needs of returning women students, Janice Hays asserts that they often encounter ideas and viewpoints that contradict well-established personal constructs. Obviously, survival in the university depends on resolving these conflicts. Toward this end, peers and female instructors play key roles, with peers serving as sounding boards and instructors providing support, understanding, and reassurance (176). I fear Barbara did not get this from her peers, and I know she didn't get it from me.

Still, because Barbara paralleled Mary Jo in so many ways, I turned again to *Women's Ways of Knowing* for some insights into the women's differing responses. Barbara's behavior appeared to parallel subjective knowers, for like them she seemed to "assume that there is only one right answer to each question, and that all other answers and all contrary views are automatically wrong" (Belenky et al. 37). This belief in the source of knowledge helped explain Barbara's difficulties with analytical thinking and writing. Belenky and her colleagues found that subjective knowers feel they are

> recipients but not sources of knowledge, [they] feel confused and incapable when the teacher requires that they do original work. . . . These women feel confident about their ability to absorb and to store the truths received from others. As such they perceive themselves as having the capacity to become

richly endowed repositories of information. They may be quite successful in schools that do not demand a reflective, relativistic stance. (42–43)

Belenky et al. found these characteristics in very young women students, although these ways of thinking tended to quickly disappear "in pluralistic and intellectually challenging environments" (43). When they did not change, the students either dropped out or flunked out. Sadly, in this too there were parallels. At the end of her first semester, Barbara resigned her teaching assistantship and dropped out of graduate school.

Melva: Rejecting Community and the Loss of Self-Efficacy

Many of the factors influencing Barbara's resistance might also explain Melva's. Although she agreed with the need for pedagogical change in the classroom, Melva found it difficult to address these issues in her written assignments for Teaching College Writing. Her response journals seldom met the minimum length, and for the first two months of the semester, she did not turn in any of the weekly research logs required (and necessary) for the development of her action research project. Each week in my comments on her journals, I reminded her of the necessity of completing the logs and offered to discuss any problems during office hours. Melva did not respond until midterm, when she explained that the research project worried her, not because the research took so much time but because it marked for her "a beginning point for making a commitment to study a writing/reading issue from the vantage point of teaching."[41] In response, I offered her the option of relying more heavily on library research for her final project because she had neither access to a composition classroom nor sufficient free time to conduct observations. But Melva assured me that she had "sufficient motivation to seriously engage an issue."[42]

This commitment appeared evident in the peer-response sessions for essay 2, an analysis of the students' composing processes. Transcripts from the tape-recorded discussions of Melva's peer-response group suggest that although she continued to lead her peers, she was beginning to benefit from the group interaction. While Chris was reading her draft, Melva suddenly exclaimed, "Ohhh!" The rest of the group stopped talking and asked, did you get an insight? "Yes," she laughed excitedly. "Not for you, for me." As the group laughed in response, Melva explained that a phrase in Chris's draft, "perplexed and humbled," triggered something she had completely blocked out: "The year I spent at the office of the League of Women Voters completely changed the way that I write, that I wrote. I think I'm probably trying to undo some of what they did. . . . I hadn't really thought about that."[43]

After the group finished discussing Chris's draft, Pattie and Melva began to talk. Melva asked Pattie if she was learning anything from peer response because she realized that initially, she had rejected everyone's suggestions. "What you were asking for was more of *me*, as opposed to this political, analytical stuff, okay, the way that I write. . . . more personal voice."[44] Melva's comment reflects the concern Anne Aronson discovered among returning women students, especially women of color, that such writing "embodies the self" (64). Aronson's case studies of nontraditional women students concluded that when writers feel this way, their writing "becomes a site where the self can be damaged by overtly or covertly hostile audiences and discourse communities. At stake is participants' basic sense of self-worth, and more specifically their sense of competence and authority as knowers, thinkers, and language users." Such writing becomes what Aronson terms a "danger zone," for it threatens both their personal construct and sense of self-efficacy. To avoid entering the danger zone, these women employ two different types of resistance: "to control the environments in which one writes so that self-disclosure is safe, or alternatively to limit the degree to which one self-discloses in writing when the environment is potentially dangerous" (Aronson 65). Melva's control of her group members' discussions suggests movement along the former path, while her refusal to revise, despite sound suggestions and apparently strong rapport within her group, indicates movement along the latter. Melva appeared to be considering these issues. In the conclusion to her second paper, an analysis of her composing process, she wrote:

> Before taking this course, I had not thought about studying or changing my writing behavior. I had, in fact, lost touch with writing as an art. A competent rendering of facts and information is not always the best writing. Changing writing patterns is very challenging work. The important first-step is recognizing patterns and practices that need improvement. A critical next step is investing time to apply alternate ways of getting the writing done. A final, but equally valuable recognition for me is that my writing power lies in my willingness to put me in the writing. I will need to decide each time that I write whether I want my work to be merely competent or really good. This course has given me the insight to ask that question.[45]

Many of these ideas were repeated in Melva's portfolio analysis in which she said she was "grateful for this semester's challenge to rethink [her] reasons and style for writing." This state of mind also seemed evident in her revised version of essay 1, which she completed before midterm. But after midterm, Melva apparently changed her mind; in the final revised version of essay 2, her conclusion was quite different from the original cited above (the changes are boldfaced):

> Before taking this course, I had not thought about studying or changing my writing behavior, **which does, in fact, serve me quite well in my work and in my personal correspondence.** This course has **raised some issues about the usefulness of feedback and expectations of others about writing— some insights have been helpful.**[46]

Gone were the references to changing her writing. In the earlier version, Melva had cited three key factors: "recognizing patterns and practices that need improvement"; "investing time to apply alternate ways of getting the writing done; and the "willingness to put [herself] in the writing." Had she decided there was no need for improvement? Had she been mimicking the "party line" (as Shor describes it) in an attempt to demonstrate her understanding? Did she lack the time to make those changes? Or was she unwilling to risk making changes that involved putting herself into the writing? Melva's changed stance parallels a similar case cited by Susan Wall. In "Rereading the Discourses of Gender," Wall discusses the efforts of a female student who tried and failed "to move outside of the restrictions of her epistemological perspective" (179). Rather than explore points of view that would have contradicted her personal construct, the student chose to write around them, revising instead of analyzing her newfound perspectives.

This refusal to analyze seems related to Aida Hurtado's contention that "many feminists of Color [sic] see knowledge as relational and recognize that what is true in one context is not necessarily true in another" (386). Although the personal voice was praised and encouraged in my seminar, Melva recognized that it was neither used nor respected within the academic milieu where she had to write. In this regard, race might not seem so much an issue as context. Yet, Hurtado reminds her readers that for women of color, each social interaction requires the assessment of what is said, to whom, and how it is said. Every tactical judgment involves risk because each interaction requires assessment of who can be an ally, a friend, or an enemy regardless of a person's skin color, sex, or sexuality. (387)

This degree of rhetorical awareness is something most white people are seldom attuned to. Certainly, I was not.

What I noticed was Melva's irritability and frustration surfacing as the semester drew to a close. As the tape of the final peer-response session begins (the one that would examine the students' drafts of their action research paper), Melva can be heard saying above the clamor of the others, "Now listen, I haven't proofed it, I haven't proofed it!" to which her group members reply, "I haven't either!" Then she continues, "I haven't any conclusion, I haven't any transitions, okay? So don't grade me for those things!" Again, her group members reassured her and tried to calm her down. Chris said she was looking forward to reading Melva's draft, and Pattie said she liked the green paper Melva used, but none of this helped. When Chris gave her draft to Melva, Melva exclaimed, "I can't read this! I can't see it!" Melva and Pattie (who were usually partners) exchanged drafts instead. After reading Melva's draft, Pattie praised her use of field notes, to which Melva angrily replied:

> I put them in there because *she* was on my case about turning them in. I was keeping all my notes in a spiral notebook and didn't have time to type them up and turn them in weekly, so I just had to keep the stuff together and organize it for myself. I finally turned in everything to her today—all my notes and classroom observations—but she was really on my case about how little I had done. . . . To do this right, you have to have ongoing observations, and my work schedule doesn't permit me to go sit in on [another teacher's] class.[47]

When I heard this, I did not consider that Melva's anger might be related to our different skin colors. Rather, the tenor of her earlier comments suggested a frazzled, typically harried graduate student at the end of a busy semester. However, Hurtado's comments regarding the risk of social interactions led me to question my attitude and compare my relationship with Melva to that with Barbara and Mary Jo. Melva's refusal to revise or to heed the advice of her peers coupled with her anger at my requests to submit her work on time reminded me of Barbara. But Barbara's obnoxious classroom behavior irritated me, whereas Melva's insightful comments, pleasant demeanor, and easy camaraderie within her group led me to enjoy her presence. Indeed, my reminders to Melva about the course requirements as well as my offer to change the parameters of the research assignment were made out of concern, not hostility. If Hurtado is correct, perhaps because for women of color, "each social interaction requires the assessment of what is said, to whom, and how it is said," this situation played a negative role not only in the teacher-student relationship but also in Melva's desire versus her ability to change.

At this point, such possibilities are merely conjecture. It is more logical to point to Melva's personal construct as a successful black woman who had mastered the conventions of formal academic prose and suggest that the requirements to change this style represented too great a challenge to her feelings of self-efficacy.

Bob: Context and Resistance to Composition Pedagogy

By the time Bob finished Teaching College Writing, he believed that the new approaches to writing pedagogy were valuable and appropriate. However, because he still felt that most graduate courses were boring and irrelevant, he asked me if Reader Response Theory (offered the following semester) would be equally useful. I warned him that the readings were more theoretical during the first half of the course but promised that we would make practical applications each week in class, and so he enrolled. Given his changed attitude toward collaborative learning and reflective writing, I believed that Bob might continue to benefit from the group work in Reader Response. On the first night of class in his introductory paper, he was quite open: "A number of years ago, I made the decision to make any career secondary to my wife and children. . . . I will never be a well-known, honored teacher, but I will have the knowledge that I did my best with my family."[48] These feelings were reiterated in a subsequent paper in which he declared, "I don't really know how I would function without [my wife], for she really is part of me," an extremely direct statement of feelings for a man (especially a very traditional, conservative man) to write to virtual strangers. When asked to describe his most successful moment, Bob focused on his marriage, which he termed a "unity," and his happy family life.[49]

Based on these feelings and his openness, I grouped Bob with Kim and Joan, both of whom valued teaching and family life. Kim was energetic, talkative, and enthusiastic; she would get the conversations going.

Joan was much quieter. In that regard, as well as the fact that she was an inexperienced writer from a rural setting and just beginning graduate school, she paralleled Bob. All together, the three seemed like a workable combination. Unfortunately, the reader-response texts and the practical assignments were not what Bob had anticipated, nor were the group's personalities as congruent as I had assumed.

The pedagogical focus of this course—reader-response analyses of individuals' language features—brought up issues Bob did not want to address and that to him seemed irrelevant to teaching literature. Kim and Joan soon found that Bob's recurring topics were his frustrations as a teacher and his belief that students were incapable of independent or intelligent thought—the same themes that had emerged the previous semester. Another related and preferred topic, as well as an additional source of frustration, was the theoretical texts we were reading by Wolfgang Iser, Norman Holland, Stanley Fish, and Bleich. Every week, Bob expressed feelings of anger and inadequacy in his journal. Because his group members had just met him, they were unaware that he had expressed similar feelings the previous semester. They saw only frustration expressed with sarcasm, which they tactfully pointed out in their responses. Nonetheless, Bob chafed under their scrutiny. At the end of the first month of classes, he wrote:

> I have had some thoughts about all this analysis of each other's writings we've been doing. First, studying language features and freewriting seem to me to be mutually incompatible. I find myself so hypersensitive to everything I put on this paper, that I feel no "freedom" to write at all. I keep thinking, "How will this be interpreted?" or "I know what I mean here but who knows what will be read into this?" I find myself resisting this. Why? Well, I guess I don't like to be "figured out."[50]

Because I had come to know Bob the previous semester, I tried to respond positively to his journals, praising him for his directness and fluency, agreeing with some of his criticisms, and attempting to establish links between the theory he was reading and applications to his teaching. But Bob had been trained in the New Critical tradition. He had great difficulty reconciling his doubts that readers—especially high school readers—brought meaning to a piece of literature. His primary interest in teaching literature was in its explication rather than in the students' comprehension, so he viewed a reader's response as irrelevant.[51]

By midterm, Bob was actively resisting the content of the course as well as the in-class activities, which consisted in large part of the group's reader-response analyses of their members' language features. At that point, Bob was not resisting collaboration per se but the focus of the group work: He did not like to be analyzed, and he did not see the relevance of this approach to teaching. But after midterm, when the focus of the students' writing changed to personal responses to literature, Bob's openness decreased as his resistance increased. This resistance created a vicious circle. First, he told his group members that their analyses of his language features were wrong;[52] in response, Kim and Joan suggested that Bob was being evasive.[53] The result of these comments was evident in his subsequent paper, which comprised less than two handwritten pages, so his group decided he was definitely evading the topic. Bob addressed these charges in the following paper, a response to "Ruth's Song" by Gloria Steinem in which the students were to compare the stereotypes in that story to their own experiences:

> I think this class has been the experience in my life when I've felt like I've been stereotyped on a fairly regular basis. From week to week, I hear the words *male* and *control* used in tandem. I don't remember feeling this way in last semester's class, . . . but this semester I've been annoyed more than once by references to "male" behavior. . . . I feel upset that I am lumped with all the cruddy males in the world. I wish that [my wife] could be here to defend me! Boy do I sound silly! In another month it won't matter anyway. . . . The class will be over.[54]

At the time, these comments struck me as overly sensitive since only one of the eight books in the seminar, Elizabeth A. Flynn and Schweikert's *Gender and Reading*, actually dealt with gender differences. But, in retrospect, I realized that the most outspoken person in the class had been Missy (from chapter 6), a young woman who equated feminism with confrontation, and that second place went to Bob's group member, Kim (from chapter 7), who not only considered herself a feminist but who also raised these issues on a weekly basis. During the final month of the semester, Bob's traditional views increasingly clashed with Kim's feminist stance. In response to Raymond Carver's short story, "What We Talk About When We Talk About Love," Bob wrote that the main characters' marriage

> will fail because they are trying so hard to feel like they're in love. Ironic, isn't it? For marriage to work, people need to be committed to one another re-

gardless of feelings & emotions. . . . [My wife] and I have a deep, certain, mutually beneficial relationship, not because of emotion, but because of commitment.[55]

I found this response a little confusing, but Kim was appalled: "Your definition of a fulfilling relationship sounds horrifying to me."[56] Joan was even more confrontational: "You've always been evasive before on this subject," she accused, "but here it seems like maybe your home life isn't exactly what you would prefer it to be."[57] That was the last straw for Bob. Rather than address the issues raised by his group members, he began to write less and to respond impersonally to the readings. He explained his actions in his final essay:

> As the course progressed, I became more and more uncomfortable about being misunderstood. I would say this lack of comfort turned into a fear and, when it did, I began to change my writing habits in this class. . . . I depersonalized my writing. In a nutshell, I was being evasive because I was very uncomfortable with being misunderstood or seen in a way I considered inaccurate.[58]

Were Kim's and Joan's readings inaccurate?

As I looked over my field notes on Bob, I noticed I had initially labeled him Mr. Negative. As I reread those notes and Bob's essays, I could see that my attitude had definitely affected my reception of his group members' analyses. Although I had been somewhat confused by Bob's description of his marriage as "mutually beneficial . . . not because of emotion, but because of commitment," Kim's and Joan's responses reflected their frustrations with him rather than any insights about his marriage. Having read Bob's essays for ten weeks, they detected traits suggesting that he was fairly traditional and somewhat controlling, but their conclusions that his marriage was "horrifying" and not "exactly what [he] would prefer it to be" were not only inappropriate but unfounded. In my weariness at what I considered Bob's obstinance, I had allowed his group to do what Bleich consistently warns about—I let them move beyond an analysis of language features to an uninformed psychoanalysis of Bob's personality.

Bob had written repeatedly about his relationship with his wife and always with love and respect. When he complained about being "lumped with all the cruddy males in the world," he had gone on to say he wished his wife could be there to defend him. Even his response to the Carver piece, when read in context, revealed a strong belief in faithfulness and commitment to one's spouse. But I did not see this at the time. I was so tired of Bob's constant complaining that I felt he deserved whatever he got. It was only upon reflection that I began to realize how seriously his group had gone awry. Bob was resisting in the Girouxian sense of the term—he resisted what he perceived as the dominant ideology, a personally intrusive feminist analysis of his life and his language. For most people, a strong marriage and a successful career are integral to their personal construct and feelings of self-efficacy. Bob's group attacked both.

Like Mary Jo, Bob resisted exploring the areas raised by his group because they challenged his beliefs about himself, his teaching, and his relationships, all key to his self-image. But in Mary Jo's case, the findings came from a peer she respected, so she was willing to accept the interpretation and wrestle with the problem. Bob's issues related to the two most important areas of his life—his marriage and his career. If these interpretations had occurred in a different context, he might have been willing to examine them more closely. However, when these findings emerged in a class whose foundations he doubted and emanated from two increasingly antagonistic women whose political beliefs clashed with his own, consideration was out of the question.

IMPLICATIONS FOR TEACHING

Phyllis Kahaney, who has conducted numerous teacher-training workshops over the years, maintains that an average of 20 percent of the participants make significant changes in their teaching, 60 percent make moderate changes, and 20 percent resist change altogether (192). Kahaney attributes the ability to change to three factors:

> (a) the ability to articulate a problem . . .(b) access to a benevolent authority (a text, a teacher) that reflects the shape of the resistance back to the change-maker; and (c) a community in which change can take place and in which the new behavior can be practiced and reinforced. (192)

Mary Jo was able to overcome her resistance because she had access to all three factors. The same was true of Bob at the end of Teaching College Writing; however, that context changed in Reader Response Theory, and so Bob's resistance returned in full force. Melva was able to articulate the problem, but she seemed to believe she lacked the other two elements, whereas Barbara apparently felt she had access to none.

These case studies suggest that even when the above factors are present, they will not facilitate change unless they in some way correlate with the individuals' personal constructs and sense of self-efficacy. In his analysis of elements contributing to teacher change, Diamond concludes that when personal construct is taken into account, we need to realize that learning to teach, especially to teach in different ways, "is often hard and sometimes costly" even with sufficient modeling, support, and engagement. Each teacher must compare new ideas and approaches with his or her own beliefs and determine what to accept or reject. In other words, changing teaching is "not the easy reproduction of any ready-made package of knowledge but, rather, the continued recreation of personal meaning" (64). To aid in this construction, Diamond suggests that faculty acknowledge their students' fears and ideas and encourage them to explore them through reflective writing. But this, too, will fail if the elements within the "package of knowledge" do not coincide with the individuals' views of the world and their sense of self.

To believe that if we present the package of knowledge in just the right way, learning will occur, and the student will be transformed, is to fall prey to what Richard E. Miller terms the "teacher's fallacy" (24). No one possesses such magical powers. But most people do possess human traits that can help students along the path to learning. The first is empathy. Faculty need to be aware that learning—especially learning new ways to teach—may involve "nihilism, doubt, and destructiveness" (Helmers 66). Through the use of reflective journals, we can become aware of our students' doubts and fears, but rather than rejecting them as naive, we need to listen, empathize, and offer support. Although this dictum applies to all students, it may be particularly important for returning women and students of color, who may be more skeptical than most faculty realize.

To help our students overcome these feelings, I offer three suggestions. First, learn from the case studies in this chapter, and pay special attention to the construction of collaborative-learning groups. In Mary Jo's case, feedback from a permanent group of like-minded individuals helped awaken her to the need for change; conversely, Bob's and Barbara's negative experiences underscore the necessity of permanent groups comprised of members who share complementary skills, put forth a similar degree of effort, and are willing to work together to develop relationships built on trust. As Vera John-Steiner, Robert J. Weber, and Michele Minnis point out in their analysis of collaboration, working and talking together are not enough—successful groups are built on shared values and perspectives (775–76). When constructing groups, keep in mind also the gender of the members and ensure at least a gender balance. In her critique of collaboration, Evelyn Ashton-Jones warns that a gender imbalance in writing groups can contribute to "chilly conditions for women" in the university classroom (22). Bob's case suggests that gender considerations apply to men as well as women.

Second, be a mentor. Ten years ago, returning adult women constituted 48 percent of the female students at the postsecondary level; that number continues to grow (Aronson 58–59). Graduate students who work with a mentor have a better chance of surviving graduate school and succeeding in the academic community. Within the field of composition, which has a predominance of female faculty, male students are nevertheless twice as likely as females to have benefited from mentorship.[59] Other fields may not be so "feminized," which is all the more reason to help female graduate students succeed.

Finally, Mary Jo's ability to overcome resistance and Barbara's and Melva's inability to do so serve as reminders that learning and change take time. When graduate students are asked to reconceptualize their role in the classroom and those of their students, they are going against the view of higher education held by most of their professors. A single pedagogy seminar cannot overturn the mind-set held for over two centuries. Nevertheless, faculty should try to instantiate these pedagogical changes in every class. To ensure that graduate students are prepared to take over the professoriate, they will need sufficient time and opportunities to recognize and understand why change is necessary.

5. Overcoming Resistance

*W*hereas chapter 4 described conditions impeding the ability to overcome resistance, this chapter examines factors facilitating change. Both male and female graduate students will resist composition pedagogy if it contradicts their personal construct and threatens their feelings of self-efficacy; however, students of both genders can overcome resistance if their sense of self-efficacy is restored. Three factors contribute to their acceptance of change: age, writing experience, and engagement in composition pedagogy. Although this might appear to be a linear progression, overcoming resistance is a complex, multilayered process.

Overall, resistance typified the behavior of one-quarter of the graduate students I encountered in Teaching College Writing. The majority of resisters were male; moreover, the men's resistance differed in duration and degree. As a rule, the women's resistance, characterized by questions or writer's block, began to subside after the first peer-response session and disappeared by mid-semester. In almost every case, the men's resistance was more extreme—characterized by anger, sarcasm, or inappropriate language—and persistent, usually lasting most of the semester. However, by following their reactions, I found that these behaviors were only starting points on a learning curve that eventually led to a degree of understanding.

This chapter begins by expanding the parameters of resistance and then moves on to describe the context for the students' varying behaviors. Because the types and degrees of resistance corresponded not with gender but with the students' age and writing experience, the chapter is organized chronologically, moving from the youngest to the oldest "resisters." Using this organizational pattern, I trace the factors characterizing these students' resistance and examine the similarities and differences between genders. In so doing, I hope to provide a road map so instructors can recognize the signs of resistance and anticipate its demise.

EXPANDING THE DEFINITION OF RESISTANCE

Before I began this project, I assumed that my female students would welcome composition pedagogy, and the male students would resist. I based this belief on research suggesting that male students have been socialized to favor individualism, to be highly competitive, and to identify with authority. Because of their socialization, male students might view collaborative learning as an abdication of the teacher's authority; therefore, they would be likely to assume authority within a group setting, dominate conversation, or ignore the contributions of their female group members. Indeed, arguments against collaborative learning often cite these situations to support the contention that group work only reinforces the male-dominated status quo.[1]

Other studies led me to believe that female students would be particularly receptive to this pedagogy.[2] Carol Gilligan's *In a Different Voice* was one of the first to point out that whereas men are socialized to work individually and competitively, women learn to build relationships. They tend to be sensitive to others, to listen to their opinions, and "to include in their judgment other points of view" (16). Women's socialization seemingly prepares them for group work, for their language is based on "negotiation, rather than application of absolute standards . . . and emphasize[s] the communal aspect of intellectual life" (Gere 73, 75). In both *Women's Ways of Knowing* and *Knowledge, Difference, and Power*, Mary F. Belenky, Nancy R. Goldberger, Jill M. Tarule, and Blythe M. Clinchy argue for a pedagogy that builds on these elements, maintaining, "Educators can help women develop their own authentic voices if they emphasize connection over separation, understanding and acceptance over assessment, and collaboration over debate" (Belenky et al. 229).

Contrary to these earlier studies, I found that graduate students' behaviors could not be so easily categorized. Some of my female students' responses contradicted research suggesting that nontraditional pedagogy such as collaborative learning would be second nature, while most of the men's responses ultimately refuted research implying they would wholly reject new ways of teaching and writing. For both genders, the reasons for resistance differed from those in the previous chapter. Although those students resisted writing theory and pedagogy largely because it contradicted their personal constructs, which are internal and highly impermeable to change, the students in this chapter may have overcome their resistance because these approaches initially affected their feelings of self-efficacy, which are context-specific and thus more amenable to change.

Ruth Ray's study of graduate students' introduction to action research,

The Practice of Theory, further expands the concept of resistance. Ray maintains that students may resist new methods of teaching and research for *rhetorical, pedagogical,* or *epistemological* reasons (155). Drawing on Carol Berkenkotter, Thomas Huckin, and John Ackerman's case study of Nate, Ray explains that Nate's *rhetorical* resistance was exemplified by his hesitance to join the academic discourse community, and *pedagogical* resistance emerged as a result of his former teaching experiences, while *epistemological* resistance may have resulted from markedly different writing experiences prior to his admission to Carnegie Mellon University (154–55).

As I followed my graduate students' learning, I found that resistance for *rhetorical* reasons was characteristic of young, inexperienced teachers and writers new to the graduate program. These students appeared to question the new theories and pedagogical approaches to writing because of their uncertain status and relatively conservative approach to writing. Insecure about succeeding in graduate school, they were afraid to take risks, to tamper with what had worked before. In class, their resistance was obvious—they disliked freewriting, agonized over drafts, resented working in groups, and openly expressed anger and frustration. These graduate students felt that by requiring multiple drafts and asking them to participate in peer response, I was trying to change their writing style. Because they believed their students should not be subjected to something with which they themselves felt personally uncomfortable, they tended to avoid these teaching methods.

Students resisting for *pedagogical* reasons were inexperienced teachers and experienced but superstitious writers. They believed that good writers were born, not made; that good writing was the result of inspiration; and that to question or disturb the "muse" was blasphemous if not disastrous. Resistance of this type was difficult to reconcile, because it was illogical yet deeply rooted in the writer's process and personality. In group work, these students seemed to ignore their peers' suggestions and do little or no revision between drafts; however, upon closer examination, I found that for these writers, revision connoted expansion, because they had already labored over each word while drafting. These students were perfectionists in their writing and their teaching. Afraid of losing control in the classroom, they maintained a teacher-centered class, often avoiding group work because they believed their students could not write well enough to profit from collaboration. Correlating good writing with good thinking, they assumed that those students who did not measure up were either lazy or dumb.

Like their peers, graduate students who resisted for *epistemological* reasons were also inexperienced teachers; however, these resisters were experienced writers secure in their own process. Because of their prior successes, they were skeptical of theories of writing and learning at odds with how they wrote and reluctant to engage in activities such as peer response because they felt these were not only intrusive but unnecessary. They displayed their resistance by playing what Peter Elbow describes in *Writing Without Teachers* as "the doubting game: arguing, questioning theories, trying to poke holes in them, raising objections, and quibbling over minor points" (177). Nevertheless, because they were confident writers, these students were somewhat more willing to try freewriting, drafting, and collaborative learning in their classrooms because they wanted to help inexperienced writers become aware of their composing processes.

Because the reasons for resistance for both sexes are parallel, in this chapter, I paired males and females exhibiting similar behaviors. These case studies move along a continuum of writing experience, one of the most salient factors in determining and coping with resistance. The more experience these students had, the more willing they were to take risks with their writing and subsequently in their teaching.

THE CONTEXT

Of the six graduate students discussed in this chapter, five took just one of my pedagogy courses. Paul, Susan, Jeff, Ken, and Pattie took Teaching College Writing, and Gail took Reading-Writing Theory. Susan, who specialized in composition, enrolled in Radical Pedagogy four years after her first composition seminar. Like my other graduate seminars, Reading-Writing Theory and Radical Pedagogy teach writing as a process.

The ages and writing experience of the paired case study students were quite similar. Gail and Paul were 23–24 years old, first-year students who did not know what to expect of graduate school and (perhaps as a result) were taking an overload. Gail was single and supporting herself with a teaching assistantship; Paul was a married, full-time student supported by his wife. Susan and Jeff were in their late twenties. Both of them had worked in a variety of jobs and attended a number of universities before deciding upon the graduate program on my campus. Susan was single and teaching part-time at a local community college. Jeff was married; both he and his wife were TAs in their respective departments. Pattie and Ken were in their late thirties, returning students who had worked for years as writers, Pattie in business and Ken in journalism. Pattie was beginning her master's degree because she was divorcing and would need to return to the workforce. Ken was married; disillusioned with journalism, he was beginning the M.A. and then planned to go on for his Ph.D. Taken altogether, these students are representative of a certain percentage of their peers whose prior experiences strongly influence their perception, reception, and application of composition pedagogy.

PERSONAL CONSTRUCT AND WRITING EXPERIENCE

When examining the possibility of changing the way they practice or conceptualize teaching, graduate students, like experienced teachers, are quite often influenced by their personal constructs. As Christine Farris found in her study of TAs, "Instructors teach writing as a limited function of who they are; what they value; what they have read, taught, and been taught; and whom they teach" (*Subject* 152). When students begin graduate school, they have already experienced at least sixteen years of fairly traditional pedagogy; however, these beliefs are not necessarily static. Farris concludes that a new TA's theory of instruction may "be viewed as a dynamic rhetorical transaction between individuals and experience rather than as a coherent and explicit set of assumptions about the nature of writing" (29). If this is true, then the quantity and quality of both past and present experiences will impact the construction of that theory. In the following vignettes, I further describe the students whose personal construct initially led them to resist composition pedagogy: Gail and Paul, Susan and Jeff, and Pattie and Ken.

Rhetorical Resistance: Gail and Paul

Since I began directing the writing program, I have consistently argued that new TAs should not be hired in the middle of the school year. Unless they have taken the presemester workshop and Teaching College Writing, these TAs begin teaching without a solid grounding in theory and pedagogy, without the support of their fellow TAs, and without the knowledge engendered by participating in the "mastery experiences" practiced in these courses. Despite my protests, a new TA is periodically hired at midyear; not surprisingly, these graduate students, as well as the students they teach, suffer the consequences. Such was the case with Gail.

Gail's first semester of teaching had been miserable. She didn't know what she was doing, so she relied on the syllabus and lesson plans of her office mates without understanding the theories behind them. Because she wanted to be better prepared for her second year as a TA, Gail enrolled in my reading-writing seminar the following summer, at which point I discovered the extent of her discomfort. On the first night of peer response, I planned to audiotape the students' discussions for analysis. When I mentioned my intent at an earlier meeting, Gail made no comment; however, when I began to tape this peer-response session, she asked me not to. The drafting process had been so painful, she said, that she just "couldn't take" being taped. Despite guidelines on the peer-response sheets, Gail argued that she did not know what she wanted to say in the discussion and would feel uncomfortable if her comments were recorded. Reluctantly, I honored her wishes.

Gail felt that collaborative learning was personally intrusive in part because she "didn't like any feedback on [her] writing."[3] Perhaps in consequence, she did not believe group work was appropriate in the context of a graduate seminar. As a graduate student, Gail felt exposed and forced to intrude on the writing of her peers; as a new TA, she believed her tenuous authority had been breached, for group work placed her in direct contact with her students. In Gail's response journal, she explained some of these feelings:

> I went into this class with some trepidation—realizing that it would be a stressful environment. My fellow teachers probably won't understand what's stressful about it. All I can say is that for a natural introvert basing class discussions on her own freewrites is hell (and lack of confidence has nothing to do with it, it's a matter of privacy) and introducing a new cure-all theory of education is like sending an earthquake through a place that was always home.[4]

But that was not the only reason Gail resisted group work. After analyzing her drafts and freewrites, I learned that she objected to tape recording her peer-response conversations because she did not want anyone to see her paper until she got it "right." Gail was unaccustomed to drafting and unfamiliar with the theories she was encountering; consequently, when she learned that her midterm essay was to describe how she would use reading in her writing classroom, she panicked. These feelings led to embarrassment over her draft and anger at me because I had put her into that position.[5]

Gail's feelings were similar to Paul's. Both were new graduate students who had succeeded within traditional lecture-based classrooms in which they were assigned essay topics and told what to learn.[6] Neither had ever been asked to compose multiple drafts or to collaborate with their peers, so it should not have been surprising that both Gail and Paul felt my way of teaching was not only difficult and frustrating but also intrusive, disruptive, and pedagogically inappropriate. Their role as students was to receive knowledge, memorize it, and give it back to the professor. Gail and Paul wanted to be told how to do their work, and they wanted to hear it from an authority. Needless to say, this mind-set also meant they did not believe in collaborative learning or respect a professor who asked them to engage in it.

Like many graduate students, Paul held fairly traditional assumptions about writing. He believed that good writing did not include personal experience and that an individual's ability to write was inborn. Responding to readings about collaborative learning and the student-centered classroom, he wrote, "Ideally, these things shouldn't have to be discussed at all. . . . [They] would occur if the students were to have a coup, after which anarchy would reign in the classroom."[7] He dismissed collaborative learning as fallacious and unnecessary because "the education system is set up to provide information" and denounced theories about writing-as-a-process as "fairly simplistic." Paul said he found freewriting his journal entries useless—"the work became almost an excuse to avoid writing well." He regarded freewriting as "artsy-fartsy [sic] new age . . . no guts behind it. The sound of it reminds me of pansies dancing around a mulberry bush or something." To illustrate his contempt, some journal entries even descended into the scatological, the worst of which began, "Oooh. Sorry. I just paused to take a dump," and then continued with the details.[8]

This behavior infuriated me. I did not mind Paul's skepticism—I had dealt with that before—but I strongly resented the way he expressed it. He obviously had no respect for the readings and even less for me. But Paul's disrespect was not limited to me. During the semester he was enrolled in Teaching College Writing, I encouraged the students to choose their own peer-response partners and to change partners periodically to get a variety of feedback. For the first peer-response session, Paul chose to work with Sr. Gisela. At the time, I assumed he did so because they were sitting near each other and because they were taking many of the same classes together, but after listening to the tape recordings of their interactions, I began to suspect there may have been other reasons. In addition to being a first-semester graduate student, Sr. Gisela was also a woman and an inexperienced writer. When they worked together, Paul displayed behaviors similar to what feminist researchers fear will occur in mixed-gender groups: He dominated the conversation, directed the tasks, and reported their findings.[9] When Paul and Sr. Gisela responded to each other's drafts, they were always the first group done, finishing in half the allotted time. Eventually, I began to wonder if Paul chose Sr. Gisela because this pairing allowed him to avoid peer response altogether. As he so delicately put it, "All I had to do was ask her a question, and she wouldn't shut up."[10]

Pedagogical Resistance: Susan and Jeff

When Susan enrolled in Teaching College Writing, she had just been hired to teach a section of basic writing at a community college even though, like many adjunct instructors, she had no pedagogical training or experience. She was simply given her books and shown her classroom. Aware of her inexperience, Susan was anxious to learn more about teaching. Initially, she was also sympathetic to her students' writing apprehension and willing to try some "new" teaching strategies such as group work and short, reflective writings.[11] However, after reading her students' freewrites, Susan was so appalled that she equated their inexperience with stupidity, at one point even referring to them as "Neanderthals." This attitude led her to reject collaborative learning as far too advanced for basic writers: "They need the structure of some lecturing, as they seem to either fail to read or fail to understand the assigned material otherwise." Not surprisingly, Susan also rejected peer editing as "premature," viewing it as a matter of "the blind leading the blind."[12] Week after week, Susan resisted the teaching strategies we practiced in Teaching College Writing; one after another, her teaching logs began, "I spent most of today lecturing."[13] According to Patricia Ashton, such behavior typifies teachers with a low sense of self-efficacy. When a teaching strategy is not successful, these teachers blame the students rather than themselves, an unconscious strategy allowing them to avoid self-blame (149). Susan's reliance on lecture rather than group work reflected that feeling.

Susan's attitude also reflected her educational experiences. As she noted in her journal, "Nearly all of my learning has been teacher-centered or self-taught." Throughout high school and college, her courses were lecture-based, discussion was teacher-centered, and collaboration was regarded as cheating.[14] Susan's beliefs about teaching related to her beliefs about writing. She admitted that she had "always been a little confused about the idea of rewriting. . . . For me, rewriting has always been an inconvenience."[15] Susan resisted revising—and the peer-response sessions preceding it—because they interfered with her creative "muse":

> I do feel there is some magic in the writing process. I enjoy that moment of inspiration and the process of discovering my own thoughts and feelings through writing. Collaboration diminishes that. Maybe I have bought into the romantic notion of the isolated writer, but I feel it must be this way for the work to truly be my own.[16]

Given Susan's beliefs that basic writers were Neanderthals who could not profit from small-group work and that collaborative learning was creatively disruptive, it follows that she would resist these methods in her teaching and her writing.

Jeff was one of three fiction writers enrolled in Teaching College Writing during fall 1994. This was not the first time Jeff had taught, but it was the first time he had taken a pedagogy course. Until this point, he had modeled his teaching on his experiences as a student. As an undergraduate science major, Jeff had been trained to believe in a positivist methodology: There were right answers, and there were wrong answers, and only the teacher knew which was which. He described his teaching strategies as hiding behind the lectern, lecturing on the day's readings, and outlining on the board how a paper should be correctly written.[17]

Because of these experiences, Jeff began Teaching College Writing openly skeptical of the de-centered classroom, a belief reflected in his teaching. Once again, he was "running the classroom from the podium." Like Susan, Jeff was uneasy allowing students a voice in their discussions or in editing their peers' papers. These feelings and experiences are not atypical, yet they appeared contradictory in light of Jeff's subsequent training as a creative writer. Even though his primary experiences had been in workshop settings, Jeff had difficulty believing the same approach would work with expository writing. If his creative-writing students failed to comprehend an assigned story, he did not worry. He would use misunderstandings to illustrate that "art does not rely exclusively on analysis or even close reading." Faced with the same misunderstandings in a composition course, however, he would outline the essay on the board and lecture about how its different parts contributed to the overall meaning.[18] This dichotomy may have been related to Jeff's concern with teaching grammar. A native Hawaiian, he had learned to speak pidgin English outside of school but to speak and write standard English in the classroom. He explained that in this environment, it was a given that "In order to get one good job, you got to learn to talk like one *haole* (*haole* meaning *Caucasian*)."[19] Like the minority students Lisa Delpit describes, Jeff perceived the expressionist and social constructivist approaches informing creative-writing pedagogy as antithetical to teaching expository writing. Intellectually, he believed that the two were similar, "but somehow, there is a skepticism that resides in me which does not allow me to act as if I believe it."[20]

Epistemological Resistance: Pattie and Ken

Pattie and Ken were not just skeptics—they were also cynics. Nontraditional students in their mid-thirties, both had held jobs involving a considerable amount of journalistic writing, which ultimately led them to graduate to school to retool. Like Susan and Jeff, Pattie was a perfectionist who feared tampering with what she considered a successful composing process; unlike them, she resisted nontraditional teaching strategies because she doubted their epistemological basis. Pattie had been writing—and publishing—since she was ten years old,[21] so by the time she entered Teaching College Writing, her attitudes about writing were fairly well-established. Despite her experience, Pattie's confidence had been decimated by fourteen years of marriage to a man who belittled her talent and her intelligence. I learned of these feelings after the first meeting of Teaching College Writing when Pattie called me because she doubted her ability to complete the writing requirements.

If Pattie had not called, I would never have guessed she was insecure. In her first journal response, she commented that the female authors "seem to have been paid by the word as it seemed obvious that more attention was paid to the number and length of the words used than in the clarity of their ideas." Neither of the readings had reached her or taught her anything, she said. John Trimbur's explanation of collaborative learning was "of interest," but she was not "in favor of this type of scheme" because in her experience, the most capable people in the group usually ended up doing most of the work. Pattie explained her resistance when she wrote, "I was educated by the old school where each individual did their [*sic*] own work and that was that." She believed the classroom should reflect a hierarchy of knowledge with the teacher possessing all of the power:

> To be involved in a group of my peers does not give me a feeling of comfort. How can I possibly consider them to be credible judges of my work when they are in the same situation as I am and I don't know what I am doing?

Given this stance, it followed that Pattie also disagreed with social constructivist theories of learning. "While some ideas may come from social contacts," she declared, "writing is a solitary act."[22]

Ken's attitude and experiences paralleled Pattie's. After majoring in journalism, he had worked as a reporter for five years and free-lanced for eight years before beginning graduate school. During that period, he had published thousands of articles and won numerous national press awards. When he became disillusioned with journalism, he returned to college to finish his bachelor's degree, where he won prizes for his undergraduate essays.[23] These experiences had clearly influenced his beliefs about writing. Like Pattie, Ken believed writing was a solitary act whose process he had internalized.[24]

When Ken began Teaching College Writing, he quickly revealed his skepticism. He questioned the practicality of prewriting and criticized Donald Murray for being boring and repetitive, claiming, "Reading Murray was like reading the phone book." Ken did not like Peter Elbow any better, noting that "a lot of [his] ideas seem only of partial relevance," too advanced for freshmen, better suited for English majors, and full of wishful thinking.[25] But Ken reserved his most scathing criticism for Anne Gere's *Writing Groups*—a text I had added to the reading list to defuse Ken's reputed cynicism. In a journal entry of almost four single-spaced pages, he disputed Gere's social constructivist theories regarding authorship, reiterating his beliefs that writing was an individual activity and that the writer's products were his sole property—he owed nothing to anyone else.[26]

Despite these feelings, Ken's teaching reflected the very strategies he criticized. When teaching students to write objective essays, he asked them to get into groups and revise a poorly developed model paper.[27] When he held student conferences, he asked his students to bring a draft of their paper and worked with them on its revision, trying, he said, "to offer them the same sort of response they're getting in class from their peers." In evaluating these sessions, he admitted he may have given the students too much advice, noting it was "a bad habit (and particularly hypocritical in me, since I'm always whining about individuals writing their own papers)."[28] This approach contrasted sharply with Ken's views of collaborative learning spelled out in his first paper for Teaching College Writing, in which he complained:

> I worry about collaboration. I worry about it a lot. I worry that by teaching people one process, I am keeping them ignorant of others that might better suit them. I worry that by compelling students to collaborate I am alienating them from their own voices.

In the essay's conclusion, he became even more specific:

> Look: I want to give collaborative learning my best effort. But the very heart of me is built out of ideals of individualism I can't abandon. I can't. I'll take collaborative learning as a free association of equal individuals, or I won't take it at all. The irony is that to make it work I need an environment in which those equals can learn to trust each other, rely on each other, and learn from each other.[29]

At that point in the semester, Ken conflated collaborative learning with collaborative writing. He seemed to believe that working in small groups would result in people other than the author writing the paper or in those others coercing the author to change his content or point of view. Despite his years of working for newspaper editors, Ken did not equate that process with peer response. He needed to experience collaborative learning to gain a better sense of how it could work.

WRITING EXPERIENCE AND SELF-EFFICACY

In her study of TAs' self-efficacy, Susan H. McLeod concludes, "A teacher's sense of efficacy will determine the amount of effort she puts into her teaching, her task choices, her degree of persistence when confronted with difficulties, her motivation to continue" ("Pygmalion" 377). When applied to the teaching of writing, the source of this efficacy (or lack thereof) can be traced to the teacher's writing experiences. Experienced writers may express a strong sense of efficacy when teaching composition, because they know what works for them; conversely, inexperienced writers often lack a strong sense of efficacy as teachers of composition because they find writing difficult and frustrating.

Peter Elbow and Pat Belanoff maintain that one of the primary reasons people find writing difficult is because they tend to believe in and use a single approach to composing (12). Elbow and Belanoff try to demonstrate that different writing tasks require different processes—an idea that even skilled writers find difficult to accept. Graduate students are no exception. They are much more accustomed, as Murray notes ruefully, to believe that they must compose with a clear-cut purpose, message, and audience in mind than they are to experiment with various ideas and approaches. Moreover, very few students (or faculty) reflect on how they write. Because they have never tried it, some reject freewriting out of hand and resent requests to reflect on their writing or to compose multiple drafts. As Donald Schon explains, when we present students with new theories of learning, we are asking them to "let go of earlier understandings and know-how, along with the sense of control and confidence that accompanies them" (*Reflective* 120). To avoid this feeling, they may resist these theories.

Reading Elbow and Belanoff's explanation of freewriting or Murray's ruminations on process writing will not convince these students to try them. They need to practice these methods, to engage in "mastery experiences," and to reflect on their effects if they are to be persuaded to try them in their classrooms. The following vignettes illustrate not only how composition pedagogy can affect graduate students' feelings of self-efficacy but also how resistance varies by gender.

Inexperienced Writers: Gail and Paul

At the beginning of our Reading-Writing seminar, Gail described her composing process quite succinctly: She wrote a single draft at the last minute from an outline based on what she determined "her teachers wanted."[30] Given this approach—which had always worked for her—

writing drafts and working with a peer partner did indeed send "an earthquake through a place that was always home," for I neither lectured nor did I tell students what I wanted them to say. Instead, I asked them to freewrite to explore ideas and to exchange these reflections with their peers. In her first freewrite before the midterm essay, Gail complained that she had "absolutely no idea what to write on" because she did not know what she believed about her own teaching and writing.[31] In a subsequent journal assignment, she explained her discomfort:

> Given the connection between thinking and writing I can see why I don't like discussing my writing process in class—it's like opening up my brain and studying how it works or like analyzing me. At least with other subjects, even literature, when you write you have the subject matter as a buffer between yourself and your writing. When studying writing and in personal writing, you don't have that.[32]

Gail's feelings were hard for me to understand. I did not view the discussions of journal entries as intrusive because we were using them as springboards for discussion rather than to psychoanalyze or test the students' comprehension. But I realized Gail's difficulty when first drafts of the midterm essays were due. Before class, Gail came to my office and told me she was having trouble with this paper. "I don't know what to do," she said. "I've never had so much trouble writing a paper. I've done draft after draft, I've tried freewriting, but I just can't come up with anything I like." Part of Gail's problems could be attributed to her previous writing experiences. Marcia B. Baxter-Magolda, in her analysis of gender-related patterns in intellectual development, explains that if a person was used to writing only "what the teacher wanted," the mode of thinking this required most likely precluded analytical thinking or complex reasoning (19–20). Developing an essay describing her understanding of the reading-writing relationship and applying it to her teaching was outside Gail's experience; therefore, trying to develop ideas while engaging in a new way of writing only increased her frustration while decreasing her feelings of self-efficacy.

Paul's confusion was even more pronounced. In his first essay for Teaching College Writing, in which he was to describe an ideal teacher, his first draft began:

> Looking at what the assignment is, and trying to figure into this whole (bullshit) theory of freewriting and teaching the notion that "teaching, like

parenting, is a learned imitative behavior. We teach as we were taught" and all that. My difficulty is that I cannot get beyond what the instructor wants. Does she really want me to write what I feel? Or what I think?

From there, he answered his own question: "According to the articles I've read for this course, I shouldn't look at what the instructor wants at all. . . . So who do I choose [to write about]? That is as good a place to begin as any."[33] And so he did, writing four more pages on three different teachers before deciding which one had been most influential. Although Paul claimed that freewriting was "an excuse to avoid writing well," analyses of his drafts support Belanoff's findings that drifting off for a few lines or even a few pages—what she terms "chaotic freewriting"—helped him focus his ideas (18).

Nevertheless, when Paul began writing his second paper, "On Becoming a Teacher," his resistance returned in full force. His first draft followed the same pattern as those leading up to essay 1: He questioned and complained, ending with "Why do I want to teach? I want to help people. I want to argue. I want to be an educator—But, Christ, why? WHY?"[34] Paul had no difficulty explicating literature and presenting his findings in impersonal academic prose, but like many male students, he had little or no experience writing reflectively (Gannett 159). In his second draft, after meandering for two pages, he exploded with three pages of angry complaints about his inexperience, ending:

> What am I supposed to do about this class, huh? I'm really fed up. A week ago I wrote a paper comparing Donne's "La Corona" to Eliot's "Ash Wednesday." It was a good paper. And now I come to this class and I have to write about a subject I can't look up in a book, can't fake my way around, and have no experience of, except a little inkling of a topic that I found difficult to stretch to 2 pages, much less 5. . . . OH WHAT THE HELL! DAMN THIS ASSIGNMENT TO HELL. BEGONE WITH IT. BURN IT.[35]

Clearly, this type of writing had damaged Paul's feelings of self-efficacy.

Superstitious Perfectionists: Susan and Jeff

Like Barbara (in chapter 4), Susan's composing process could be described in two seemingly unrelated words—procrastination and perfectionism—both of which had caused her "untold hassles."[36] Because she wanted her writing to be perfect, she kept putting it off in the hopes of finding the right time to write, a behavior typical of apprehensive writers (L. Bloom

163). Paradoxically, because of this tendency, Susan often left herself with too little time to revise. Susan's experiences in Teaching College Writing helped somewhat because she had to bring her drafts for peer response, but it took her awhile to adapt to this approach. Although she claimed that the group work in our class had "been really good" and that she was learning "how to teach using groups as well as how to better participate in them," the drafts of her first two essays showed no evidence of her group members' influence. In essay 1, she deleted one paragraph and added two more; in essay 2, she added one sentence to her first draft and deleted another. Nevertheless, for both papers, Susan maintained she was benefiting from her group work.[37] This may not have been evident in her writing, but the experience was influencing her teaching. After participating in peer response for essay 1, Susan tried small groups again with her basic writers, and this time it was more successful. In her teaching log, she explained the difference: "You're right about modeling and narrowing down the focus of what they were looking for. The first time I tried this, I just told [the students] to exchange papers and give each other responses. What did I expect? This was way too unfocused."[38]

By the time she began to write essay 3, Susan's composing process had begun to reflect her change in attitude. In her journal, she admitted, "I'm . . . not quite sure what I want to say in this paper, and I don't think I found out in the first draft. I'm eager to see how the others in my group respond to it."[39] Their influence was evident in the difference between her second and third drafts: The latter was expanded by six pages of quotations, explanations, and examples in the body and three pages of solutions to teaching problems in the conclusion, all of which Susan attributed to her group members' feedback.[40]

By building in class time for drafting and peer response, I was able to help Susan recognize the necessity of revision. As she concluded in her final journal entry:

> The group work has been really good. . . . I often feel wrapped up in a paper and am unable to separate myself enough to analyze it well; the group helped me step back and think about it more objectively. Early on, I saw group work as detracting from the originality of the individual. I now see how wrong that was. . . . The peers are not trying to change what the authors write but are instead trying to help them clarify and refine their work.[41]

Susan modified her resistance because she was willing to spend some time reflecting on her process. As she wrote in the introduction to her portfolio,

> Re-examining the process of writing has allowed me to change my ideas of how to write. . . . This has been beneficial to me in this class and will be beneficial to my writing in the future. More importantly, though, it has changed my thinking and my criteria. The true beneficiaries of these changes in philosophy will be the students I teach.[42]

Like Susan, Jeff was a superstitious perfectionist. In an early freewrite, he admitted that although he was a creative writer, "I would like to learn how to rewrite. . . . I am . . . a poor rewriter. I don't ever know where to begin, I am always afraid of making things worse."[43] This process was evident in the composition of Jeff's first and second essays in Teaching College Writing. His drafts revealed no revisions, only additions. Group work did not help, he said, for his peers only confirmed what he already knew was wrong with the draft.[44]

Jeff had long aspired to be a creative writer. Originally, he composed only when "inspired," at which point he would write until he could write no more: "I had decided that this was my personal writing style, based on the myth of writer as anguished artist who worked in fits. . . . I did not think of writing as a process. I thought writing was a magic trick." After talking with novelist John Barth, Jeff believed he had abandoned these myths, but the process he described still fell into the category of "anguished artist": "Wrote about 800 words yesterday, good words, and met quota of two pages. More like 2 and ¼ pages." Jeff described this process as involving patience and time, sitting at the computer for "at least six to eight hours, and sometimes if you are near completion of a story, ten to twelve hours."[45]

As a writing theorist, I believed Jeff's process stifled his creativity, but I was more concerned with how this process affected his teaching. Jeff believed that creative writers were better than expository writers; therefore, what worked for the former (workshopping, experimenting, risk-taking) would not work for freshmen, who needed to learn the basics before they could be allowed to compose independently: "Deep down," he said, "I believe my job is to keep them from getting worse than they came in."[46] Such fears suggest a low sense of personal efficacy in the classroom.

Cynical, Experienced Writers: Pattie and Ken

Pattie's writing process was much like Jeff's. Perhaps because of her early training as a journalist, she "never considered writing as a process." Although she found the idea "fascinating," she, too, had no idea how to revise. Like Jeff, she said, "My biggest fear is that the second draft won't be as good as the first one, that is assuming, of course, that the first one was any good." Pattie did not revise; she expanded. Her composing process involved perfecting every word of a so-called draft before showing it to her peer group. The amount of time this process entailed, coupled with her belief that no one in her group could provide useful feedback, led Pattie to believe that there was no such thing as a draft—when she was done, she had a final product.[47] However, when she brought her first draft of essay 1 (on educational experiences) to workshop with her group members, her opinion began to change:

> While discussing the first essay, I was at a dead end with regard to the topic of my third vignette. Listening to Chris read her story provided me with an idea that never would have occurred to me had she not included something similar in her story. . . . Writing truly is a singular activity, but I have found that the discussing of one's writing is necessary in order to move forward.[48]

This discovery was reinforced during the writing of the second essay, an analysis of her composing process. Because of her perfectionist tendencies, Pattie had once again tried to ensure the draft was perfectly worded. This focus, as well as the time it required, prematurely stifled her creativity. Instead of allowing her mind to explore new ideas, she worried about perfecting those she had already generated. Consequently, she had a tendency to hit what she referred to as the "proverbial brick wall,"[49] which led her to polish rather than develop her writing. But once again, Pattie's group members came through, suggesting that she bring in excerpts of her earlier writing to "demonstrate change or refinement" and to "include copy from previous papers or freewrites" to illustrate her problems with revision.[50] Feedback from her group helped Pattie over her brick wall so she was able to go home and revise. Analyzing her composing process also helped her to realize that she did indeed have one; she concluded that the assignment had provided "a wealth of knowledge about the writing process and skills that I never knew I had."[51]

Pattie's case represents one of the biggest problems experienced writers bring to teaching: They know how to write but they have seldom considered how they learned or what they know, so they tend to believe that writing cannot be taught. For too many teachers of writing, this ignorance causes a sort of amnesia. They enter the classroom believing they have always known how to write or that their writing abilities must have come naturally. For experienced writers, this latter statement contains an element of truth. Most of them are also experienced readers, which aids in the acquisition and development of their literacy skills (F. Smith, *Understanding*). However, without a conscious awareness of one's process—of its sources, strengths, and weaknesses—it is very difficult to empathize with, let alone to analyze the processes of inexperienced writers to help them develop their own strengths. As Elbow and Belanoff point out, "Writers learn the most by becoming students of their own writing processes" (446).

This line seems particularly applicable to Ken. His first paper for Teaching College Writing, basically a critique of collaborative learning, was clearly written for me, yet it was equally clear that Ken misunderstood my intent in promoting group work. When asked what had helped him compose and develop the paper, he replied:

> Well, the feedback from [his group member] Melissa was the most useful thing. Actually, she kept hammering away at the conclusion, saying it was weak, until I broke down and rethought it. Until that point, I'm not sure that I exactly knew what the conclusion was supposed to be. This, to me, is ideal collaboration, in that the conclusion is mine—she never really said how to change it—but just her stubborn insistence that it was insufficient pushed some, I don't know, competitive buttons and caused me to work harder on it.[52]

That was, as I pointed out in my response to his paper, exactly what I believed collaboration could and should accomplish. In the process of communication or even miscommunication, ideas would be developed or fleshed out because one person would realize that the other was not getting his point. Ken's diatribe and my response to it helped clear the air. In his response to Ulric Neisser's chapters on schema theory, Ken's conclusion suggested a changed opinion regarding the social construction of knowledge: "I guess this is obvious, what else could collective knowledge be but mass schema developed from a lot of individual schema."[53]

APPLYING THEORY

By the time students enter graduate school, most professors assume they possess the background knowledge and motivation to learn individually. Because of this belief, "the teaching of writing to graduate students is held to be redundant or superfluous" (Sullivan, "Writing" 288). These beliefs are based not only on "institutional praxis" but also, as Patricia A. Sullivan found, on the professors' misperceptions about composing processes. Among the reasons given for not teaching writing were the beliefs that it could not be taught, that it ought not be taught because it would "inhibit the students' creativity," and that it need not be taught because the students should pick up everything they needed to know by reading (294). If this sounds familiar, it's because the same sentiments were voiced by graduate students in this chapter.

There are at least two problems with these assumptions. First, they preclude the elements Frank Smith maintains are necessary to learning—demonstration, engagement, and sensitivity—thus making learning unnecessarily difficult. Second, these assumptions provide graduate students with an implicit model for learning that (as we've seen) they unconsciously assimilate: they come to believe that learning—especially learning about writing—must be individual, solitary, and difficult. If these misconceptions are not challenged, graduate students will teach as they were taught, thus perpetuating these beliefs and impeding their students' learning.

Such prior experiences form graduate students' schema regarding how learning should occur in the seminars they take and in the classes they teach. However, if faculty understand that schema can be updated and that demonstration, engagement, and sensitivity foster the learning process, it follows that by using these methods in the graduate classroom, we help our graduate students reformulate their schema regarding teaching and learning. The following examples illustrate this possibility.

Gail and Paul: Writing Experience and Self-Efficacy

When I began teaching the Reading-Writing seminar in the summer of 1990, I had been using constructivist pedagogy in my classrooms for over ten years. Although I occasionally encountered students who just "didn't get it," I tended to view any resistance as the student's problem, not mine—a view that enabled me to maintain my own sense of self-efficacy (Ashton

143). Because I had not closely examined the effects of my pedagogy, traced my students' progress, or sought their opinions on my teaching, I was unaware of any other reasons for discomfort or discontent.

This relative state of bliss came to an end when Gail enrolled in my Reading-Writing seminar. On the first night of class, Gail told me she disliked sharing her freewrites; on the second, she said she felt uncomfortable with group work; by the third, she was complaining about the reading, freewriting, and active learning.[54] My first reaction was amazement, but as the complaints continued, that feeling changed to annoyance. My first instinct was to blame the student; I remained in that mode throughout most of the summer session. But at the end of the summer when I began to analyze Gail's writing, study her journals, and compare her work to that of her peers, I began to gain some insight into her feelings and behavior. Gail's responses were the impetus for continuing this action-research project.

Working in a permanent small group with a peer who was supportive and possessed complementary skills helped Gail overcome many of her negative feelings. Her peer partner, Angie, had six years experience as a high school teacher but considerably less writing experience. Angie's teaching had accustomed her to providing positive feedback on a one-to-one basis; this same experience had convinced her that she needed to expand her teaching strategies. Therefore, she was open to change, anxious to learn about collaborative learning, and quite willing to participate in group work.[55] Although Gail was an inexperienced teacher, her first year as a graduate student in English had already given her more writing experience than Angie. So, even though she disliked peer response, Gail was able to read Angie's work critically and provide constructive feedback. These complementary strengths contributed to the women's gradually increasing friendship and trust.

When I looked at the first draft of Gail's midterm paper, her resistance was evident in both the tone and content. In this version, she recounted her personal problems with collaborative learning. Indeed, her feelings were so strong that she was unable to move beyond them to write an objective essay, but ironically, collaborative learning played a valuable role in Gail's revision process. If I had told Gail that her essay was too personal, she might have ignored me. However, when Angie said that she "would really like to know how many other students share this view and what could be done (if anything) to make sharing your writing less uncomfortable,"[56] the suggestion sounded less threatening because it came from a peer. At the end of that peer-response session, when I asked the class to comment on the experience of sharing their writing, Gail admitted that she had been skeptical: "Up until this point, I felt this was just like any other writing course. But I have never gone through anything like this with my writing." She was pleased and relieved that the feedback from her group had helped her decide what direction to take in her revision.[57]

When Gail returned to class for the second peer-response session, she brought with her two more drafts because she could not decide which was better, so Angie read them both. When she finished, Angie noted that Gail's voice was stronger in the shorter version, she marked the best paragraphs, and she pointed out those needing development. This session was useful for Gail as a teacher and as a student. In responding to Angie's paper, Gail was gaining experience working one-to-one; in her response to Gail's, Angie was providing the type of positive feedback Gail needed. As she left class, Gail turned to me and said, "I'm so relieved. This was so much better."

After working with Angie, Gail began to see that drafting meant she did not have to be perfect and that feedback from a supportive but objective reader could help her to focus. Collaborating with Angie also helped Gail work through her fears about peer response. Angie's teaching experience and concern for her students manifested itself in a concern for Gail and in her responses to Gail's writing. Her comments consistently suggested that Gail share her concerns about group work with her students and that she use her own feelings to meet their needs and make them comfortable. This feedback helped Gail broaden her understanding and lessen her fear.

Gail's discomfort helped me become aware of these feelings and the factors contributing to them. As a result, I began to work more closely with my students and tried to structure my courses so I could better recognize and address their fears. Gail's experience in this course also raised her awareness. In subsequent semesters, she became more willing to use collaborative learning in her classroom and, as I learned from one of my colleagues, she gained the confidence to take more risks with her writing.[58] Certainly one factor in this behavior was Gail's increased experience teaching and writing at the graduate level, but another factor may have been her experience with reflective journals. Janice Hays maintains that such writing "requires active response from each learner and encourages her to formulate and explore her own ideas about what she is learning and thus discover that she indeed has ideas." In the process, reflective writing helps develop metacognitive skills (169).

During the first two months of the semester, Paul's resistance waxed and waned. The timing of the first peer-response session marked the initial change in attitude. Despite his limited interactions with Sr. Gisela, this session seemed to dispel some of his misgivings about collaboration. Paul said he did not mind sharing his work and that "it was a good feeling to get feedback on something [he'd] written." To my surprise, when asked what would have helped him to revise, he responded, "more critical peer editing."[59] During this period of collaboration, his negative attitude also disappeared from his journals. Paul's anger and resistance reappeared when he began to compose the second essay, but after purging his feelings in his first and second drafts, his third draft was better developed.[60] For this essay, Paul worked with a male peer-response partner, Auggie. The difference in Paul's interactions with Sr. Gisela and Auggie is instructive.

Although Sr. Gisela offered positive feedback, Paul rarely acknowledged her comments beyond muttering "uh-huh" or "okay,"[61] conversational behavior typical of mixed-gender interactions (Ashton-Jones 13). But when he started working with Auggie, Paul's behavior changed. As with Sr. Gisela, Paul gave Auggie useful advice about how he might revise his paper. In turn, Auggie responded with questions and comments about how Paul's paper was coming together. Contrary to the previous interactions with Sr. Gisela, Paul explained what he was trying to do, described plans for revision, and asked Auggie how he viewed particular parts of his essay. For the first time, the peer-response session sounded like a conversation between equals. Instead of struggling to fill ten minutes, they talked for almost a half hour.[62] This essay, due the eleventh week of the semester, coupled with the peer-response session with Auggie, marked a final turning point in Paul's resistance. Although he periodically quibbled with some of the weekly readings, henceforth, his attitude was generally more positive.

Why had Paul been so angry? None of his other professors elicited such feelings, but they were male and fairly traditional in their instructional strategies, so my de-centered classroom was probably a factor in Paul's behavior. A number of other factors may also have contributed: insecurity in graduate school, overwork from four graduate seminars, inexperience with the reading assignments, difficulty with a new writing process, discomfort with personal writing, inability to generate topics, and embarrassment when forced to present an imperfect draft for inspection by relative strangers—in sum, diminished feelings of self-efficacy.

The essay assignments were clear, but the topics were unfamiliar. The journal questions were also clear, but the criteria for evaluation were not, so Paul resented the low scores he received for what were sometimes literally scribbles. Although they had specific questions to address during peer response, working with Sr. Gisela presumably resulted in silence because of her gender and lack of writing experience. Paul may have regarded these sessions as worthless because he received little substantive advice. However, when he began to work with Auggie at midterm, Paul found a peer in gender, ability, and experience as well as someone familiar with collaborative learning; consequently, they were able to communicate and to benefit from the feedback. By the time he began the final paper, Paul was more accustomed to process writing and actually looked forward to receiving feedback.[63] Working with Auggie again, Paul began to develop a degree of trust and camaraderie that seemed to influence his feelings about process writing and collaborative learning.

In his analysis of writing blocks, Mike Rose claims that "in some cases, writer's block might be an inevitable part of compositional growth" (*Writer's Block* 104). This seems to describe Gail and Paul. Whereas Gail had to overcome her need to give the teacher "what she wants" and to write from an outline, Paul needed to revise his perception that writing was "poetic discourse," a belief Rose found can "result in premature editing" (104). These students also had to reconsider their prior experiences with objectivist pedagogy and learn to take risks with their thinking and their writing. Their resistance was not merely a matter of gender, for both Gail and Paul initially resisted composition pedagogy, viewing drafting, peer response, and exploratory writing as a waste of time. Nevertheless, by the end of their respective semesters, these students' experiences helped them begin to change not only their personal constructs regarding what was appropriate in the classroom but also their feelings of self-efficacy. Through demonstration and engagement, Gail and Paul became sensitive to the learning process.

Susan and Jeff: Experience and Self-Efficacy

Although Susan ended Teaching College Writing asserting her newfound belief in collaborative learning, that feeling began to lessen the following semester when she tried to write without the luxury of drafts and peer response built into her seminar's syllabus. Consequently, she left the university and began to work full-time in a bank staffed primarily by women who had separated into competitive, rival cliques. When Susan had a question, she was often rebuffed and forced to find the answer for herself. Luckily, some groups were friendlier than others, and eventually these women helped Susan solve problems; gradually, she began to realize that working with a group was easier than working alone. Two years later, this realization, coupled with her dislike of the business world, led her back to teaching.[64]

Susan told me that the intervening years had given her time to reflect on her teaching. This was obvious when I visited her class during the first weeks of school. She began by having the students freewrite on the strengths and weaknesses of their drafts. When they had finished, she addressed these concerns, directed their attention to a series of peer-response questions she had written on the board, and asked if there were any additional questions. This strategy involved the students in the decision-making process and let them know she valued their input. As soon as the peer-response criteria were finalized, Susan divided the class into groups and had the students apply the questions to their partners' drafts. This was quite a change from the woman who regarded her students as Neanderthals or the blind leading the blind. Susan's teaching reflected Farris's findings that self-reflection is instrumental in making "implicit theories of discourse explicit and more flexible" (*Subject* 165). Some TAs just need more reflection than others.

When I interviewed her after she finished my Radical Pedagogy seminar, Susan told me that this course had strongly influenced her views on teaching composition. Reading about the feminist classroom and women's ways of knowing had opened her eyes and upset her acceptance of traditional pedagogy. Working with her classmates as a permanent large group had further enhanced her perspective on collaborative learning. "Usually we don't get to know each other in graduate courses," she told me. "The atmosphere is usually so competitive rather than collaborative. But in here, we got to know each other and to appreciate each other's perspectives."[65] Four years after taking Teaching College Writing, Susan was once again working in a collaborative environment, but rather than giving lip service to collaborative learning, she really was sharing her ideas and her drafts, providing feedback, and incorporating some of her peers' suggestions into her own writing.

In contrast, Jeff's discomfort with collaborative learning and the de-centered classroom was painfully obvious. The first time I visited his class, he had decided his students needed additional time to develop their fluency and the use of details, so he had developed a series of freewriting topics designed to generate ideas and stimulate the imagination. This sequence of freewrites, which took the entire class, included useful prompts, which the students seemed to enjoy; however, Jeff neither interacted with the students nor asked them to share the results. This pattern continued in subsequent classes. Although the exercises he assigned paralleled those used in creative-writing courses, Jeff could not make himself take the next step and allow his students to discuss their ideas or to workshop their papers.[66]

Finally, during the fourth week of the semester (when we discussed theories of collaborative learning), Jeff tried peer-response groups, but after class, he picked up the drafts and edited them at home. During the following class period, he began calling the students up to his desk to discuss necessary revisions, but to his surprise, he found they already knew what to do, for their peer editors had pointed out the same problems. Indeed, Jeff realized that the peer editors had done a more-thorough job than he had, because he had rushed through every paper while they focused on only one or two. "In the space of 50 minutes," he wrote, "I had turned from a peer editing naysayer into a peer editing supporter."[67]

Because of this epiphany, Jeff decided to focus his action research for Teaching College Writing around the hypothesis that collaborative learning was a better strategy than traditional models of teaching. For this project, the students conducted action research by choosing a pedagogical issue (usually one they had trouble with), focusing on a particular student, and collecting data through interviews, observations, reflective journal entries, and analysis of the student's written texts—that is, they followed the same methodology used in this study.

Jeff monitored the progress of one student, Cheri, whose background, training, writing process, and beliefs closely mirrored his own. For the rest of the semester, Jeff watched as Cheri began to write and revise, incorporating the advice of her peer-editing partners. As he observed the effects of collaborative learning on Cheri's writing, he began to change the focus of his teaching. He organized group tasks and involved the students in developing additional activities "so they could avoid problems during the actual essay writing process." Surprised at their success, he stopped planning lectures and began fine-tuning peer-response sheets that provided students with "guidelines and strategies for reading each other's papers." Instead of hiding behind the podium, he began interacting with the students, serving as a "facilitator" rather than a "dictator." Intrigued with the factors affecting group dynamics, he experimented with "the composition of the groups, to see if differences in age, skill level, or sex made any differences." Then he observed these effects on Cheri and her writing. With each discovery, Jeff turned his attention to another facet of the curriculum in an attempt to strengthen the integration of reading, writing, and collaborative learning. With each success, Jeff's feelings of personal efficacy regarding his teaching were reinforced and passed on to his students, who continued to live up to his newly raised expectations.[68]

In his research report, Jeff admitted that he was "amazed" at the progress shown by his students and by Cheri in particular. As the semester progressed, he moved more and more out of the "editing loop." The students worked independently with their peer groups and appealed to him for consultation rather than guidance. During these sessions, Jeff noted that Cheri "spoke more confidently and surely about her work."[69] In his final paper, Jeff describes the results of this experience:

> This is a conversion story. This is the story of my conversion from a teacher-centered teacher to a student-centered one. This is not a dramatic and absolute conversion story, like the biblical story of Saul. The divine light of collaborative learning did not blind me and cause me to fall off my pedagogical horse and see the errors of my ways. I am bearing witness to a conversion of resistance, a dragging of heels, akin to dragging a dog through the office door of a veterinarian. A reluctant convert of collaborative learning convinced through weeks of observing the writing and attitudes of one of my own students. . . . [T]he story of my life is that I don't believe anything until I take it on and my skepticism runs deep. Only now I'm beginning to acknowledge that I can teach.[70]

Numerous factors enter into people's teaching styles. Chief among them are their prior experiences and their approach to writing, for "how teachers teach writing, or anything else for that matter, is a function of who they are, what matters to them, what they bring with them into the classroom, and whom they meet there" (Perl and Wilson qtd. in Bishop, *Something* 102). If teachers believe that writing stems from inspiration, they will resist the concept of writing as a process and reject the notion that peers can help that process along. If teachers believe that good writing means perfect writing, they will demand perfection of their students: They will focus on commas, not content; they will penalize those who fail to master the conventions; and they will stand firm in their belief that writing must be hard work. Engaging graduate students in analyses of their writing and their teaching helps broaden their views of what writing entails. The resulting understanding leads graduate students to improve their writing, their teaching, and their perceptions of themselves as professionals.

Pattie and Ken: Action Research, Empathy, and Self-Efficacy

The importance of action research is also evident in Pattie's final paper, "The Anxieties of the Privileged," a case study of an insecure undergraduate female writer. Like most of my students who have conducted an action-research project, Pattie selected a student whose fears and talents paralleled her own. "Tiffany" was a senior education major with a high grade-point average who began confiding in Pattie as they sat together in an upper-division literature course. On the first day of class, Tiffany told Pattie she was scared to death; she felt so stupid that she didn't know what she would do if the professor called on her[71]—fears echoing those Pattie expressed after our first seminar meeting. In both cases, these fears stemmed from a lack of self-confidence rather than a lack of ability. Both women were the only daughters of successful parents, and both had been socially active, high achievers in high school, yet both felt "inadequate" and "under pressure" and believed they had to "prove themselves" to their parents. These feelings did not diminish after high school; they only increased.[72]

Tiffany and Pattie were excellent writers, yet they continually worried that their work was not up to par. Both women used their journals as a means of expressing themselves, because they lacked the confidence to speak up in class. Perfectionists, they labored over every word when writing and worried that revision would hurt rather than help their papers. As the semester progressed, the two women became friends as they grew "increasingly aware" of these similarities. More importantly, as Pattie discovered her writing process and began to recognize the value of her group's feedback, she tried to pass on these lessons to Tiffany. She encouraged the girl to speak up in class by praising her and telling her how smart she was. "You give off such a feeling of panic and anxiety which causes you to appear less than what you are," she told Tiffany, "which is a very intelligent and insightful student." After volunteering to read a draft of Tiffany's term paper, Pattie pointed out how well organized and convincing it was. Because she knew that Tiffany planned to teach high school, Pattie further prodded her by asking what she would do with a student like herself.[73]

Eventually, Tiffany worked up the courage to speak in class. Afterwards she told Pattie,

> I really thought a lot about what you said when you asked me what I'd do if I had a student like me in class. I guess it never occurred to me before. I don't know that I'd call on them, but I think I might try to do what you did for me and that is to encourage them and give them the confidence to speak.[74]

The above passage suggests the mutual benefits—what Pattie Lather refers to as the "emancipatory power"—of action research. Because of this research project, Pattie and Tiffany gained knowledge about themselves and each other. In the process, they learned that one of the keys to successful teaching is the ability to relate to and empathize with one's students. This is not a lesson learned by reading or by listening to a lecture; rather, it requires crossing the invisible boundaries between professor and student. Since the publication of *Women's Ways of Knowing*, numerous scholars have concluded that the dialogue inherent in teacher-student relationships aids in the construction of knowledge as well as the development of self-confidence.[75] Although most would agree that empathy is important when dealing with younger children, this feeling is important at all levels of education. In their study of successful graduate programs, Jennifer G. Haworth and Clifton F. Conrad conclude, "Students who had 'connected' learning experiences sharpened their professional identities." They began to think like a teacher, developed feelings of professionalism, and decided on a professional focus (68).

The effects of action research were evident in Pattie's and Jeff's changed attitudes and behaviors. Conversely, the absence of this assignment may have contributed to Ken's resurgent resistance in the second half of Teaching College Writing. At midterm, his teaching and his response journals led me to believe that his experience in small groups had resolved his resistance to collaborative learning. However, the following week, he was suddenly faced with the dilemma of how to deal with a student whose argument paper advocated his own suicide. This problem was exacerbated, in Ken's eyes, by collaborative learning, for in sharing his writing with his peer group, the student had made his suicide threat public. So, in addition to dealing with a disturbed student, Ken had to worry about the effects of this threat on the rest of the class.[76]

On my advice, Ken took the problem to a psychologist in the university's counseling center, who suggested he let the student "get this out of his system."[77] Unfortunately, as a result of this supposedly therapeutic writing, the student set a date for his own death—a fact communicated to Ken once again by a member of the student's peer-response group.[78] I helped Ken deal with this by accompanying him to the counseling center, where the psychologist decided the student needed help. To accomplish this, Ken and I worked out a plan. I came to his class as if to observe it. After everyone arrived, Ken put the students in groups, then he asked the suicidal student to speak with him in the hall, where he convinced him to go with him to the counseling center. At that point, I took over Ken's class for the rest of the period.

Needless to say, this was a traumatic experience for a novice teacher. Ken dealt with it, in part, by talking to me (as his teacher and teaching supervisor) and to the school psychologist and by recounting the incident in his teaching log. He did not, however, discuss how this had affected him; he merely restated the facts. But in his next reading journal, due one week after the suicide-threat incident, Ken inadvertently revealed his feelings in a renewed attack on the proponents of collaborative learning, which went on for three single-spaced pages and concluded, "I'm weary of this argument. I do have to say, though, that I've never before felt myself under such overt ideological pressure to conform to a system of ideas I just really don't believe."[79]

Given our joint efforts to help his student, the intensity of Ken's response and its underlying resentment surprised me. I found it difficult to reconcile his apparent resistance to theory with his continued use of small-group work in his teaching and his willingness to share his drafts during peer response. Luckily, an examination of Ken's second essay, "On Becoming a Teacher," offered some explanation. In his first draft, written a week before the suicide threat, he had compared two of his high school teachers; in the second draft, written a week later, the tone and content were quite different. Whereas the first version had begun with some humorous character sketches, the second included a page of angry sarcasm about his students and his teaching:

> I typically divide my class into work groups who solve problems and then report their findings back to the whole class. The spokesman for his group is a scrawny kid who sports the abrupt, up-thrust haircut of the recently de-institutionalized, and who begins every report by saying: "Let me think. I got to think a second. Just let me think a second." Meanwhile the class groans and sighs like a forest in a windstorm. And I rage silently to myself: "For Christ's sake, give it to the Polish guy. Nobody understands him either, but at least he won't bore us to death!"[80]

The final draft of Ken's paper, due the week after our suicide intervention, retained the angry sections, although they were tempered by a dialogue between the two high school teachers advising Ken how to teach.[81] When I asked what he liked about the paper, he replied, "the diction." The rest of the paper, he felt, was weak. "I didn't know what to say," he went on. "Maybe the topic was one that threw me (though it shouldn't have) but I felt no real 'closeness' to the subject. I felt I put together a mechanical exercise."[82]

I agreed with Ken's self-evaluation. The language throughout was sharp, crackling; its sarcasm distanced Ken from his subject. Reading it, I felt that he disliked his teaching and his students, but given the events occurring as he was drafting the essay, perhaps those feelings were understandable. Dealing with a student's suicide threat would be difficult for an experienced teacher; for a first semester TA, it was frightening and frustrating. These conflicting emotions helped to explain the detachment I sensed in Ken's teaching logs. More importantly, his logs offered some explanation for the disparity between Ken's early resistance to the theories behind collaborative learning, his continued reliance on group work in his teaching and in his writing, and the reemergence of resistance following the suicide threat.

Although Ken found theoretical flaws and questioned the epistemological soundness of group work, he had discovered that collaborative learning worked, for he could see that his students were improving their writing. The suicide threat happened to coincide with a second round of reading on collaborative learning focusing on practical applications, which Ken practiced and understood. Consequently, his discomfort with the student's proposed suicide may have been translated into what appeared to be renewed resistance but which may have been merely a general frustration with teaching and all it entailed. An examination of the drafts of Ken's final essay appear to substantiate this conclusion. In his first draft, he described the effects of this experience:

> Almost immediately [after learning of the student's threat] I found myself under a black cloud. I became clumsy, unreliable, inept. I've always been absent-minded; now I was dangerous. I lost a set of car keys and over a two-day period, compelled by a rage that defied rationality, I tore my house apart. At one point during those two days, alone in my school office, I ripped drawers from my desk, raging to myself until I realized that my raised voice had begun to echo down the silent hallway.[83]

Because the essay topic was graduate students' stress, the description is particularly telling. One of Ken's group members, Kimmy, said, "I forgot about the stress of TAs and got into this kid you were talking about." His other group member, Melissa, agreed: "I got the impression that the essay is less about TA stress, and more about the emotional struggle of humanity brushing against humanity—of your struggle as a human being trying to comprehend the pain of a young man."[84] I think Ken's group members were right. He may not have been complaining about group work or the theories underlying it but about the multilayered responsibilities of being a teacher.

Trained as a journalist to remain distant and objective, Ken was unaccustomed to this degree of interaction. Although he had left journalism because he disliked who he was becoming,[85] those years had built up a residue of skepticism and cynicism not easily overcome. As we became better acquainted, I learned that these feelings were exacerbated by an unhappy marriage, which left him with a rather jaundiced view of the world. (His favorite essay was Emerson's "Self-Reliance.") The student's suicide threat pierced that protective layer of cynicism and forced Ken to deal with long-repressed feelings, "to struggle," as Melissa said, "as a human being trying to comprehend the pain of a young man."

Like Paul, Ken's fear and frustration were expressed as anger. Judith V. Jordan, a clinical psychologist specializing in women's growth and development, explains that although men and women are equally capable of recognizing another's pain, their responses are generally quite different. Whereas women tend to identify with the other's feelings, men have been socialized to "act or master rather than 'merely feel' in response to affective arousal" (156). Mark Tappan, whose research focuses on moral development, expands on this analysis. According to Tappan, men find it difficult to change "from a predominant justice focus to a predominant care focus in response to moral conflicts and dilemmas," not only because of socialization but also because the "sociocultural context" does not sanction such expressions, at least not in public (9). In Ken's case, the result was anger and sarcasm directed at the injustice of our classroom readings rather than expressions of sympathy and understanding for the suicidal student. Ken's group members were right on target.

IMPLICATIONS FOR TEACHING

In *The Practice of Theory*, Ray urges faculty to "openly acknowledge [resistance], study it, and reflect on it collaboratively with other faculty and students, trying to understand more fully the role it might play in both learning and teaching" (156). In studying the writing and resistance of my graduate students, I found that sharing their writing was apparently the most threatening aspect, but ironically, writing was also the catalyst for change.

It has long been accepted in composition studies that writing aids learning. However, this theory is seldom applied to graduate course work. Consequently, the composition-pedagogy seminar is often graduate students' first encounter with reflective writing. Reflective response journals provide resistant students with the opportunity to question the theories they are encountering and also to explore and explain their resistance rather than reject out of hand what they read. In so doing, journals provide students with a site in which to "articulate a problem," one of the elements Phyllis Kahaney posits is essential for change (192). Response journals are also instrumental in the establishment of discourse communities within the classroom and between students and professor. In class, journal entries provide a basis for discussion and a means for connecting more easily with peers during group work. Outside of class, the journals provide a link between me and my students, for I am able to respond to their queries, question their assumptions, and clear up misconceptions. In sum, reflective journals provide what Kahaney maintains are the second and third elements necessary for change: they give students "a community in which change can take place and the new behavior can be practiced and reinforced," and they offer "access to a benevolent authority" (192). Drawing on Lev S. Vygotsky's theories, Kahaney concludes, "When action—of the self, of self and other, of self, other and culture— is married to a kind of reflectivity it is nearly impossible to continue on as one has" (198). The ability of the students in this chapter to overcome their resistance suggests the potential of reflective journals.

Because my students' journals were due weekly, we established a regular dialogue; because (after Paul's semester) they were not evaluated until submitted as part of the semester's portfolio, they also created a safe place for the students to vent. And vent they did. A certain percentage of both male and female students resisted—the men were just louder and longer. Albert Bandura explains that when people doubt their abilities, such feelings can "disrupt optimal use of cognitive skills, whereas a strong sense of self-efficacy enables people to make the most of their capabilities" (465). Across genders, three elements helped lessen the students' resistance: demonstration of and engagement in composition pedagogy and participation in action research. By facilitating learning rather than transmitting information, assigning responsibility to the students by requiring them to teach and design assignments, teaching them to collaborate in small-group activities, and assigning action-research projects, I modeled the pedagogy I wanted them to learn. After engaging in these activities, the graduate students began to regain their feelings of self-efficacy. These changes are not anomalies. In her studies of teachers' motivation and self-efficacy, Susan H. McLeod found a strong positive correlation between composition pedagogy and student achievement, self-concept, and relations with peers ("Pygmalion" 376).

Nevertheless, after analyzing the various case studies, I recognized specific areas of my teaching in need of correction. In chapter 4, I advocated the careful formation of permanent small groups, paying special attention to the racial and gender balances. When I started forming permanent groups, I tried to follow this dictum by organizing students on the basis of what I perceived as common interests and similar levels of expertise determined after reading their introductory freewrites. But after a semester or two in which my decisions were clearly flawed, I realized the students deserved a voice in this matter. Consequently, I introduced a series of pregroup activities so that the class might become acquainted and request their group members. Since that time, I have observed considerably less resistance and much-stronger discourse communities.

Resistance ceased altogether after I began assigning action-research projects. As this study has demonstrated, action research plays a major role in graduate students' professional development. Carefully studying one's teaching or documenting the changes occurring during a semester can be enlightening and empowering for faculty and graduate students alike. Action research "challenges the conventional belief in the separation between researchers (those who make knowledge) and teachers (those who consume and disseminate it)," essential steps in reconceptualizing teaching as a scholarly activity (Ray, *Practice* 174). At the same time, this methodology helps graduate students realize that rather than consuming the knowledge generated by others, they are actually constructing their own. In the process, they are not only identifying and modifying their behaviors, they are also changing their relationships with their undergraduate students. Instead of being merely "subjects," the undergraduates become "co-researchers" as they help to inform their teacher-researchers (175). Instead of viewing undergraduates as anonymous, empty vessels to be filled, TAs begin to recognize that their students possess useful information. This realignment of teacher-student relationships in turn empowers the undergraduates. By viewing their students as "thinkers/knowers" and alleviating "adversarial" teaching techniques, TAs affirm and empower their students to prosper as learners and simultaneously serve as positive role models (Stanton 41).

Lather has described action research as *emancipatory pedagogy*, a term encompassing the possibility of change on both sides of the desk. Because of graduate students' previous academic writing experiences, they tend to resist and misunderstand this approach. When I first began assigning action-research projects in Teaching College Writing, the graduate students did not know what I meant about observing and taking field notes, and reading Ruth Ray's guidelines and rationale—which I found particularly helpful—did little to clarify their misunderstanding. At midterm of that first semester, it occurred to me (as I was rereading Smith's *Understanding Reading*), that my students needed *demonstration* and *engagement* if they were to become *sensitive* to the students and situations occurring in their classrooms. Although my students turned in weekly field notes, they were too general, so I designed a series of questions to help them focus. For each week of the semester, I developed a research question that required the students to apply the theory they were reading to their analyses of classroom activities.

After introducing students to current composition pedagogy via their initial readings, I ask how these compare to how they were taught and what teaching issues these approaches suggest for their research. After reading about collaborative learning, I ask them to compare the theories to their (in-class) experience with peer response and to observations of their students' group work. In response to Smith's psycholinguistic explanation of reading, I ask students to hypothesize about their focus-student's reading processes and to schedule an interview with him or her to gain more background information. Bishop' *Ethnographic Writing Research* offers guidelines for "writing up" an interview. In addition, my students must analyze their subject's reading and writing processes by studying his or her drafts, journals, and freewrites. At midterm, they analyze their data and determine what other information they need. After reading about basic writers, I ask them to reflect on the effect of race and gender on their own writing and that of their student-participant. The following week, they profile their student, based on models provided by Mike Rose in *Lives on the Boundary*. When we read Thom Hawkins's strategies for collaborative learning, they have to analyze the comments on their subject's peer-response sheets and their own role in the efficacy of group work. Similarly, after reading about grading, they are asked to analyze the effects of their grading and response on their subject's progress, process, and attitude.

During the last month of the semester, TAs choose a mini-ethnography from Bishop most relevant to their research, outline it, and then adapt the outline to their own project. The following week, first drafts are due. The students bring copies for everyone to exchange, read, respond to, and discuss as a class the following week. With this feedback, the students revise their drafts and exchange them the next week with their peer-group members. In their journals, they discuss the effects of the research on their student-participant's learning and behavior and on themselves as teachers, an entry that often serves as the reflective conclusion to their projects. Using various texts, models, and journal questions, I have been assigning action research since 1993, but it was not until I introduced the above combination that my students began to fully comprehend and appreciate the project.

Graduate students' misperceptions of teaching and writing typify those of most faculty and many of their peers. Teachers, like anyone else, are "influenced both by their individual psychological makeup and by the cultural, historical, and institutional contexts in which they live and work." When teaching graduate students, faculty can become aware of these factors through dialogue, by modeling pedagogical approaches, by providing students with the opportunities to experiment, and by observing their responses to these opportunities (Tappan 10). Indeed, by engaging in the activities they want their students to learn, teachers themselves may learn a great deal about how to teach them. Unless we provide graduate students with opportunities to teach and write in a variety of modes and contexts throughout the semester, we will lack sufficient insight into their motives and beliefs—and so will they.

6. Building Confidence

This chapter focuses on graduate students who, for various reasons, lacked confidence in themselves as teachers or as writers. Among the women, these feelings were manifested in different ways. Some were literally silent or tentative in the classroom, afraid to express an opinion for fear it might be wrong. This group, however, expressed themselves clearly and strongly in their writing. Other women were more voluble. To hear them, one would assume they were completely confident, but when they sat down to write, their fears escaped onto paper. A third group of women claimed to have a single, unified voice: In both their speaking and their writing, they believed their voice was objective, impersonal, and argumentative. But this voice was not their own. Theirs was a stereotypically masculine voice, devoid of feeling and personal expression. This latter description also characterized the writing of the men (both gay and straight) in this study. Because of their socialization, this voice came somewhat naturally to the men who were straight, whereas the gay men found this restricted voice quite unnatural. Straight or gay, they found it difficult to open up or reflect.

More than two-thirds of the women in this study fell into one of the three categories above, whereas almost all of the men displayed a consistently objective voice. For different reasons and to varying degrees, these students' language and sense of self had been engendered by their families, peers, education, and socialization. The women had been raised to speak using a "feminine" voice characterized by silence, hesitation, or deference and by the use of personal experience, anecdotes, and asides to illustrate or animate a story or a discussion. In undergraduate classes, silence might not be an impediment, for at that level, students are generally expected to be quiet and prove their understanding by reproducing information from lectures or textbooks on tests or in their writing. At the graduate level, however, seminars are more likely to be discussion based: The professor poses questions, and the students demonstrate their intellect and their comprehension verbally.

Within this context, the verbally adroit appear to be the best students;

consequently, until called upon to prove themselves through their written work, silent or timid women seem the weaker students, while their male counterparts who eagerly volunteer or speak without being called upon are presumed their intellectual superiors.[1] Because many graduate courses require only a final paper, such gender-related behaviors may taint the view of classmates and professor so that by the end of the semester, first impressions are firmly in place—the outspoken males are judged the stronger students, the quiet females the weaker. Needless to say, these perceptions are erroneous and unfair. But as Gesa Kirsch demonstrated in *Women Writing the Academy*, unless these students gain confidence, unless they can force themselves to speak as well as they write, such perceptions may affect not only their graduate careers but also their professional lives.

Composition pedagogy offers one solution to this problem. By de-centering the classroom, engaging students in learning, and encouraging reflective and narrative writing, this pedagogy helps marginalized students develop feelings of self-efficacy that lead to the development of confidence, as exemplified in their own unique voices. To illustrate the process, this chapter explores the various reasons and tensions contributing to the development of voice. I establish a context for this discussion by defining the terms and introducing the students featured in this chapter's case studies. In the body of the chapter, the first section examines the relationship between gender and voice as they pertain to personal construct, while the second looks at the influence of education and socialization on feelings of self-efficacy. Together, these provide the background for the third section, which discusses the potential impact of composition pedagogy on these graduate students' sense of self as exemplified in their written and oral language. Donald Murray has written, "When we discover what we have said we discover who we are. In finding your voice you discover your identity" (7). In the case studies that follow, I hope to demonstrate not only why such discoveries are so problematic but also how we can help our graduate students to find and develop their voice and with it, the self-confidence necessary for success and respect in the academy.

ENGENDERING VOICE

In their research on the development of women's voices, Belenky, Clinchy, Goldberger, and Tarule maintain that voice is closely related to a woman's sense of mind, self-worth, and feelings of isolation from or connection to others. . . . [W]omen repeatedly used the metaphor of voice to depict their intellectual and ethical development; . . . the development of a sense of voice, mind, and self were [*sic*] intricately intertwined. (18)

In *Women's Ways of Knowing*, Belenky and her colleagues exemplify this concept in the different epistemological positions defined by the women's voices. Although these positions could be viewed hierarchically—moving from silence to received knowledge, subjective knowledge, and procedural knowledge to constructed knowledge—the authors insist that voice is not a static concept. A woman's voice may vary depending on her knowledge, experience, and sense of security in any given situation.

The research that became the basis for *Women's Ways of Knowing* began in the 1970s when the feminist movement was impacting women's lives and, presumably, their voices. When this book was published in 1986, these findings still held true. Unfortunately, in recent years and in subsequent studies, the findings of Belenky et al. continue to be relevant. In *Women Writing the Academy*, Kirsch reports that women still have difficulty establishing their authority in the classroom, in part because their voices are not those identified with authority. These "cultural definitions" make it difficult for women in the academy to write assertively, yet in their own voices. Although men are generally less likely to suffer problems with voice and authority, their socialization impairs them in other ways. Because they have been socialized to be strong, stoic, and competitive, male students are considerably less likely to reveal uncertainty or express their feelings. Feminist researchers maintain that young men learn to guard their personal boundaries closely.[2] Although these socially inscribed boundaries contribute to men's identification with power and authority, these same invisible strictures can impede male students' ability to express themselves, to analyze their feelings and behaviors, and to empathize—elements of self-awareness essential to successful teaching.[3]

These issues negatively affect men in general, but society's constructions of masculinity have an even greater effect on gay men. Because homosexuality is still considered beyond the bounds of "normal" male behavior, this group tends to view itself as disenfranchised in terms of power and authority. Donna Qualley explains that because men are supposed to be strong and masculine, and women soft and feminine, when members of either gender wander too far beyond those "norms," they are considered perverted. Men are supposed to be strong but not rigid, while women should be flexible, not weak. Thus, men are viewed as lacking masculinity if they appear "soft," and women are considered unfeminine if they seem too rigid or hard (29). Although this model was designed to emphasize the stereotypical assumptions regarding women, it also applies to men who do not fit the traditional stereotype—and who suffer from it by being marginalized and disempowered.

In *The Double Perspective*, David Bleich explains that

> one's *sense* of one's gender (the psychological issue of gender identity) follows, in part, from the fact of biological gender; as this sense is brought more deeply into society through growing up, the person's language will be a function of both the biological fact of gender and one's sense of it. (125)

Quite often, this sense is reflected in an individual's voice. Self-confidence and the accompanying feeling of self-efficacy are evident in a strong, unified voice; conversely, a lack of confidence may be indicated in a weak or bifurcated voice. As future professors, graduate students will need a strong speaking voice. As scholars, they will need a similarly strong written voice. We can help to unify and strengthen our students' voices through our teaching and our classroom relationships.

Belenky et al. maintain that

> educators can help women develop their own authentic voices . . . if they accord respect to and allow time for the knowledge that emerges from first-hand experiences; if instead of imposing their own expectations and arbitrary requirements, they encourage students to evolve their own patterns of work based on the problems they are pursuing. (229)

Kirsch reiterates these calls for "connected teaching," that is, a noncompetitive, collaborative environment using strategies such as active learning, peer-response groups, and portfolio evaluations (*Women* 131). In sum, both groups advocate the same strategies introduced by composition pedagogy.

THE CONTEXT

All but one of the students discussed in this chapter, Jimmy, were students in Reader Response Theory (described in chapter 4). All but Missy took at least two other graduate courses with me either before or after the Reader Response seminar. Melissa, Jimmy, Jenny, and Auggie were students in Teaching College Writing and Reading-Writing Theory. The Reader Response Theory course, like the others I offer, teaches writing as a process.

Melissa, Jenny, and Auggie were new graduate students beginning their master's work shortly after receiving their bachelor's degrees; they were all in their early twenties. Missy was approximately the same age, although when I met her, she was starting her second semester of graduate course work. This group had a good deal in common: They were of similar ages, held similar interests, and lacked prior teaching experience. Jenny and Auggie were TAs, and Missy and Melissa applied for graduate teaching assistantships during the semester they were my students. Melissa was single, whereas the others were married without children. Jimmy stood apart from this cohort. He had already earned a master's degree in French and had taught high school; he was also a single gay man. However, like the others in this chapter, he was a TA and a full-time student taking two courses per semester. Through their voices, each student revealed varying degrees of confidence. The following case studies demonstrate how composition pedagogy helped to strengthen and unify those voices.

GENDER, VOICE, AND PERSONAL CONSTRUCT

Gender and socialization strongly influence the development of personal construct, and the results can be seen in each person's voice. The primary sources for language socialization are the family, from whom children learn how to speak in public and in private; the community and its surrounding culture; and the school, which either reinforces the family's teaching or introduces additional strictures. In *The Double Perspective*, Bleich addresses the role of gender identification in this process, a developmental factor beginning between the ages of two and five, and explains how it is represented in students' awareness of and identification with voice (127–28). Analyzing the language use of male and female graduate students, Bleich found that when reading narrative prose, male students were prone to recognize voice in a literary passage, whereas females "experienced [voice] as a 'world'—without a particularly strong sense that this world was narrated into existence" (128). Bleich views these varying senses of voice as stemming from the initial stages of gender identification: Early on, boys begin to recognize that their language is different, or separate, whereas girls retain a sense of identity (with their mothers) that allows them to relate. Consequently, the boys recognize boundaries where the girls see relationships (153). Another way to view these gender differences is to question the source of such identifications. During their reading experiences, men may recognize the narrator's voice because they identify with the ability to narrate and create a world, whereas women overlook or fail to identify voice because they often feel they do not possess it.

A gendered voice is acquired at an early age. After studying twenty-four audio- and videotaped interactions between parents and their children ages two to five, Jean Berko Gleason demonstrated how children acquire their sense of language and gender identity through interactions with their parents (254). Because of boys' more aggressive dispositions, the language directed at them is usually more negative and prohibitive, whereas girls' less aggressive natures elicit less harsh interactions (254). Indirect language similarly influences children's gendered behaviors. Gleason found that although both boys and girls are expected to be polite, their parents' language patterns provide gendered role models on which the children's language use is based. Parents interrupt their daughters' talk more often than their sons', and fathers break into their children's conversations more often than do their mothers (260). Mothers are more likely to use indirect questions for requests, whereas fathers tend to use imperatives, gendered patterns that children assimilate by age four (261). Bleich illustrates the endurance of such patterns in his case study of Ms. K., whose "underlying strategy of language was related to how and when each parent spoke and what that meant regarding when and how she should speak (and write)" (*Double* 233). By analyzing her writing and her family background, Bleich learned that Ms. K. used language indirectly because she related this speaking style to her mother and her mother's lack of authority within the family structure (*Double* 234). Conversely, in studying the writing of male writers, Bleich noticed a tendency to demonstrate and retain their own sense of authority. Based on these analyses, he suggests that individuals' use of language reveals both their level of self-awareness and their sense of personal authority: "Each person's language use, in other words, has a simultaneous individual and social reference" (210). The following case studies illustrate various manifestations of this dual influence.

Melissa: Personal Construct and Silence

When Melissa was a child, she was nicknamed "Pig Pen" after the cartoon character in "Peanuts," because her room was always filthy, her hair never brushed, her clothes torn and dirty. A tomboy, her favorite activities were playing ball, watching the *Brady Bunch*, and getting into trouble. She insisted on wearing her baseball cap to church (where her father was pastor), and she acted out in school. Her parents were continually being called in for teachers' conferences, and Melissa found herself more often in the principal's office than in the classroom. Compared unfavorably to her older, overachieving brother ("a genius and straight A student"), Melissa suffered from the stigma of underachiever. Not surprisingly, she hated school, rebelled against her teachers, and "cultivated a reputation in the school as 'unmanageable,' 'angry,' and 'unmotivated,'" labels that only reinforced her behavior and her negative personal construct. Melissa's academic nadir occurred in eighth grade when she received Ds in English and was consigned to the remedial track, which led to more despondency, more *Brady Bunch*, and more ballplaying (the only thing she believed she was good at). Melissa described the results:

> I began to develop an inferiority complex. I carried this complex with me into graduate school this winter. . . . Crawling out from beneath such oppressive labels proves difficult, and consequently I sometimes continue to believe what people thought of me long ago.[4]

Melissa's attitude and behavior began to change when she was thirteen, and her family moved to another state. There she enrolled in a large high school where no one knew her brilliant brother and where she was quickly removed from remedial classes. One of the individuals contributing to this transformation was Mrs. K., an English teacher and cross-country coach, who praised Melissa's writing ability and encouraged her to join the track team. "Suddenly," Melissa wrote, "I had a basis for my identity. For the first time in my life, some one was recognizing my ability and encouraging me to cultivate that ability. And I began to change." That year marked the beginning of Melissa's quest for perfection. It also marked a change in her relationship with her family: "After years of apologizing for my behavior, after wondering hopelessly what would eventually become of me, I was doing something my parents could boast and feel proud about." Her parents' pride further motivated Melissa to work hard and succeed, yet her early experiences had left their mark. During secondary school, she recalled, "A teacher putting a 'C' on several of my more personal pieces would send me into a tailspin of insecurity and deplete my feelings of self worth."[5]

As Belenky and her colleagues have so thoroughly detailed, women lacking in self-esteem are quite often silent, for they believe they have nothing of import to offer (24). This behavior is generally reinforced in the school's treatment of girls. David Sadker and Myra Sadker, who have documented this treatment in over two decades of research, summarize the effects: "From grade school through graduate school female students are more likely to be invisible members of classrooms. Teachers interact with males more frequently, ask them better questions, and give them more precise and helpful feedback" (1). Female students are "taught" to be silent and invisible in a variety of ways. Boys receive more attention because they are louder. Male figures dominate textbooks, and when girls question the absence of female characters, they are often ignored. Females are also more likely to be ignored when they report incidents of sexual harassment or demeaning behavior. Thus, even when subjected to insulting jokes or remarks, girls tend to stay silent (8–10). The Sadkers conclude, "Women who have spent years learning the lessons of silence in elementary, secondary, and college classrooms have trouble regaining their voices" (10). This described Melissa at the beginning of her graduate studies.

Jimmy: Personal Construct and Stifled Creativity

Jimmy's personal construct might be attributed to his parents' reaction to his homosexuality. At age sixteen, when he revealed his sexual orientation, his parents kicked him out of the house, an experience that convinced him it was better to stay "in the closet."[6] These feelings, he realized, had definitely affected his writing:

> I find that not being able to create using my personal voice, not being able to open the closet door, has often made it difficult for me to become engaged in my writing. . . . I had always considered myself a creative writer who, because of the . . . precarious circumstances of being gay, had, ironically, written very little creatively. Being gay, though certainly not everything I was, though certainly not the core of my being, was, nevertheless, a very great part of me, of my experiences, of my feelings and expressions and desires. To write

as if I were not gay or to try in some way to conceal that fact in my writing had always seemed a sort of superficial act to me and therefore one which was uninteresting, unenlightening, and ultimately untrue.[7]

Jimmy believed his composing process was a direct result of his fear of failure. A self-described perfectionist, he could not begin writing until he had developed a "frame" for his paper. Once started, he agonized over every word. Jimmy attributed his feelings and this process to the fact that he "was rarely taught to think for [him]self, to perceive [him]self as an independent thinker whose voice mattered." Thus, he did not consider himself a writer. To do so, he said, would be too threatening because it would require perfection and responsibility.[8] As he wrote in his first teaching log, "This idea [of writing] fills me once again with those ever-churning fiends of fear, those tyrannosauric tyrants of insecurity and worthlessness who have settled—indeed, have holed up in permanent residence—somewhere in the maelstrom called my stomach."[9]

Jenny: Personal Construct and Sexism

Jenny's anxieties were not nearly so traumatic or stifling as Jimmy's, yet the disparity between Jenny's public and private voices offers another example of how perfectly competent and intelligent young women can nonetheless harbor self-doubt. Jenny's parents were educators; her father was a high school administrator and her mother a teacher. Because her father's job required him to dispense discipline daily throughout the school year, Jenny's mother became the disciplinarian at home.[10] Thus, Jenny's mother became the primary role model for her strong, outspoken voice—a voice Jenny cultivated and through which she projected a veneer of confidence. At school, however, Jen did not receive the same degree of reinforcement. In algebra and trigonometry, for example, her teacher—"who continually flirted with many high school girls"—would note errors on her papers by writing "a blonde mistake" or "blonde mistake #2." At first, she tended to dismiss such comments, but over the course of the year, this man's sexist remarks angered and hurt her.[11]

Jenny was an attractive young woman. A soccer player during her undergraduate years, she had maintained her athletic figure and enhanced it with long, blonde hair. In other words, she looked like a cheerleader, the type society tends to dismiss as beautiful but dumb. Jenny had experienced this discrimination throughout her life. So, although a modicum of insecurity might ordinarily emerge in any graduate student's writing during his or her first semester, Jenny's tendency to tell "blonde jokes" and to disparage herself for acting "blonde" suggests that she had internalized some of these beliefs, as exemplified when she wrote, "I don't think I particularly write well, but I know I sound more intelligent on paper than I do when I'm speaking."[12]

Missy: Personal Construct and Muted Feminine Voice

Although she was initially unaware of it, Missy's voice also showed distinct variations. Missy believed she possessed a "masculine" voice, which she equated with an argumentative stance.[13] Unfortunately, she carried this stance to extremes. She argued with all of her male professors, but rather than finding her aggressiveness a sign of independent thought (as they might with a male student), they merely found it annoying.[14] In one of the seminars, Missy's strident and incessant arguing provoked an ordinarily calm graduate student to such a fury that her classmates "thought the guy was going to kill her." After that session, another of her classmates declared, "Missy is such a bitch!" The speaker was Sr. Gisela.[15]

The source of Missy's voice was revealed during the second half of the Reader Response seminar when the students began to write about more personal subjects. Describing recurring arguments with her parents, Missy claimed that her mother had "always been childish and selfish; I've always been a little more practical. She says I'm a dried up old stick with no sense of adventure."[16] In an essay about her "most significant accomplishment," she steered away from the personal and described the time she cooked a twelve-course dinner, concluding:

> I still feel that I am barely competent most of the time, but now I have a new fear/insecurity to go along with it. Now I worry that people come to our house because they get good food, not because they like me. I am always certain that people hold me in silent contempt. The insecurity that I feel permeates every aspect of my life, like a silent watchdog, waiting to remind me of my failures and loneliness if I get too self important.[17]

Some of these feelings were explained in subsequent essays in which Missy revealed she had been raised to be "the charming companion to a wealthy gentleman." Consequently, she learned "to trade on [her] looks." She was so indoctrinated in this way of thinking that it was not until

145

she reached her mid-twenties that she "realized there could be more." This realization led her to reject her "sexual attributes," to shave her head, and to adopt the aggressive style of argumentation she became infamous for in graduate school. At the beginning of the Reader Response seminar, Missy believed she had rid herself of all "female" attributes, which she equated with weakness and dependence, and adopted instead a "feminist" outlook that, paradoxically, she equated with the stereotypically male traits of strength and independence.[18]

Auggie: Personal Construct and the Socialization of Males

In her academic writing, Missy's voice resembled Auggie's. As an undergraduate, Auggie had majored in political science and paid for his education by enlisting in the ROTC. Neither of these fields was to his liking, but he felt compelled to focus on areas essential to career success. After graduation, Auggie worked for five years as a counselor for the mentally retarded and then returned to graduate school to pursue his real interest—teaching English.[19] Nonetheless, his undergraduate education seemed to affect his perceptions of what constituted academic language. In his first graduate seminar, Reading-Writing Theory, Auggie's response journals were consistently impersonal, mixing succinct and insightful syntheses of the readings with practical applications for the classroom. Although he did not follow the "typical male" pattern of questioning and critiquing the readings, his impersonal responses typified those Cinthia Gannett found among male journal writers (75), so my first insight into his personality did not come until the last month of the semester.

When we began a unit on reader-response theory, I asked the students to write two personal essays and to share them with their group members for analysis and response. Auggie's essays showed two distinct but related characteristics: a preference for absurdist humor and an avoidance of personal revelation. Describing his wife, he wrote, "I am married to a unique individual. A cliche, right? No. C. is truly amazing. No matter how grumpy I am, she simply handles my barrage of mad absurdity." In contrast, he was quite open about his love of sports: "I have become emotionally involved with Hockey [sic]. The speed, grace, and guts of the game is like an addiction." Auggie was aware of these dichotomies, explaining it was "A gender thing. A German thing. . . . I tend to use humor when discussing personal issues, especially emotional ones."[20]

After his third seminar with me, Auggie finally explained these tendencies by describing their source—his family's language style:

> My writing is reserved and so is my family. I see my family's cool demeanor as the primary influence on my writing style. I've never told my sisters nor my dad that I loved them. I've told my mother a few times. I remember when I did, it felt like someone was taking out my appendix with a corkscrew. The same is true for my family: only my mother has expressed her love to me a few times. This detached demeanor extends throughout the spectrum of emotions, from anger to love. We don't fight openly; we only sit and let time heal with slow, ugly scabs. . . . [O]ften times disagreements in our family are one-sided as the one angry is so reserved the offending party is unaware.[21]

Each of these vignettes suggests the various ways gender roles are learned at home and how these constructs can impact the development of oral voice and written voice. Melissa's hesitant speaking voice typifies girls' classroom demeanor, while the disparity between Jenny's confident exterior and insecure writing voice suggests how society's focus on female appearance can lead young women to doubt their intelligence. In response to what she perceived as her mother's weakness and the academy's reification of strength, Missy tried to shut off her personal (female) voice, whereas Auggie's and Jimmy's experiences had taught them never to reveal the personal. As future teachers, they will need to be aware of and reconcile these disparities. The next section suggests some ways to do so.

EDUCATION, SOCIALIZATION, AND SELF-EFFICACY

A family's verbal interactions strongly influence the development of its members' personal constructs as manifested through their voice. Personal construct provides the lens through which we perceive our self-efficacy, a perception further shaped by education and socialization. In *Gender and the Journal*, Gannett maintains that "gender as a social construct powerfully writes itself onto all of our lives" (11). Although Gannett acknowledges that such a discussion must avoid essentialist reductions, she emphasizes that gender plays a distinctive role in the development of individuals' personal constructs and feelings of self-efficacy. These factors do not exist in isolation; rather, their effect is dependent upon the social context in which they occur.

Language can engender by privileging males and muting females, for example, through recognizing the writings and accomplishments of the former and ignoring those of the latter or more commonly through the use of the masculine terms and pronouns (Gannett 56). A more extreme example can be found in the correlation between physical and sexual abuse and the silence of the victims; less extreme examples are evident in daily conversation as males listen to males and ignore or interrupt the contribution of females or denigrate women's talk as gossip (Gannett 68). Such conversational patterns, established early in life at home, are reinforced in school.

Numerous studies have demonstrated that the schools play a major role in women's feelings of alienation and subsequent silence. Abstract rather than personal styles of speaking are valorized in classrooms; perhaps because of this, teachers pay more attention to males while the comments of female students are either interrupted or ignored. Although the studies Gannett cites were done in the 1970s and 1980s, more recent research by Sadker and Sadker reveal that these conditions were still prevalent throughout the 1990s. In the elementary grades, girls are still being told to speak quietly and defer to their male classmates. By the time they graduate from high school, too many of these young women have internalized the message that they should be "passive and deferential." Although we might expect that such treatment would cease at the post-secondary level, it is actually more pronounced. According to Sadker and Sadker, university teaching is "the most biased" (168).

At the college level, only half the students in a traditional classroom are likely to contribute to discussion; of this number, "twice as many females [are] voiceless" (Sadker and Sadker 170). In contrast, male students are "twice as likely to monopolize class discussions" and to interrupt those females bold enough to interject a comment. When the women do speak, too many still evidence language patterns observed when gender studies began thirty years ago: They speak hesitantly, quietly, and with self-deprecation. Sadker and Sadker sum up this state of affairs when they observe, "The college classroom is the finale of a twelve-year rehearsal, the culminating showcase for a manly display of verbal dominance" (170).

Less often discussed are the effects of socialization on male students. According to Sadker and Sadker, boys learn to take risks that often land them in trouble, so boys are more likely to be labeled behavior problems, "to fail a course, miss promotion, or drop out of school" (197). This type of risk-taking not only imperils their educational accomplishments but also makes them more prone to accidents, suicides, and murder. Because risk-taking can be either dangerous or advantageous, male students may channel this behavior in positive ways and emerge as academic or athletic stars or continue unchecked and fall to the bottom of the class. Wherever they land, because of their gender, they are still pressured to succeed (198).

Boys learn these behavior patterns at home, where even in the late 1990s, they were generally regarded as the pride and focal point of the family (Sadker and Sadker 199). This type of attention leads many of them to feel a sense of entitlement and to engage in competition to get what they feel is theirs. But there is a downside to this role. Sadker and Sadker found that boys receive harsher punishment, often taking physical form, from both parents and teachers (202–4). And just as girls' expectations and achievements may start high and end low, boys could be said to decline on a different front. When they are young, boys are willing to express fear and uncertainty, to value friendships, and to express their feelings freely (204). However, they quickly learn to repress those feelings, even to deny having them; instead, they tend to explode into anger or withdraw in silence (205). Those males who find the courage to openly express emotions may be ridiculed, shunned, or accused of homosexuality (207). Fairly quickly, boys learn that their gender is preferred and that activities or behaviors associated with girls should be avoided.

Sadker and Sadker conclude this sad recital by arguing, "Until this changes, everybody loses." In the following vignettes, I offer examples of the effects of institutional sexism on my male and female graduate students to underscore the continuing existence of what Sadker and Sadker have researched for two decades. I do so, however, to set the stage for how we can help, at the graduate level, to institute change.

Melissa: Traditional Pedagogy and Self-Efficacy

When Melissa began graduate school at age twenty-four, her first course was my seminar in Reader Response Theory. Luckily for her, I required weekly journal entries, for otherwise, I would have had no hint of her intellectual abilities. Even though Melissa's journal entries were among the most insightful in the class, her behavior typified the lack of confidence described by Sadker and Sadker. She rarely spoke in class; she even had trouble making eye contact. Similarly, her early prose was punctuated by questions, qualifiers, and tentative statements such as "I struggle to understand" and "where do I draw the line?"[22] A self-described perfectionist, Melissa was her own worst critic even though her papers were among the best in the class. Throughout that semester, I made a point to praise her writing and encourage her to speak up. Although I did not succeed in engaging her in class discussions, my praise coupled with Melissa's strong sense of self-efficacy regarding her writing skills gave her the confidence to apply for a job in which a strong voice would be essential—a graduate teaching assistantship.[23]

The following semester, when Melissa learned that she was one of only two applicants chosen from a field of ten to be a TA, her feelings of self-efficacy were further bolstered. Describing her first day of teaching, she noted,

> My first reaction to situations like this is to completely destroy myself verbally (getting back to perfectionist issues). However, I decided I would not beat myself up over mistakes made on the first day—I'm sure every teacher isn't perfect their first day in the classroom.[24]

At a time when most new TAs' fears run rampant, Melissa's reading and teaching logs were upbeat. There were no misgivings, no hesitations, no apologies or qualifications. In an early journal entry, she discussed possible reasons for her confidence:

> The classes where I kept and shared journals, read my work in class, and spent time one-on-one with the professor were important learning experiences. . . . I was finding my voice, and through my journal writing now I continue to discover who and what I am.[25]

This confidence was evident in Melissa's first essay in Teaching College Writing, due the sixth week of class. A narrative collage of three different learning experiences, the paper flowed beautifully. Melissa attributed its success, in part, to the feedback from her peer group consisting of Ken (from chapter 5) and Kimmy, a graduate student in Education. After their first meeting, Melissa wrote, "Having Ken critique my paper was a very good thing. For perhaps the first time ever in a group setting, I felt like I received helpful suggestions."[26]

A tape recording of the group's interactions revealed Melissa's role as an active participant as well as her comfort within the confines of this small group. When Ken questioned Melissa about her paper, she answered easily, explaining her writing decisions and admitting doubts about the strength of her conclusion. With these issues resolved, Melissa began to describe what she found in Ken's paper. At first, she was hesitant, qualifying her responses, second-guessing herself, and suggesting that perhaps she did not understand his conclusion because she was not reading closely enough. But as she continued, her voice grew stronger. After telling Ken his style was "passionate and forceful," she reiterated the problems she saw in his conclusion, then closed by offering humorously sarcastic suggestions for clarifying some unintentionally negative images. Overall, she did not hesitate to offer constructive criticism despite the fact that she was dealing with a writer at least ten years her senior and with at least a decade's experience as a journalist.[27]

The following week, however, Melissa's tone began to change. Doubts and hesitations began creeping into her teaching log: "I feel fairly unsure about my grading technique. . . . Today's class left me feeling rather discouraged. . . . I always feel like I'm forcing my voice, like I'm almost screaming to be heard."[28] Initially, these fears did not appear in Melissa's reading log, where she remained clear and positive. In fact, in this log Melissa revealed that as a result of her recent reading and writing experiences, she had begun to change her composing process. Instead of laboring over every word, she had freewritten the first draft of an essay for another seminar, and she was pleased with how the paper was turning out: "I'm not sure Professor X will like it, but I think it's pretty good."[29]

Melissa's premonitions were correct. Within minutes of turning it in, Professor X called her into his office and demanded she rewrite it. He was not responding to the content, however; he was displeased with the first sentence, for Melissa had begun her essay with a subordinate clause. This, he told her, was simply not done. As we discussed the professor's actions, Melissa revealed that he had been questioning her judgment all semester, criticizing her writing and quizzing her about grammar. In the previous weeks, his in-class comments had more than once reduced her to tears. She had always believed she was weak in grammar, and so she had tolerated his comments, but this latest attack unnerved her.[30]

The effects on Melissa's confidence were reflected in her writing. Her reading journal became filled with apologies: "I'm kind of stymied . . . I'm not making sense here . . . I'm sorry about all this stumbling around."[31] Her teaching log began, "I REALLY didn't want to come to school today—I dreaded whatever Professor X was going to say about my paper, and so didn't even want to be around."[32] By the following week, Melissa was able to express anger at the professor's treatment, yet her writing continued to suffer. Her teaching logs revealed self-doubts while her response journals were full of apologies for what she perceived as her inability to comprehend the readings. The most obvious sign of her shaken confidence came in her second essay for Teaching College Writing, due shortly after this incident began.

Whereas her first paper had been a model of fluency, clarity, and conciseness, the second was somewhat disjointed. Melissa said she hated writing this paper. She had avoided writing, then struggled mightily, composing multiple drafts and discarding them all.

> I can't really articulate why I don't like this essay at all, but if I must come up with a weak part and if I must be specific, I would say that my message seems flaky and unimportant. . . . I don't know, again, what is wrong—it just isn't right to me. Besides, my writing is wrought with grammatical errors, I'm sure.[33]

To bolster her confidence, I pointed out that her introduction and conclusion were engaging, that her use of student examples provided strong illustrations, and that her message—that teachers influence their students' attitudes and thus their performance—was valuable, so much so that I wanted to use her paper in a packet of readings for future TAs. The only revision I suggested was to use stronger transitions, yet this comment alone caused Melissa to burst into tears. When I asked her why, she apologized and admitted that Professor X had "decimated" her confidence.[34]

Because the third essay was to be a case study focusing on teaching, I suggested she contrast composition pedagogy to traditional teaching to illustrate how the former developed confidence and how the latter could deplete it. At first, Melissa said she was "unsure about undertaking such a task." However, after thinking about it and discussing it with her group members, Melissa decided to proceed with the project. As a result, she said in her journal, "I went through Wednesday and Friday's class periods with a changed attitude. This guy isn't going to get me down."[35]

Jimmy Comes Out: Self-Efficacy and Personal Voice

Like Jeff and Susan in chapter 4, Jimmy's perfectionism and educational experiences had influenced his beliefs about teaching. He resisted using collaborative learning, preferring instead to hold onto his tenuous authority. At the beginning of the semester, Jimmy attempted to engage his students in discussions about the day's readings by putting them in a circle and throwing out questions; however, he did not possess the strategies necessary to involve the whole class in a substantive discussion, so he usually answered the questions himself. Faced with a classroom of equally inexperienced freshmen, he soon became disheartened and frustrated.[36]

Jimmy took this teacher-centered approach for a number of reasons. He held undergraduate degrees in French and English literature and a master's degree in French. In his foreign language classes, instruction had been based primarily on memorization, translation, and recitation; consequently, Jimmy had no models of collaboration and interaction to emulate. When he taught French in high school and in the community college, he had been similarly directive, so he had no reason to think this approach would not be successful in freshman composition. Lecture and discussion were the approaches he encountered when he took literature courses, and he had done well there, so he saw no reason to change when he began to teach English.[37]

Slowly, Jimmy began to change his approach during the semester he took Teaching College Writing. Narrative writing assignments helped him do so. Essay 1, requiring three narrative collages, coincided with the tragic end of a love affair after which Jimmy said he felt himself "seized to speak the restless life I had always lived—to express a growing belief, a materializing faith in who I was, and to voice this faith to the world." In other words, he came out of the closet. This essay marked the first time Jimmy had written a paper for more than a grade: "This made the process easier. It was the first time in a long time that I truly felt my writing to be an extension of me." He closed the paper by emphasizing the necessity of finding and being true to his personal voice.[38]

A second factor contributing to Jimmy's understanding was participation in a permanent small group for peer response. I placed Jimmy with two other TAs—Carolyn, a straight female (from chapter 7) and Richard, another gay male. Like the other groups in this course, they met six times during the semester to read and discuss each draft of the three required essays. As soon as they became acquainted, I asked Richard to help Jimmy with his teaching, for Richard had quickly adopted constructivist pedagogy. To make that intervention appear more natural, I suggested that both men visit each other's classes, share lesson plans, and work together to develop pedagogical strategies. These collaborations seemed successful: At midterm Jimmy wrote that Richard had "been a sort of savior" with regard to his teaching.[39]

Although Jimmy's group was not altogether supportive or cohesive, he benefited by participating in collaborative learning. Carolyn and Richard were rather conventional writers, unaccustomed to Jimmy's increasingly flamboyant style and uneasy with his disclosures.[40] Moreover, as the semester progressed, Richard became unusually protective of his teaching materials, refusing to share or discuss them with his group members and eventually going so far as to copyright them. By the end of the semester, Rich had ceased talking to Jimmy altogether. Nevertheless, for Jimmy, the group provided a valuable outlet. Before participating in collaborative learning, his writing had been "generally sporadic, and usually produced only for the approval of [an] authority figure" who was held in "absolute awe. . . . My writing is in essence not controlled by my voice or by my thoughts, but rather by the expectations of my authority reader who continuously edits every word I write before I've written it."[41] Writing for an audience of his peers helped Jimmy overcome many of these feelings and develop his confidence:

> I would never have been able to write [so openly] without the support and understanding I felt within my small community of writers. I felt less isolated as a writer than I ever have before. Moreover, working collaboratively helped put many of my writing issues in perspective. I suddenly realized that other writers were experiencing the anxieties which I was feeling.[42]

Jenny: Mentorship, Dialogue, and Self-Efficacy

Jenny was as voluble as Jimmy but in a positive way—she was outgoing and talkative, seemingly full of confidence. In Teaching College Writing, she was equally at ease, willing to offer her opinion and participate in group activities. But outside of class, Jenny's demeanor was less secure. During her first semester as a TA, Jenny taught three days a week at 8:00 and 11:00 A.M. Every day she came to my office between 9:00 and 11:00 to discuss what she done in her first class and to get advice on how to improve the second one. Sometimes, she just wanted feedback on her lesson plans, but other times, she wanted my help. "This bombed in my 8:00," she'd say. "What can I do to make it work?" And so we would use this hour to brainstorm variations on her original lesson. Jenny would go off to teach at 11:00, then drop by at noon to tell me how the new approach had worked. These sessions were prompted partly by a desire for friendship and mentoring but also by a degree of insecurity and a genuine desire to learn. As she told me recently, "I couldn't have survived that first semester without you. Day after day, your advice saved my [teaching] life."[43] I looked forward to our daily talks. I have always preferred the TAs who are interested in teaching, so the combination of Jenny's interest and personality furthered our relationship. These conversations also contributed to Jenny's gradually increasing feelings of confidence: "Teaching makes me feel like a success. . . . When I see students' light bulbs going on it gives me such a high!" [44]

Jenny's experiences in Reader Response Theory offer further examples of how collaborative learning and critical inquiry facilitate the development of voice and self-confidence. Whereas group work had been informal during Teaching College Writing, in Reader Response I assigned students to permanent groups based on common interests but arranged to ensure a gender mix. I placed Jenny in a group with Linda, Auggie, and Missy because of preexisting friendships and because they all seemed to possess compatible personalities. Of the four, Missy was the wild card. She had not been one of my students before, but I was aware of her friendship with Auggie. Apart from these characteristics, Missy was bright and outspoken, so I felt she would provide some spice to the group discussions.

"Spice" was an understatement, for Missy's argumentative behavior at times introduced turmoil, tension, and dissension into the group interactions.[45] Although she may not have recognized it at the time, these exchanges were good for Jenny. The often-heated group discussions forced her to examine and defend her ideas, yet this peer response provided Jenny feedback from three different types of writers. Group work also strengthened her relationship with Auggie, which led to their collaboration and peer response outside the classroom setting.[46] Such interactions are rare. Although graduate seminars can become contentious, the primary combatants are usually males who tend to out shout and interrupt their female peers. But within a group of three females and one male, Jenny had the opportunity and support of her peers to enter into the fray. These experiences helped introduce Jenny to the language and discourse of the academy. As Jill M. Tarule explains in her analysis of

CASE STUDIES OF RESISTANCE AND CHANGE

collaborative learning, by engaging in these debates, students like Jenny not only feel more "enabled and empowered" but also more "entitled" to participate (285). This combination helped unify Jenny's voice by enabling her to recognize her strengths and accept what she perceived as her weaknesses.

Missy: Collaborative Learning, Voice, and Self-Efficacy

Whereas Jenny was primarily concerned with teaching, Missy was enmeshed in the politics of the academy. Like many of her female peers in academe who believe that "they can 'cross-dress,' that they can master the male idiom, that they can engage in either adversarial or disinterested modes of discourse and succeed by whatever standards" (Sullivan, "Feminism" 40), Missy spoke with great pride of her masculine voice and her "male-thinking brain." She wanted to be respected for her intellectual capabilities so much that she shaved her head. In doing so, she felt she had "extracted every attractive attribute of [her] physical person and become a real human being—not just a woman." Missy had done a reverse Samson. In cutting off her hair, she felt "the power of NOT being a sex object for the first time in my life."[47] Missy, like other women in academe, viewed possession of feminine attributes as professionally dangerous,[48] yet, ironically, and apparently unconsciously, she displayed a distinctly female voice in her writing. Her responses were a mixture of opinion and analysis, thought and feeling:

> I am a hundred people, all fighting for their 15 minutes of fame. . . . I am T's wife. . . . I am also S's daughter. . . . I am cool, but I try to be warm and fail. . . . Though I think of myself as a great seductress, I really fear and detest men. . . . What I want to be is a bone marrow donor and a professor of Literature [sic], but I never believed I could do it, so I never tried.[49]

This was not a strong, impersonal, masculine voice; this was the very personal voice of an insecure, young woman. However, Missy appeared more confident in her academic responses. She was not wholly objective, yet her divergences from straightforward summary were more sarcastic than personal, such as when she wrote: "Trying to get through [Louise Rosenblatt's] *The Reader, The Text, The Poem*, with its five examples for every point she makes, is a little like reading a radio repair text for the mentally retarded."[50] The other difference between the two papers was length: Although both were to be written in the same amount of time, her academic responses were three times longer than the personal ones. Like many of her male counterparts, Missy appeared more comfortable and confident critiquing a text than writing about herself.[51]

Although initially put off by her argumentative stance, after reading and responding to her work, Missy's group helped her recognize the sources of her disparate voices. Jenny was the first to recognize "the dichotomy within [Missy's] personal history and political orientation." The group also helped Missy move beyond blame to a better understanding of her mother and herself. Although she claimed to end the semester "as much under my mother's influence as ever," Missy said she was "learning to better deal with her power over me." As with Jimmy, narrative writing helped Missy discover that "the motivation behind my drive to succeed [is] the desire to please her." Another factor was the discovery that her straightforward style was not masculine but feminine, for it was modeled on her mother's pattern of speech. At the same time, however, Missy was able to conclude, "If this semester has taught me anything it is that I am NOT like her, but am a real person with my attributes and abilities." She reached this conclusion "largely with the help of this class."[52]

Although some women believe they must adopt a masculine voice to succeed in the academy, Nadya Aisenberg and Mona Harrington maintain that women often find this voice unnatural and feel like impostors when using it (66). Male students wrestle with the opposite problem. Throughout their lives, they have been taught to develop an impersonal, objective voice, so altering their voice to allow personal reflections or admit feelings can be quite daunting. To quote William Perry, they are "caught under the pressure always to preserve their masculinity" (22). Such changes require a great deal of self-confidence as well as a similar amount of trust in the individual(s) encouraging such risks. I became aware of how deeply ingrained these language patterns were as I became better acquainted with Auggie.

Auggie: Men's Feelings of Self-Efficacy

When Auggie enrolled in Reading-Writing Theory, he participated in collaborative learning for the first time in his educational experience. Unlike many of his male peers, he did not resist group work or reject the theories underlying it. He viewed it as a positive aid to teaching: "Collaborative learning . . . is a new and powerful concept for me. This is especially true given my reticent personality. Collaborative methods allow students to take control of their learning and, thereby, go farther with it."[53] Auggie's belief in a de-centered classroom became evident the following semester when he became a TA, for he used groups in a variety of innovative and pedagogically sound ways. Nevertheless, his teaching logs suggested a continual struggle between this approach and the traditional, authoritarian pedagogy he had been trained in. Like the other students in this chapter, Auggie's actions and his writing revealed two conflicting sides of his personality.

Describing his first day of teaching and attempts to assert his authority, Auggie wrote: "with horns and tail I took my haunching position in front of the class." An initial freewriting assignment—"to describe the instructor's desk at the front of class"—suggested a similarly authoritarian focus. Despite these concerns, however, Auggie's teaching could be described as constructivist. He wrote with his students and shared his description of the desk; then he asked the students to introduce themselves and tell him their concerns and expectations for the course.[54] Still, Auggie's teaching logs continued this objective/subjective dichotomy. They were always written in an impersonal voice, yet they included self-criticism of his teaching and an awareness of his tendency to revert to Socratic inquiry when students did not respond quickly enough. Auggie's reading journals also continued in the mode of summary rather than response, but as he grew more comfortable with this mode, his logs began to include touches of humor.[55]

Auggie's personal writing was similarly split. In his first essay for Teaching College Writing, he intended to illustrate the qualities of a good teacher by describing how his high school coach had helped him deal with the trauma of learning his girlfriend was pregnant. But Auggie could not focus on this issue. Instead, he wrote around it: His first draft devoted three pages to baseball practice, the quality of the team, and the coaching; one-half page to his girlfriend's pregnancy; another half page on the coach's advice; and a final paragraph describing the resolution of the problem (the girlfriend was not pregnant after all) and gratitude for his coach's help.[56]

Auggie worked with Linc and Bob (from chapter 4), conservative men in their late thirties who found peer response an alien, awkward experience. Linc's initial responses to Auggie's paper focused more on his own experiences than on the content of the paper. When Auggie tried to raise questions, Linc cut him off; when Auggie was finally able to ask if humor detracted from the point, Linc ignored him and continued dissecting what he perceived as Auggie's stylistic flaws.[57] Lacking substantive feedback, Auggie made primarily stylistic revisions to his second draft. Although he added three paragraphs comparing coaching to teaching, ultimately this editing further distanced him emotionally from the key event—the trauma of his girlfriend's pregnancy—so that by the final draft, his girlfriend and her "problem" covered less than half a page, and the resolution was omitted altogether.[58]

Auggie's writing remained fairly impersonal throughout that semester. Part of this might be attributed to his educational background and part to his reserved Germanic heritage, but another factor may have been Auggie's aversion to revising,[59] which resulted in only minor changes between drafts and was not supported by his early work in peer groups. For essays 2 and 3, Auggie again worked with an all-male peer group, who focused their comments on organization and style rather than the development of content. The only change I observed was the gradual inclusion of a humorous voice bridging the strictly objective and the potentially embarrassing.

By the end of his first semester of teaching, Auggie seemed to have reconciled his struggles with these new perspectives. This process may have been aided by his final paper examining the ways teachers stereotype their students. Such behavior, he wrote, "can limit responsibility as well as personalities. If Mr. Underachiever or The Martyr do not do well the teacher can hardly be blamed: it is these students' nature to fail." Auggie's solution was to further de-center the classroom: "It is up to the teacher to break the cycle of dehumanization inside his/her classrooms by allowing for physical and mental contact."[60]

APPLYING THEORY

Over the years, I have found that during their first semester of graduate school, regardless of gender or gender preference, many students feel like frauds. They believe they know less than their classmates and that their inadequacies will soon be exposed. Those students who continue in the program eventually lose some of these fears as they gain experience with the conventions of the academy; nevertheless, many of the female students never believe their successes are more than flukes. In their research of female academics, Aisenberg and Harrington found that as these women progress through graduate school, they "still report feeling 'inadequate,' 'uncomfortable,' 'an impostor,' 'mute.' To state views boldly in public debate, to challenge the intellectual views of others, still pose problems for professional women" (64–66).

One reason for these difficulties relates to the language of the academy. Most women find it difficult to express themselves simultaneously "as a woman, as a feminist, and as an academic" (Gannett 16). When I discuss this phenomenon in my graduate seminars, the women nod knowingly, but the men look puzzled. Because the male voice is expected to be forceful, objective, and authoritative, writing in this way presents few problems to most men, but many women have difficulty with this juggling act. Clearly, the results of a lifetime of socialization are not going to disappear in a semester, but a number of feminist theorists suggest that changing the way we teach can help women discover their voice and with it their confidence. The previous chapters examined the influence of collaborative learning, reflective writing, action research, empathy, and trust in the development of feelings of teacher efficacy. These strategies are instrumental in facilitating the development of women's voices and feelings of self-efficacy, or confidence in the classroom. Narrative writing can have similar effects. In *Women Writing the Academy*, Kirsch argues that narrative writing helps women get in touch with their thoughts and ideas; nevertheless, female academics must recognize that in order to gain authority, they will have to master the conventions of their discipline as well (52).

This latter area is where the juggling act begins, for these conventions represent a voice and a format unnatural to most women. To attain it, Belenky et al. suggest that women first "'jump outside' the frames and systems authorities provide and create their own frame" (134). This process involves an active attempt "to *integrate* knowledge that they felt intuitively was personally important with knowledge they had learned from others. . . through a process of intense self-reflection and self-analysis" (134–35). Women who successfully learn to construct knowledge for themselves are able to do so after they "get to know the self and to reflect on the contexts that confined and defined them" (135). The following examples suggest the possibilities of this approach for students of both genders.

Melissa: Composition Pedagogy and the Unification of Voice

When Melissa sat down to write her final paper in Teaching College Writing, her renewed confidence was evident in the drafting process: She wrote the first twelve pages in two hours, then easily expanded that to eighteen. After this initial explosion, she began shaping the paper. The thesis clearly illustrated the direction it would take: "Unknowingly, Dr. X taught me something—that traditional pedagogy leads to non-thought, to non-learning, and perhaps most importantly, to the silencing of my voice. I'm sure this was not his intention, but I am grateful for the lesson." From there, she went on to describe Dr. X's teaching and its effects. Classroom discussion was virtually nonexistent, she said, for "it was easier to remain silent than to risk a blunt and humiliating response from Dr. X. . . . I spoke less and less in class; by the semester's end, I wasn't speaking in class at all."[61]

With such a focus, this paper could have easily degenerated into a diatribe or a lament. Instead, with the help of her group members, Melissa took it to a higher level. Ken believed she was "too emotionally close to the material" and suggested she move from a straight chronology to a more objective view by comparing the traditional classroom to what she was learning about composition pedagogy. Both group members supported Melissa's overall approach, praising the essay as "much stronger than [essay 2]—better organized, better written, even for a first draft."[62] This feedback gave Melissa the impetus to tighten her focus and incorporate secondary sources, strengthening her argument; it also helped restore her self-confidence.

During the drafting of essay 2, when her confidence had been "decimated" by Dr. X, Melissa had seldom spoken during group work.[63] Instead of responding to Ken's suggestions with sarcasm or explanation, as she had during the first paper, she merely murmured "okay" and sat silently. But during peer response for this final paper, Melissa took control. After each of Ken's suggestions for revision, she followed up with questions and explanations. When Ken's answer was relatively general, she persisted until he clarified his response. Following the discussion of her paper, Melissa decided they should move on to Ken's. During this conversation, she did not hesitate to offer constructive criticism: She suggested he change his paper's focus, noted his overuse of semicolons, criticized a passage denigrating a student, and resumed her use of sarcasm, summarizing their discussion by saying, "but otherwise, I thought it was a piece of shit."[64] Once again, Melissa was holding her own against a potentially authoritative male voice. Within the security of her group, Melissa was clearly an equal.

Melissa acknowledged that because of the support she received from me and her group members, her final paper "came together without much struggle."[65] She analyzed why her fellow students tolerated and accepted oppressive teaching methods, showed why these methods were ineffective, and offered solutions to the problem:

> The other students probably hadn't felt the freedom that process learning and critical thought can provide; thus the role of received knower didn't feel odd or stifling. . . . Only when they encounter such teaching methods will they sense the change—in themselves, in the way they think, and in the way they learn. And this transformation of Self [sic] will only occur when more teachers begin to use progressive pedagogy; only then will students be able to challenge the traditional methods of learning.[66]

In the process of writing this paper and analyzing her experiences, Melissa began to realize that she was not powerless. As a TA and someday as a professor, she would have the opportunity to interact with students every semester. In this capacity, she said,

> It becomes my responsibility to teach them to think and to learn on their own, through process writing, collaborative learning, and critical inquiry. . . . I must press forward with my own agenda: an agenda that empowers students to speak and write freely and learn, on their own.[67]

Melissa's conclusions underscore Tarule's findings that by connecting personal experience with the means for constructing knowledge, we help our students gain "a sense of efficacy, even authority, instead of a sense of being silenced and a damaged self-esteem" (298).

Jimmy: Composition Pedagogy and Self-Confidence

Despite upheavals within his peer-response group, Jimmy remained undeterred in his quest to find and develop his own voice. For his action research project in Teaching College Writing, he developed a case study of one of his students, Walter, to determine the source of his writing ability. To understand this student's attitude and behavior, Jimmy drew on what he had learned about himself and his writing. Jimmy's realization that he was a perfectionist helped him to recognize that trait in Walter. Just as Walter had come to view writing as a process that "never ends," Jimmy finished the semester with the same awareness:

> It's hard for me to accept the fact that writing can never be complete, can never be perfect. I can't be the perfect writer—or the perfect teacher or researcher for that matter. And yet, there's also a wonderful feeling knowing that you're always capable of improving, of reaching out just a bit farther or reaching in just a bit deeper.[68]

The following semester, Jimmy took my Reading-Writing seminar, after which he completely revised his freshman composition syllabus. In an essay explaining the rationale behind these revisions, Jimmy illustrated how his attitude toward teaching had changed over the course of two semesters: "Students should also be given the opportunity to explore how reading and writing reflect real life. They should be allowed to find their own voices, to empower themselves, to actually have a part in the self-teaching process." He vowed to help them by moving away from the traditional approach of lecture and discussion and involving students in their own learning:

> I have been a victim of such a [traditional] system, and the difficult, sometimes painful struggle out has not been easy. Now I am ready to help students in their struggle. And together, we will find new ways of reading, new ways of writing, and new ways of uniting the two—new ways, in brief, of theorizing about the world we live in.[69]

Some observers might be put off by Jimmy's openness, his theatricality, or his methods of engaging his students, for they remain uncommon in the academy. But imagine the confidence it must take to go against those traditional models. Until and unless they come out, gay males must not only conform to society's expectations for "masculinity," they must also constrain any tendencies to reveal "feminine" characteristics in their professional lives and in their language use. Even if they do come out, these men must decide whether to risk the censure of the academy by expressing themselves and their sexual preference through their language or whether to play it safe and succeed on terms other than their own. As Jimmy explained, "Most gays and lesbians have the freedom to be openly gay only in what one might term 'safe environments.' Consequently, most gays and lesbians are only 'free' in such environments. The rest of our existence is spent in fear, in isolation and pretense."[70] By changing the way we teach, we can help these students to feel free, at least, in our classrooms.

Jenny: Composition Pedagogy and the Development of Voice

Two key features of Jenny's early writing were self-deprecatory comments referring to her comprehension, writing style, and grammar use, and a straightforward style exemplified by simple, declarative sentences and colloquial usage. Jenny attributed these language features to a lack of self-confidence, a fear of failure, and a basically simple nature,[71] but her group members saw a great deal more. Linda, a professional writer and editor, suggested that Jenny's self-deprecation might be "habitual, almost un-thinking" because of modesty about her appearance and success: "brains and good looks, individuality and good looks, social conscience and good looks DON'T MIX. This self-deprecation is socially imposed and is perhaps not altogether a bad defense mechanism."[72]

Although Jenny acknowledged the influence of these factors, she still felt inferior to her classmates, which led her to apologize and to readily express "confusion or frustration" when reading theory.[73] But Auggie in-terpreted such comments as "interest in coherence or succinct thought" and suggested that Jenny's desire for organization and simplicity (rather than inability) contributed to her tendency to write clearly and concisely.[74] On this point, even Missy agreed: "Your use of short declaratives is, I would say, pithy. I like it; you seem alert and to the point."[75] Analyzing Jenny's preference for colloquial language, both Linda and Auggie described them as "reader friendly," a trait they linked to her desire for clarity in the theoretical works we were reading.[76]

Because she respected most of her group members, Jenny began to accept what they said and view her writing more positively. These feel-ings, coupled with the group's input and their growing familiarity, led to positive changes in Jenny's writing as the semester progressed. Her voice became more direct, her style and syntax grew in variety and com-plexity, and the tone of self-deprecation began to diminish. These changes produced something of a snowball effect: The more Jenny's writing matured, the more praise it elicited from her group members. Missy noted, "Now you are becoming more comfortable with us as group members who know your mental abilities and so you are dropping that shield."[77] Auggie also pointed out this dichotomy:

I must say that there are two Jenny's, the self-deprecating and the confident, competitive one. The former seems to dominate the two. This is unrepresentative of reality since you have an incredible amount of positives including energy, friendliness, and competence. This is Kafka vs. Whitman.[78]

Despite the positive feedback from me and her group members, Jenny found it difficult to overcome a fear of "looking stupid" when she wrote.[79] Considering that these fears had accumulated after years of being dismissed because of her appearance, one semester was hardly sufficient to change Jenny's conception of herself as a writer. Although she graduated with a specialization in composition, which required twelve hours of course work utilizing similar pedagogical strategies, at the end of the M.A. program, she still did not believe her writing was valid or substantive. Of course, these twelve hours represented only a third of her M.A. classes.

Jenny's lack of confidence in her writing echoes some of the women Kirsch interviewed for *Writing the Academy*, who found it difficult to "transcend gender" when attempting to establish their sense of authority. Perhaps, like these women, additional years of writing to an audience she knows, about a subject she understands, will help Jenny improve her feelings of self-efficacy. Yet, as Kirsch notes, even experienced, published writers will "evaluate themselves according to institutional definitions of writing and research" (70). Add to these biases the fact that Jenny remains pretty and blonde, and the possibility of a change in writing-related confidence seems dim. Like some of Kirsch's subjects, these factors may overshadow Jenny's successes to such an extent that she may never be able to "credit herself with the ability to write" (70).

Missy: Composition Pedagogy and Self-Knowledge

Despite doubts about her own writing, Jenny was instrumental in helping Missy understand her language use. At the end of the semester, when Missy wrote her final essay examining her language features, she acknowledged the emergence of a personal voice, noting that in her responses to literature,

> I had fully expected to return to my less personal style of the [academic] writings, but I did not. Instead, I found that my work had a much more personal and anecdotal feel to it, and that I could not return to the New Critical method of discussing a piece of literature without feeling anything

I had learned as a child. I felt a lot, and by the end of the semester, almost all of these feelings were emerging beyond my control.[80]

As she traced the source of these feelings, Missy acknowledged that the group's feedback had led her to reexamine her relationships, their influence on her writing, and her need for "power and control." "Though I had not realized it at the beginning of the semester," she wrote, "I am a control freak. This accounts not only for my interest in strength . . . but also dictates my belief structures much more than I would have realized." This burgeoning understanding led Missy to question the basis of her political stance and to realize that she was really not a feminist. By the last few weeks of the semester, she "had ceased to equate [her]self with feminism at all" because she realized that her definition lay in the belief that feminism was "a political stance that focused upon opposition."[81]

This changing point of view was facilitated by reading feminist reader-response theory, by the narrative writing assignments, and by Missy's group members' responses to her writing. Linda implicitly pointed out the discrepancies in voice when she observed that Missy's expressions of feeling focused on a desire for equality. Jenny commented that Missy's expressions of feeling were not only characteristic of women but positive characteristics at that: "Would a man mull over this? This might be a deviant to your male thinking brain."[82] Ultimately, Missy revealed that "over the course of the semester I have seen clearly how my 'feminist' impression of myself in the responses to academic readings has altered into a more humanist approach."[83]

Missy would be the first to admit she was not transformed during that semester of reader response. In her final essay, she acknowledged that she was still a bundle of paradoxes: "I am no more certain of who I am now than I was four months ago. . . . I am still not sure who I want to be."[84] Perhaps because of these feelings, she remained somewhat insecure. In fact, she felt this trait had "grown worse" as she became increasingly frustrated with the demands of her graduate course work—evidence cited by Belenky et al. of increased self-awareness and movement to a more complex way of knowing. Writing personal narratives and listening to those of others, such as Missy did in Reader Response, facilitates this journey.

Of course, a single semester of personal writing was not sufficient to effect these changes. Missy continued to feel more comfortable with academic discourse than with personal narrative, which she found "discomforting." Nevertheless, she began her journey as a result of the writing and response in our graduate seminar:

> I learned to accept my mother and my husband on their own terms, not simply as extensions of myself. I went a little crazy, in pursuit of the perfect child, and made a number of changes in my writing. I became more personal, less witty, and learned that being weak isn't always a crime. I shaved my head and learned to be a human being, not just "the charming companion to a wealthy gentleman." I don't think I'll ever go back.[85]

Auggie: Composition Pedagogy and the Development of Empathy

Auggie's story underscores men's difficulty with expressing a personal voice. Although Reader Response Theory was the third seminar he had taken with me and even though he was working in a peer-response group with friends and fellow TAs, his personal feelings remained guarded by a shield of humor throughout the bulk of the course. In an introductory essay designed to introduce themselves to the class, Auggie continued his allusions to Kafka, writing: "I have had a stable childhood. When my father returned from the penal colony, I was able to quit my after school job in the coal pits & devote myself to my true love—utensil arrangement." Introducing his wife, he wrote, "I am married & have a cat. Her name is C—; his name is Watson. You figure out which is which." Of his sisters, he wrote, "They routinely brutalized me when I was young (who am I kidding; they still bully me)."[86]

In subsequent papers, Auggie continued this tactic. When asked to write about recurring arguments with his parents or his spouse, he wrote a short paper describing a time he retaliated against repeated fouls in a basketball game by knocking the perpetrator to the ground.[87] When asked to describe relationships with his teachers, he wrote a much longer response, explaining that the length was "because my family's left off."[88] Yet he was equally reticent about himself. When asked to describe his most successful moment, he wrote about the time he directed a traffic jam during a snowstorm.[89] Similarly, personal responses to three different short stories—Irwin Shaw's "The Girls in Their Summer Dresses," Raymond Carver's "What We Talk about When We Talk about Love," and Ernest Hemingway's "Hills like White Elephants"—were all brief and objective. Even an account of gender discrimination was devoid of emotion.[90]

Auggie explained some of this detachment in his final journal entry when he wrote that all semester, he had felt "displaced." Introducing gender differences into reader response, he said, was

> an awakening. It's cruel to put a male through this experience. It's like giving birth. I guess. I can tell you that I'm more than a little sensitive to minorities than I was before this class. And, I'm not talking about my language here, though I'm sure this is reflected here. I'm talking about empathy. I hate feeling small, feeling alone. I've felt alone at times around that [seminar] table. Do men do this to women? Do I? It's hard to imagine. Well, not so much anymore.[91]

The above response was easily the most personal expression of feeling Auggie had exhibited in the three semesters I had known him. Although it did not seem like it at the time, in studying Auggie and Bob's cases, I realized that gender had been an issue throughout the Reader Response seminar. Every week, at least two of their classmates introduced feminist issues into any discussion; moreover, during the second half of the semester, when we read Elizabeth A. Flynn and Patrocinio Schweikert's *Gender and Reading*, we began to include gender relations in our language analyses. I did not think Auggie had been bothered by these conversations. In fact, the only time I recalled him reacting with anything other than humor was in response to what seemed a rather innocuous comment from Melissa (ironically, one of the few times she spoke in class that semester). After Auggie described a lesson he had taught, Melissa remarked quietly, "That seems pretty authoritarian to me." Auggie turned red and said nothing for the rest of the class; afterwards, he left immediately rather than staying to chat as usual. To this day, he still mentions how angry Melissa made him because her statement had been so unfair.[92] (His reaction also effectively silenced Melissa, who had spoken up at my urging, for the rest of the semester.)

In this situation, Auggie apparently felt that personal expression was permissible. As Sadker and Sadker note, by the standards of society and the academy, men are allowed to express anger, but other feelings are considered inappropriate (205). Recognizing these traits and addressing them were long processes. By midterm, Auggie conceded that he "use[d] humor to entertain, to communicate, and to avoid."[93] At that point, he was not ready to explore the reasons, but by the end of the semester, he had begun to analyze these language traits. Describing his midterm, he wrote, "I fell victim to my very language history: I concentrated on entertaining . . . without honestly digging at the form and cause of my language." He became aware of this tendency, he admitted, because of his interactions with his group.[94]

Auggie's group members repeatedly pointed out these traits, recognizing "a hesitation" on his part, "a distrusting." Missy described Auggie's writing as "powerful but emotionally restrained," and Jenny told him his "feelings sound[ed] wishy-washy."[95] In his final essay, Auggie finally began to analyze these tendencies. He admitted that he "avoided in-depth discussion or explanation by shortened lengths of writing or mixing the matter with equal parts comedy" because he disliked expressing "feelings or even opinions." Humor was used "to hedge." Before taking the Reader Response seminar, he had followed the credo that "matters may be told most powerfully when written about 'minimalistically.'" However, his group's feedback had shown him that unless one were a Hemingway, minimalist expressions could be misconstrued.[96]

To avoid expressing his feelings, Auggie's writing became either humorous or detached. Indeed, he found that "Detachment may be seen as the guiding principle to my language, a language labeled as masculine by my group."[97] However, his group also found that Auggie's language was "sensitive to women and yet male-centered."[98] Auggie acknowledged that the source for these traits was his mother who, although "she would never label herself a feminist, has always been at least an equal partner in her marriage." Auggie admired this trait in her, in his sisters, and in his wife: "I love independent women, not because I want to be mothered, but, rather, because I don't want to be fatherly." Although he admired this independence, he did not want to be controlled by it, nor did he want to be viewed as controlling.[99]

These feelings were directly related to Auggie's anger at Melissa's remark that his teaching seemed "authoritarian," a trait the women in the class had labeled as typically masculine. In his final essay, Auggie admitted that on this issue, he held contradictory feelings. All of his group members had noted his "stated concern for an egalitarian spirit inside the classroom," but they had also pointed out "a masculine subtext to [his] outlook."[100] Such comments helped Auggie become aware that his concern for professionalism in the classroom actually caused him to distance himself from his students. After working with his group members and studying the implications of his language, Auggie realized this was an issue he needed to address. Still, he admitted, "Revolutions don't fill out quickly; I can't erase the influence of twenty years in a matter of months. But the change is there. I have been able to move away from my masculine perspective regarding my teaching."[101]

Auggie was an exceptional student, more sensitive and open to change than many of his male peers, traits he brought with him into the graduate seminar. When he workshopped his writing in the all-male groups during Teaching College Writing, his "masculine" perspectives and style of writing were not challenged. In Reader Response, however, his placement in a group with three women, coupled with his minority status as one of only three males in the seminar, created an environment in which those perspectives were impossible to ignore. If he had taken this seminar during his first semester of graduate school, Auggie might have resisted these challenges because he did not know his classmates, his group members, or me. It takes a good deal of time to establish trust as well as the right placement within a discourse community. In this case, the timing of the course work fostered Auggie's willingness to take the risk of opening up. As a result, he learned a good deal about himself.

IMPLICATIONS FOR TEACHING

During my years at the university, I have cringed at the hesitant voices of my female peers, begged my female students to speak up in class, and been dismayed by the jargon-laden prose and argumentative style of young women seeking success in the academy. I have been similarly disappointed by the impersonal voices of my male students, yet I had not considered that these men and women might share common reasons for their language behaviors. As these case studies suggest, our students' language is influenced by their interactions with family, friends, and educators. These factors are in turn shaped by gender. Even in adulthood, early experiences still have the power to influence our language and behavior regardless of age, sex, or sexual orientation (Bleich, *Double* 236). The results are revealed in each individual's voice.

An understanding of voice—and the sense of agency which accompanies it—are important for professors and for the TAs who will succeed us, for these qualities influence the quality of classroom instruction. According to Belenky et al., the development of voice and the capacity for connection are the keys to personal and intellectual growth. We can develop this ability in our graduate students and help them recognize the need for such an environment by using composition pedagogy to help students become aware of their beliefs and examine the assumptions behind them. In this chapter, these new ways of teaching and learning included writing personal narratives, engaging in collaborative learning, and erasing the hierarchical boundaries between students and faculty. Each element has broader implications for how teaching may be conceived by our future faculty.

In her interviews with female graduate students and faculty, Kirsch determined that one of the primary factors fostering the development of voice was the use of "narrative strategies." By recounting and reevaluating their experiences, these women were able to develop methods for dealing with those who challenged their authority. Narrative strategies included distancing themselves from their writing

> by describing themselves as outsiders or "participant observers" in the academic culture, by reinterpreting discouraging writing experiences as positive learning experiences, and by describing writing and research as two distinct and unrelated activities. (*Women* 64)

These strategies were evident in the writing of Jimmy, who overcame his difficulties with personal voice by writing as an outsider; by Jenny, who disassociated herself and her abilities from researched writing; and in Melissa's final essay, where she regained her confidence by using her negative experiences to underscore the need for constructivist pedagogy. Narrative strategies also enabled Auggie and Missy to understand the reasons for their distanced voices.

In their case study of Nate, Berkenkotter et al. recognized that

> the informal, expressive pieces Nate wrote provided him the opportunity to give free rein to his intellect. It appears that by ignoring many of the constraints imposed by the genre and register of academic writing expected of him, he could more easily explore new ideas. (qtd. in Ray, *Practice* 152)

Ruth Ray underscores this importance: "When entering into a field, graduate students need time to grasp information as students before being asked to analyze and critique it as researchers" (153). In this regard, gender is not an issue. Although their reasons may differ, both male and female students can benefit from personal, expressive writing.

Obviously, not every graduate student is comfortable with this approach. Graduate faculty are even more likely to resist assigning personal narrative and peer response for fear of increasing the workload and changing the focus of a course from the text to the people reading it. However, if we accept the fact that we are responsible for preparing our graduate students to enter the profession, then the use of narration and peer response merits consideration. Professional preparation no longer can be limited to the acquisition of theoretical knowledge and research skills, for very few graduate students will be hired solely to do research. As jobs dwindle and undergraduates' literacy skills decline, newly minted Ph.D.s will most likely be teaching a variety of courses to students who resent the requirements and resist the reading. In his examination of the ethics of graduate education, Richard Fulkerson reminds us that teaching

> now includes nurturing and mentoring (even outside the classroom) students
> of all ages and social backgrounds, students with families and jobs, students
> with financial and social problems, students that yesterday's Germanic uni-
> versity did not bring to campus. (128)

By incorporating opportunities for narrative and reflective writing, we help graduate students develop the self-knowledge, self-confidence, and feelings of self-efficacy necessary to change the way they teach, as well as the pedagogical skills to do so.

Of course, narration is not the only type of writing graduate students should engage in. As Kirsch points out, mastery of disciplinary conventions helps female students develop a sense of authority within the academy. To bridge the gap between personal and academic voice and instill in graduate students the belief that they deserve to participate in this discourse community, they need the opportunity to engage in discussions with their peers about these issues. If the groups are carefully constructed, they provide support and develop confidence. Collaborative learning offers this opportunity.

In the conclusion to his research paper for Teaching College Writing, Auggie wrote, "It is up to the teacher to break the cycle of dehumanization inside his/her classrooms by allowing for physical and mental contact." By changing the way we teach, we help our students gain personally and professionally. The results can be seen in the self-confidence developed by the graduate students in this chapter who, in learning about themselves, began to understand more about the kinds of teachers and professors they wanted to be. If we can accomplish all this in one semester, imagine what we could do over the course of our students' graduate education.

7. Strengthening Voice

𝒟espite advances in the past thirty years, socialization continues to play a powerful and potentially negative role in young women's progress toward independent thought and expression. These influences were evident among the majority of my female graduate students, most of whom could be described as lacking a strong and unified voice. For various reasons, these women had not reached what Mary F. Belenky, Blythe M. Clinchy, Nancy R. Goldberger, and Jill Mattuck Tarule term *constructed knowing,* "a position in which women view all knowledge as contextual, experience themselves as creators of knowledge, and value both subjective and objective strategies for knowing" (15). Constructed knowers are active learners; they work with ideas and information rather than merely taking them in. For many, the path to self-knowledge begins when they start keeping a reflective journal. The process of reading, writing, and reflecting makes them aware of what they know and more willing and able to communicate their knowledge. This self-possession is reflected in their voice, which not only interweaves personal and professional knowledge but also values listening to others and sharing ideas rather than didactic "holding forth" (144).

The women in this chapter could be described as constructed knowers. Kim, Shannon, and Carolyn began their graduate work with strong, unified voices evident in their writing, their teaching, and their speaking. Over the years, I noticed the same phenomenon in three other women students; however, they were in their mid-thirties so their attainment of this epistemological position was not so unusual.[1] The presence of strong voice among female graduate students in their mid-twenties is atypical, however. Indeed, this degree of self-possession at such a young age set these women apart from the rest of their female peers. Of the twenty-six women who participated in this study, only these three had found their voice by their mid-twenties.

This chapter explores the phenomena contributing to the development of a strong, unified voice in women—self-knowledge, empathy, positive role models, and mentors—to reinforce the argument that these can and should be essential elements of a constructivist graduate curriculum. I begin by defining voice and its relation to constructed knowing. Following these definitions, I establish the context in which I came to know these students. These sections provide the background against which to examine elements of the women's case studies. In the first section, I trace the influence of gender roles and familial expectations on the development of young women's personal constructs; in the next, I examine the effects of literacy experiences on their perceptions of self-efficacy; in the final section, I explore the correlations between feminist and composition pedagogies to reiterate that by implementing these practices in the graduate classroom, we facilitate the development of the strong voice representative of constructed knowers—the type of women necessary to instantiate constructivist teaching in our postsecondary and graduate classrooms.

STRONG VOICE AND CONSTRUCTED KNOWING

Many women have a problem with voice. They are silenced by a range of factors—family, peers, education, society—whose effects are manifested in a variety of contexts. Young women are often afraid to speak up in public or to defend themselves verbally; they tend to distrust assertive women and retreat from aggressive men. As a result, they often lack self-esteem and self-knowledge, evidenced by hesitation, qualification, or adoption of other more "acceptable" voices, feeling like frauds or impostors, and difficulty reflecting or expressing themselves in writing (Kirsch, *Women* 56ff). Women possessing a strong voice are just the opposite: They speak assertively regardless of context (or possible repercussions); they will speak up in defense of themselves, their beliefs, or others; and they maintain a clear sense of self and self-efficacy. Their writing reflects their speaking, both of which result from reflection and draw on relevant experience.

How do females develop the sense of authority enabling them to claim their voice and proclaim their ideas? One salient characteristic is "the quality of the voices of [young women's] mothers" (Belenky et al. 176). Mothers who speak their minds, participate in decision making, and function as equal partners within the family structure provide strong role models; those mothers who also communicate directly, frequently, and intimately with their daughters compound their influence. The presence of a similarly strong voice among fathers is not so crucial, for this quality is viewed as a given. More important is a father's willingness and ability to listen and communicate with his daughters (177). Within families demonstrating both characteristics, the daughters are much more likely to integrate reason and emotion in their voices (181). In *Daughters of Feminists*, a qualitative study of these young women, Rose L. Glickman reports the same phenomenon:

> In all feminist families, fathers no less than mothers exhorted and encouraged their daughters, in word and deed, to develop their minds and to strive for and expect professional achievement. The daughters speak with one voice about how their parents instilled and nurtured their self-esteem, reminded them of their worth as women, affirmed their equality with men in strengths, rights (at least in principle), and encouraged them to become self sufficient. This is the strongest common denominator in the daughters' formative years. (30)

Young women lucky enough to receive this solid grounding—and hold onto it during their tumultuous teens—often display the characteristics of constructed knowing.[2] They realize that knowledge is not static but context-dependent. This awareness leads them to analyze, question, and formulate their own criteria for developing knowledge and periodically reexamine and reevaluate their understanding (Belenky et al. 139). Because of their constant awareness, they tend to develop their own approaches for problem solving, often drawing on personal experience to make connections and develop their understanding. There is a recursive connection between self-knowledge and self-awareness. According to Belenky et al.,

> Constructivists seek to stretch the outer boundaries of their consciousness—by making the unconscious conscious, by consulting and listening to the self, by voicing the unsaid, by listening to others and staying alert to all the currents and undercurrents of life about them, by imagining themselves inside the new poem or person or idea that they want to come to know and understand. (141)

This process is enhanced through reflection and empathy. Constructed knowers value dialogue as a means of speculating, learning, and sharing ideas, for they realize the generative power of collaboration. Unfortunately, there can be a downside to this mind-set: "Once a woman has a voice, she wants it to be heard" (146). These women are willing not only to converse but also to proclaim their ideas. Despite improved gender relations, not everyone is willing to listen or to respect what a woman has to say, so constructivist women sometimes have to accede to the unspoken rules laid down by men regarding women's roles and import (148). Such situations can be particularly difficult, for these women are usually committed to their beliefs and willing to stand up for them. Nevertheless, because constructivists are equally aware of the needs of others, they weigh their options carefully:

> Constructivist women aspire to work that contributes to the empowerment and improvement in the quality of life of others. . . . [T]hey feel a part of the effort to address with others the burning issues of the day and to contribute as best they can. They speak of integrating feeling and care into their work. . . . They reveal in the way they speak and live their lives their moral conviction that ideas and values, like children, must be nurtured, cared for, placed in environments that help them grow. (152)

These elements were personified in Kim, Shannon, and Carolyn.

THE CONTEXT

At the time of this study, the young women in this chapter were all in their late twenties. As such, each could be considered a "nontraditional" student in that they were slightly older than the average when they began their graduate work. Although their marital status varied somewhat—Kim and Shannon were married with children, and Carolyn was engaged—all three shared relatively common backgrounds. Kim's and Shannon's parents insisted on equal treatment of their male and female children, encouraging them to speak freely and giving their daughters the same freedoms as their sons.[3] Carolyn's father died when she was a child so she grew up in what Glickman refers to as "mother families" (32)—an environment in which females were in control. The women in Carolyn's family treated each other as equals; they seemed to have no sense of an absolute authority to be obeyed and no concept of gender differences in language or power.[4] Growing up in an atmosphere of mutual respect, Kim, Shannon, and Carolyn developed strong relationships with their parents.

Language and literacy experiences played a major role in their development. As a child, Kim read voraciously; as an adult she wrote fiction.[5] Shannon recalled her mother reading to her nightly, a practice that introduced her to the joys of reading and that she continued with her own children.[6] Carolyn was read to by her older sister and sister-in-law so frequently that she entered kindergarten knowing how to read. In high school, she wrote for the school newspaper.[7] In every case, it was assumed that these young women would go to college and pursue a career.

Yet none of them immediately fulfilled their parents' expectations. Kim's and Carolyn's feelings paralleled the daughters of feminists whom Glickman interviewed, who felt that more was expected of them because they were women (30). Because Kim's parents had not gone to college, they expected her to surpass them and excel in her studies. Feeling pressured "to be perfect," Kim rebelled, became estranged from her parents, and dropped out of college.[8] Carolyn succumbed to similar pressures. As a member of the Jewish community, she was expected to go to college and be the best among her peers. Such expectations so overwhelmed her that she dropped out after her freshman year.[9] Shannon's situation was somewhat reversed. A member of the Church of Jesus Christ of Latter-day Saints, she was expected to marry and focus her career in the home and the church by raising her children and teaching others. After she married, Shannon entered college and continued taking course work between pregnancies and despite her husband's frequent transfers.[10]

These women were willing to take risks: They rebelled against their families' expectations and followed their own paths. Eventually, these paths led them back to college and on to graduate school where they again shared common characteristics. When writing, they were not afraid to question or challenge the "authorities," nor did they hesitate to draw on personal experience to exemplify professional behavior or comprehend complicated material. In this, their behavior differed sharply from the majority of their female counterparts who relied more on secondary materials than on their own voices and experiences. Conversely, the texts of constructivist learners synthesize academic prose and personal example, a combination lending authority to their voices. These same voices were present during small-group work. Rather than waiting to be called on or ordered about, these women assigned tasks or negotiated procedure and then shared responsibility or spoke for their group. Whether speaking to their peers, their teachers, or their students, their voices were strong and self-assured.

These students' case studies are discussed chronologically, for I discovered as I analyzed them that my own sense of self as a teacher developed with experience, reflection, and engagement. Although Kim took

Reader Response, Teaching College Writing, and Reading-Writing Theory with me, our relationship was strictly teacher-student. At the time, I was relatively unaware of this detachment, as illustrated by my lack of personal interaction in her case study. By the time I taught Shannon, I had become more involved with my students. Although Shannon took only Teaching College Writing, I felt as if I knew her better than I knew Kim because we often conferred during her teaching assistantship. Carolyn was my student in Contemporary American Women Novelists and Teaching College Writing; at the end of her master's program, we worked together on an independent study. Our relationship evolved from mentor-protégé to friends to colleagues.

As I reviewed my students' stories and my role as their teacher, I gained a clearer sense of how teacher-student interactions impact development of both parties. Graduate students are not the only ones who can profit by reflection. In tracing our mutual development, I hope to illustrate factors facilitating the development of women's voice and self-understanding regardless of their age or position.

FAMILIAL EXPECTATIONS AND PERSONAL CONSTRUCT

As the case studies in chapter 6 demonstrated, family can negatively impact children's understanding of their gender roles and construction of their personal construct, but relationships with parents can, of course, also have a positive impact. Such a thesis seems obvious, yet only recently have psychologists begun focusing on family relationships as they pertain to gender and personal construct. In their study of the psychological factors contributing to the failure and success of adolescent girls, for example, Jill McLean Taylor, Carol Gilligan, and Amy M. Sullivan conclude that strong relationships with other females are essential: "A resonant relationship with a woman, meaning a relationship in which a girl can speak freely and hear her voice clearly resounded as a voice worth listening to and taken seriously, . . . was associated with psychological health and development" (4–5). Such relationships help young women sort out their problems and validate their ideas and emotions (69).

By examining girls' development, Taylor, Gilligan, and Sullivan identified the point when these relationships tend to deteriorate. From birth through adolescence, girls are generally willing to communicate freely with their mothers; however, between eighth and ninth grades, contradictory cultural, societal, and generational tensions often introduce a rift. If their relationships withstand these tensions, the girls emerge stronger. But if they enter high school believing they have lost these ties or have been betrayed, the teenage years become a time when young women "silence themselves" internally by ignoring their feelings and beliefs and externally by keeping quiet or pretending not to care and believing, in turn, that no one cares about them (196–97).

Daughters of feminists are not immune to these conflicts, but if the relationship remains intact, the lessons of their youth reemerge. Glickman claims, "A firm, unbroken thread of individual responsibility and individual efficacy runs through the daughters' ruminations" (182). All believed they should "practice what they preach." Some enacted these beliefs in their personal lives while others tried to serve as role models (182–83). Because women now in their twenties did not grow up in the second wave of the feminist movement, they are seldom as politically active as their mothers. Nevertheless, they tend to believe that "You have to make a decision to be conscious of [feminism] and to stick to it. You have to make it happen" (190). Such beliefs characterize the women in this chapter.

Kim: The Tomboy

Kim was close to both of her parents. She felt a strong bond with her father, and she emulated the role models established by her mother, who went to work before the two-career family had become a national phenomenon, and by her grandmother, an early feminist. These dual influences and sources of support gave her the confidence to express her needs and her opinions.[11] Kim explained that her parents had raised their children to be equals—the boys were treated just like the girls with no distinctions between chores, curfews, mores, or taboos, and all were encouraged to speak their minds. Consequently, Kim grew up with little regard for traditional gender roles. When she was a teenager, she played pinball, pool, poker, and sports; rode motorcycles, went spelunking, and tried rappelling; and competed in all these endeavors with her dates and male friends. She was "a sort of class clown, always telling jokes (more often than not off-color jokes) and accepting all sorts of silly dares." Even in high school, Kim had a sense of herself as a woman who deserved respect. When one of her peers jokingly introduced her to a school assembly as "Big Boobs-a-Loose," for example, she did not cower in embarrassment or run to her parents; she confronted the offender and then went to the principal and told him such behavior was unacceptable.[12]

Because of her relationship with her parents, Kim grew up "not too hesitant to tell others what I think, and with a sense of authority." She summed up the effects of her childhood:

> My parents taught me to be strong, independent, and honest. I was always willing to talk about anything with anybody. Because of these characteristics, I felt different and unusual. These feelings of uniqueness often provided me with a source of strength and confidence.

This background was so influential that Kim felt it was her "responsibility (like it is the responsibility of all women) to do everything [she could] to fight the prejudice that faces women everyday."[13]

Shannon: The Mormon Influence

Shannon was raised in a strict religious environment in which women's roles were to bear children, run the household, and serve the church. Shannon's role model was her mother, a strong woman who treated all her children equally and served as a partner to her husband but who did not pursue a career outside the home. The mother of seven children, she would hardly have had time. From her mother, Shannon learned firsthand about nurturing. As a member of the Church of Jesus Christ of Latter-day Saints, Shannon was expected to follow her example.[14] These sources contributed to the development of Shannon's strong voice and sense of authority. Indeed, Shannon gave much of the credit to her experiences in the church:

> In my church work I work closely with many people older than me. For example, right now I'm in the Young Women's presidency, the women in charge of organizing all the activities and programs for the 12–18 year old females. The other 2 women are both in their 40s and have children closer to my age than they are. Yet we work together as equals and peers.[15]

Shannon's experiences reflect the findings of Taylor, Gilligan, and Sullivan, who argue that such nonfamilial relationships have "powerful effects" on young women because they exist "outside the burdens of conventional dictates, free from the weight and inevitable distortion of idealization and unrealistic expectations" often characterizing mother-daughter relationships (116). Still, the strong model of nurturing presented by Shannon's mother seemed equally influential: "There's a lot of truth to the saying that making people feel competent makes them competent. I lavish praise on my 4 yr. old when he makes his bed even though his actual performance is poor at best." Shannon's teaching style reflected these beliefs: "Personally, I feel uncomfortable setting myself up as some big authority figure. I am much more comfortable w/a role of mentor, facilitator, I guess nurturer. Even though I'm an authority insofar as I have more experience than [my students], I'm still very much a learning writer too."[16]

Shannon's stance echoes that proposed by Nel Noddings, who advocates "moral education from the care perspective." For Noddings, as for Shannon, good teaching entails caring for one's students, designing classroom activities that "give students practice in caring and reflecting" and praising or confirming the students' best efforts (190–96). This approach does not imply a lack of rigor. Rather, Shannon viewed it as a combination "nurturer/enforcer" in the same way she viewed parenting:

> I'm much more comfortable with [this role] as a parent because my kids are only 4½ and 2. . . . They need guidelines, & now thinking about it, my students do too. They wouldn't know where to start on improving their writing if they didn't have the textbooks & some guidelines from me.[17]

Carolyn: In the Company of Women

Unlike Kim and Shannon, Carolyn grew up without a male role model. Her father died when she was three years old, so throughout her early years, Carolyn, her sister, and her mother lived without a male in the house. Carolyn believed this context played a significant role in her development:

> I had a voice, I counted, in a home where most females, especially children, would not be allowed to speak freely. Also, my mother assumed the roles of both mother and father, so I saw that it was acceptable (from her) that I could speak and be heard. She worked full time to support us at a time when most mothers were not working at all.[18]

Like Shannon, religion also influenced Carolyn's goals, talents, and sense of self:

> In Judaism, education is strongly emphasized. I didn't consider the possibility that I didn't have to attend college. I don't categorize this belief as reli-

gious, which I am not, but cultural. In terms of religion, having a strong voice is encouraged and celebrated, for both males and females.[19]

Early literacy skills led Carolyn to pursue a career as a writer. In high school, she worked on the school paper; when she entered the University of Wisconsin–Madison, she majored in journalism. However, her family's expectations made Carolyn feel constricted, so after her freshman year, she dropped out. Lacking any credentials beyond her high school journalism courses, Carolyn nonetheless talked her way into a job as a writer for a local newspaper. She worked as a journalist for a few years until she came to her own decision about her future: She would return to college.

Unfortunately, because of her dismal freshman year, she was denied admission to the University of Missouri–St. Louis, so again, Carolyn went to the authorities and talked them into admitting her on probation. In school and sure of her direction, she excelled in her studies, yet her first year at Wisconsin continued to plague her. When she applied to graduate school, she was turned down, but again she would not be deterred. She appealed to her undergraduate professors, who supported her and helped her once more to be admitted provisionally. Again, she excelled. Carolyn found none of this exceptional: "Since I worked as a writer before I returned to school, I had to have a strong voice. Unlike a lot of my peers, I was already confident as a writer and a speaker—it just came naturally to me."[20]

LITERACY, VOICE, AND SELF-EFFICACY

The combination of strong familial support and successful literacy experiences plays a significant role in the development of young women's feelings of self-efficacy. Indeed, Belenky et al. note, "The development of a sense of voice, mind, and self is intricately intertwined." Armed with this self-knowledge, writers gain the confidence to develop their own voice, a term Peter Elbow claims is seldom associated with women's writing because it is equated with the self-confidence. People who have a voice "write with authority, with a mind of [their] own that is willing to offend" (Introduction xxxiii). This mode of speaking is not associated with women's voices for it is not how most women were raised to speak. Among daughters of feminists, however, this voice is modeled and cultivated. As Glickman points out, being a feminist parent requires a strong voice. Even in the happiest families, disputes are unavoidable, but for women striving for equality, marital discussions may often revolve around "bargaining and negotiating, cultivating respect for the mother's endeavors and weeding the soil of daily domestic obligations" (25). Those marriages that survive do so in part because the husband agrees to share chores and child care. Daughters who witness these negotiations learn from example. Kim, Shannon, and Carolyn learned well.

Kim: The Feminist

From the beginning, it was obvious that Kim held clear-cut views about teaching and did not hesitate to express them. In Reading-Writing Theory, she readily critiqued objectivist teaching, asserting that teachers needed "to realize they cannot create an atmosphere conducive to learning when they are the supreme authority with the duty of cramming their knowledge down the throats of their students."[21] Yet Kim was equally willing to accept new theories and admit when she was wrong. Although she initially scoffed at Gerald Harste, Virginia Woodward, and Caroline Burke's contention that the scrawlings of three-year-olds represented early attempts at writing, eventually she realized that children this age had already acquired a degree of literacy when she compared the research to the writing and drawing of her three-year-old son.[22]

Kim's outspokenness expanded the following year in Reader Response Theory. As in the previous seminar, Kim accepted some theorists and rejected others, but overall, she found "reader response theory crucial from a pedagogical point of view."[23] During this course, Kim revealed a strong feminist voice. Although her beliefs had been implicit in her preference for the female pronoun, they came out directly in her critique of Wolfgang Iser, for example, when she asked:

> What about the fact that what has been considered "good" literature and the criteria for judging what is "good" . . . has almost entirely been decided by white Anglo-Saxon males? Does Iser not realize that part of the reason the classical norms of interpretation have endured . . . is because these men have made sure to protect their own interests?[24]

I had placed Kim in a group with Joan and Bob (from chapter 4) because they were approximately the same age, came from similar backgrounds, and respected teaching. But as the semester progressed, Kim's outspokenness began to complicate the group's interactions. I had not realized that Bob's conservative views would clash with Kim's liberal feminism on practically every subject. Kim regarded Bob as a traditional husband and teacher whose self-image as "supreme authority" she despised.[25] Bob viewed Kim as a radical feminist who threatened the sanctity of the family and the serenity of the classroom.[26] Initially, Joan remained above the fray. However, as the semester progressed, both Joan and Bob began to focus on Kim's feminism, which they referred to as Kim's "problem" with gender issues. This only exacerbated the so-called problem:

> I tried to defend myself, insisting that my beliefs about sexism and gender issues were not a "problem," but a realistic concern about an important issue. However, they never seemed to buy my arguments, and thus, I found myself becoming more defensive and more concerned with gender issues. . . . I found myself becoming almost obsessed.[27]

These ongoing arguments raised the awareness of both Bob and Kim. During a class discussion of Kim's writing style, one student suggested that Kim's extensive editing and use of qualifiers seemed "to indicate a lack of self-confidence and a tendency toward deprecation."[28] Because of his familiarity with Kim's oral and written voice, Bob argued that on the contrary, Kim was "confident in her ideas and abilities as a writer."[29] Such feedback and support led Kim to reexamine her self-image as a writer and respect her group members' recurrent references to her "problem" with gender issues enough to explore it.

In the final essay for Reader Response, Kim concluded that there was some validity to her group members' findings. Yes, she had become obsessed with feminist issues, but feminism was not the problem. Rather, it was the key to her independence. If she expressed frustration with her husband or with any other men, it was "very much connected to [her] feelings about gender relationships and [her] desire for equality."[30] Although Kim's parents had fostered her independence throughout her childhood, when she entered her late teens, they felt she should become more demure, a double standard common even in feminist families (Glickman 29). Kim's irritation at these constraints and the "stupid roles" she was forced into was revealed in personal essays covering subjects such as ending a relationship with a jealous boyfriend, arguments with her parents, and disgust at people's belief that her husband's "helping out" at home implied he was doing her a favor.[31]

Because Kim's feminist views paralleled my own, I found her attitude refreshing, but her beliefs rankled Bob, especially when aimed at him. Kim felt no qualms pointing out that his language use and comments about teaching suggested a controlling, authoritarian nature.[32] When Bob tried to avoid controversy by turning in relatively vague or neutral texts, Kim suggested he was being evasive and asked what he was hiding.[33] Although her approach was usually tactful, Bob felt attacked nonetheless.[34] At the beginning of the semester, Bob tried to address Kim's questions, but by the end of the term, he had withdrawn almost completely and altogether rejected reader response as a pedagogical approach.[35] According to Belenky et al., such interactions are not uncommon between outspoken women and traditional men. Kim's beliefs echo those of Belenky et al.'s constructivist women. These authors maintain, "In being a woman, you have to make men see things they haven't had to see. It's not their fault. It's just the way it is." Even if their opinions fall on deaf ears, these women feel they "have a special responsibility to try to communicate to both men and women how they view things and why they value what they do" (147).

Shannon: The Nurturer

Shannon initially struck me as a dilettante. When I read her application for a graduate teaching assistantship, I found she had done undergraduate work at Brigham Young University and George Mason University and that her graduate work included courses at those schools as well as three others. Under "previous experience," she wrote "Sunday school teacher." This background, coupled with the fact that she did not apply for a teaching assistantship until her last semester of graduate school (and then only because she "wanted the experience"), led me to doubt her seriousness. However, subsequent interactions with Shannon caused me to revise this hasty opinion. I soon learned that rather than flitting from one university to another, she was actually dedicated to furthering her education despite her husband's frequent job-related transfers. She re-enrolled wherever they moved and transferred if the university did not fulfill her expectations.[36] Moreover, she continued her graduate course work while meeting the demands of her two small children. Quite often, her journal entries began, "I'm writing this at 2 a.m. after finally getting the baby to sleep." Having gone through similar experiences in graduate school,

I could relate. Other graduate students who were single and childless routinely turned in papers late or requested extensions. I had not done that, and neither did Shannon. Gradually, I grew to respect her dedication, in part because it paralleled my own.

Shannon's voice was no less distinctive than Kim's. Both were strong and assertive, yet each reflected earlier influences. In response to Ruth Ray's *Practice of Theory*, which explains the rationale for action research, Shannon began by questioning the approach and wondering how well it would be received in other fields: "It doesn't seem very empirical or like the data is quantifiable. I think this 'unscientific' approach would cause criticism by some." She reconsidered her stance after comparing it to her own experiences:

> [I]f the point of research is to give teachers classroom tools, then I suppose qualitative analysis is ok [*sic*]. It's like advice other mothers give a new 1st time mom. She gets lots of different advice, sometimes conflicting, but she can decide what to choose based on her own circumstances, goals, priorities, etc.[37]

This tendency to relate new or puzzling material to her experience as a parent was a recurring trait in Shannon's teaching and her writing; it's also typical of constructed knowers. These women understand that knowledge is relative. They realize that knowledge is constructed by "weaving their passions and intellectual life into some recognizable whole" (Belenky et al. 141). In the classroom, for example, Shannon shared journal entries and essay drafts with her students. "I wanted to make myself vulnerable to my students," she wrote, "just as my students had opened up and made themselves vulnerable to me."[38]

Shannon's nurturing constructivism is perhaps best illustrated in her action-research project describing a bright but troubling student. "Tim" began the semester declaring he did not like to write and would not participate in collaborative learning, yet Shannon soon discovered his writing was among the best in the class. As a teacher, she was challenged and intrigued by this contradiction; as a mother, she believed his outspokenness stemmed more from a need for attention than from obstinance.[39] Shannon focused her study on Tim's negativity, specifically his resistance to collaborative learning, asking whether it could be "truly liberating or just another form of coercion" or if a resisting student could actually benefit from the requirement that he participate in group work. She concluded not only that Tim's ostensible hostility contradicted "his otherwise hard work and conscientious behavior" but also that he had indeed benefited from peer response.[40]

When Shannon analyzed his drafts, she found that Tim had followed his peer editor's suggestions for revision and even admitted that collaborative learning had been helpful: "He claimed to hate class and group work yet he conscientiously participated in both."[41] To verify these beliefs, Shannon emulated my own research methodology—she gave Tim a copy of her research paper and asked him for feedback—an element of emancipatory pedagogy Pattie Lather terms *reciprocity,* "consciously us[ing] our research to help participants understand and change their situations" (57). In response, Tim wrote: "I found your paper to be accurate in almost all accounts. The only thing is the part about rejection causing a fear and insecurity. Maybe, maybe not. You may see something I don't but I'm not sure."[42] Right or wrong, Shannon's observations gave Tim food for thought.

Shannon believed her relationship with Tim had somewhat alleviated his negative attitude:

> Having a nontraditional classroom facilitated this. If this course had been simply a lecture course with required papers and little or no freewriting or journals, I would have learned almost nothing about Tim. But by getting to know [him], I learned not only about his negative attitude, but also and more importantly, that [his] negative attitude had less to do with my class than with his own poor self image. . . . I believe that group and process work, when used thoughtfully, can improve the attitude of resistant students. A negative attitude does not necessarily mean a student doesn't care, nor does it mean a student cannot be positively affected by his/her peers and teacher. In fact, because group and process work provide such a unique opportunity to learn about [a] student's individual needs, teachers can be more effective . . . than they might otherwise be in a traditionally constructed classroom.[43]

In retrospect, I'm embarrassed that I wanted to deny Shannon a teaching assistantship. Shannon's family background as well as her experiences in the church, as a mother, and as a determined continuing student all contributed to the development of her teaching, her writing, and her voice. Quite often in the graduate classroom, these factors may be overlooked or ignored. But as Shannon found in her case study of Tim— and I found in writing hers—by changing the way we teach, we may not only change our students' attitudes. We may also change our own.

Carolyn: The Critic

And yet, my first impression of Carolyn was similarly skewed. Barely five feet tall with long dark hair, Carolyn appeared quite young. At twenty-six, she had just earned her B.A. and was beginning work on her master's degree. Contemporary American Women Novelists (CAWN) was her first graduate seminar. Although I had been teaching for fifteen years, I had never before taught a literature course like this. Class discussion was dominated by two opinionated, antagonistic, and overbearing women, one openly skeptical of feminist theory, the other strongly endorsing it. Anything I said was usually contradicted by one, who was subsequently interrupted by the other. These discussions were further complicated by the presence of two men in the class who took personally any comment regarding male behavior. By the end of the semester, the combination of these conflicting points of view had effectively silenced and frustrated the rest of the class.

At some other time, teaching this course might not have seemed so traumatic, but that semester coincided with my fight for tenure, so instead of appreciating Carolyn's neutrality during those freewheeling discussions, I misinterpreted her straightforward journal responses as additional criticism. In her first entry, for example, Carolyn wrote: "For starters, I couldn't really identify with the characters [in Louise Erdrich's *Love Medicine*] other than most of them had had difficult and painful lives. Most importantly, though, I could not sympathize with them."[44] Responding to Elizabeth Flynn's essay "Gender and Reading," Carolyn dismissed it as "essentially a typical anti-male study with predictable results—women read more sensitively, males don't." In contrast, she felt Jonathan Culler's "Reading as a Woman" was "much more insightful and legitimate" because she found men's writing on feminist issues more credible.[45] Given the negative environment of that semester, these comments affected me more than Carolyn's personal insights. I overlooked that she responded positively to Bobbie Ann Mason's *In Country* because Carolyn, too, had lost her father and wanted to learn everything about him when she became a teenager[46] and that she loved Amy Tan's *Kitchen God's Wife* because of Tan's portrayal of the mother-daughter relationship. "I cried just thinking about everything my mother has been through in her lifetime," Carolyn wrote, "and what a remarkable woman she is."[47] I remembered only Carolyn's critical comments.

Even though this was her first graduate seminar, Carolyn didn't hesitate to speak during group work. Based on their introductory freewrites, I had placed Carolyn in a group with Chrissy and James because I felt all had displayed similar degrees of openness and sensitivity. However, I soon realized that while Carolyn's response had accurately reflected her straightforward personality, her group members' had been somewhat misleading. During their group meetings, James vacillated between sullen silence and injured complaints to Chrissy, who related every discussion to the fact that she was a lesbian. Within this group, Carolyn had to choose between silence and stilted discussion, yet she expressed herself nonetheless.[48] In one journal, for example, she wrote, "My next point I will probably get stomped for, as I did last week in group discussion, but I still maintain that the sexuality of the woman is a dominant theme in [Alice Walker's] *Temple of My Familiar*."[49]

Despite these contentious experiences, Carolyn decided at the end of that semester to apply for a graduate teaching assistantship. Because I felt she was overly critical, had heard she was afraid to teach, and knew she lacked prior experience, I did not support her candidacy. I persevered in my objections until finally the graduate coordinator negotiated a compromise: During the first year of her assistantship, Carolyn would not teach freshman composition. Instead, she would assist one of the full-time instructors in an introductory literature course. This experience would help model teaching strategies and provide Carolyn the time to overcome her anxieties. This decision did not sit well with Carolyn. She felt she was being discriminated against, a feeling that only intensified when she learned that no TA had ever been given such an assignment.[50] Indeed, because this position was brand-new, no one knew what Carolyn should do. She took it upon herself to contact me and her supervising instructor in an effort to make this assistantship a viable experience.

Given my doubts about her ability, I was not very friendly at first. Nevertheless, Carolyn continued to call and to pepper me with questions until I began to consider options and offer suggestions. The summer before her assistantship began, Carolyn called me at least once or twice a week. After we decided on a plan, she again took the initiative and called her supervising instructor to introduce herself and schedule a meeting. Persuading the instructor to adapt her plans to incorporate student journals, discussion groups, and time for the students to write multiple essay drafts was no easy task. Consequently, as the summer progressed and Carolyn and I continued to shape her assignment, our antagonism began to fade. Through our interactions, I began to realize that, as with Kim and Shannon, my first impression had been based on misinformation and colored by the pressure of the semester.

APPLYING THEORY

It is no accident that the elements of composition pedagogy are practically synonymous with feminist pedagogy. As Jane Stake and Frances Hoffman found in their multicampus survey of women's studies programs, feminist pedagogy advocates the use of participatory or collaborative learning, encourages personal voice in speaking and in writing, develops social and political understanding, and promotes critical thinking (30). In sum, both pedagogies hold that effective learning entails the active construction of knowledge. After studying the effects of feminist pedagogy on women's studies students, Stake and Hoffman found it had a positive effect on students' lives because these courses (as opposed to non–women's studies courses) "foster open communication, critical thinking, and multiple perspectives in their classrooms" (38). These same elements closely parallel those behaviors and experiences essential for the development of self-efficacy: modeling behavior, providing opportunities for mastery experiences, relating new information to previous knowledge, giving positive reinforcement and immediate feedback, and serving as a mentor and role model (Bandura 399–414). Such correlations underscore the potential benefits of composition (and feminist) pedagogy. The following vignettes illustrate how these benefits are manifested.

Kim: Composition Pedagogy and Feminism

Despite the ongoing disputes with her group members, Kim believed the narrative writing and collaborative learning in the Reader Response seminar enhanced her voice. These strengths were further developed the following semester when she took Teaching College Writing, where Joan was one of her group members. "Working with Joan again," Kim wrote, "did make it somewhat easier for me to openly express myself in my writing and in my discussion. . . . Also being comfortable with you, made it much easier to write about my personal experiences."[51] An excerpt from Kim's first essay in Teaching College Writing exemplifies the strength of her voice. In this account, Kim reveals that at age nineteen, a stranger abducted her and a male companion, took them to his home, and beat Kim's friend until he was unconscious. Then the man bound her hands with duct tape, tore off her clothes, and raped her. In shock, for awhile she felt nothing, but suddenly she was "back in the room." When the stranger took the tape off her mouth, Kim started talking:

> "Where's your wife?" I asked. "Are these pictures of your kids? Where are they?" At first he didn't like my questions. He hit me in the face with his fist and told me to shut up, but I didn't. I couldn't. I wanted to get out of there. I wanted to live, and for some reason I thought if I kept asking questions, maybe I could. . . . Then [my friend] started moaning. He wasn't dead. That was my chance. I convinced the man to let us go.

After their release, Kim and her friend went straight to the police. Shortly thereafter, the rapist was arrested at his home while disposing of the evidence. Since that time he has been in prison, where Kim hopes he stays. She has been instrumental in keeping him there: "I don't know why he was denied [parole]. Maybe he hasn't been the ideal inmate, or maybe the letter I wrote to the parole board describing the atrocities he committed and the fears I still have, had some effect."[52]

Kim's voice was equally strong in her teaching. During her semester in Teaching College Writing, she began teaching composition at a rural community college, so her teaching logs focused on how she carried her feminist agenda into the classroom—a dubious task given this particular locale. She designed essay topics on gender roles and obedience to authority and used collaborative learning to generate class discussion. These descriptions suggested she had internalized composition theory and pedagogy. Yet Kim appeared so confident that I began to grow irritated with her. Every teaching log seemed to end the same way: "This class went well," "I think I succeeded," or "There's nothing I could change."[53] Because these struck me as rather facile, I tried to elicit more reflection. In response to a self-congratulatory description of a discussion of gender roles, I asked: "Rather than continuing in this vein, why not discuss the students' responses?" After she mentioned a rude student, I questioned how she handled the girl. When she raved about the success of an in-class debate, I suggested she put each side's points on the board so they could see the structure and progression of the argument. In response to yet another summary ending with "I can't think of anything I'd change right now besides asking [the students] to read their papers out loud to each other," I recommended she make the groups smaller.

Apparently, my irritation was obvious, for when Kim submitted her portfolio at the end of the semester, she acknowledged that she had appeared "sickeningly confident." She went on to say that she could not help it, for her teaching had been a "tremendous success":

> I structure my class entirely after the way you do yours. Of course, my classes don't run as smoothly or come together quite as nicely as yours, but I have found these teaching strategies to be wonderfully effective. I can't imagine teaching writing any other way. I have seen significant improvement in my students' writing and in their attitudes toward writing and toward school in general. I have had several students tell me that my class is their favorite and is the only class they look forward to attending. They attribute much of that to working with their groups. Most of my students have formed real friendships with their group members, and this I think has helped them very much in their writing. They trust each other and, thus, are able to help each other with their writing.[54]

Kim's response suggests the ripple effect of our teaching. What we do in the classroom influences how our students will teach and how their students will learn.

Shannon: Composition Pedagogy and the Ethic of Care

Shannon's voice and confidence were similarly affected. During the semester she took Teaching College Writing, she also enrolled in another seminar. When her professor dismissed feminist theory as groundless, Shannon was so offended that she found herself pointing out the prejudice underlying his theoretical approach. "He really shook me," she said, "because most men that I've thought of as genuinely considering women inferior are what I would define as ignorant, not highly educated and thoughtful (full of thought) like [he] obviously was."[55] Throughout that semester, Shannon periodically blazed into my office, slammed the door, vented her anger, and then asked how to deal with this professor. I was afraid her outspokenness might affect her grade, but she could not restrain herself. "He just brought out the fight in me," she explained,

> and eventually a certain amount of nastiness. I don't think I'd probably be so out of control again—it's not academically prudent—but some of his stuff . . . upset me to the point where I felt like I had to stand up and be counted. I couldn't just let it slide like lots of the other women in the class did.[56]

Like Kim, Shannon carried her feminist beliefs into her composition classroom. She used small-group work because she believed it was important for her female students. In her teaching log, she explained that at the beginning of the semester, she had noticed that the girls seemed inhibited, seldom speaking and avoiding criticism of their peers' papers for fear of offending them. However, after working together throughout the semester, she found that the comfort of the small group "helped the women [become] more comfortable with criticism."[57]

Actually, Shannon's teaching considered the needs of all her students. The first time I observed her, Shannon's goal was to teach them how to incorporate sensory details into their narrative essays. She began class by asking the students to move their desks into a circle so they could easily share ideas with their peers. Then she instructed them to draw maps of their childhood neighborhoods or backyards to generate ideas for their personal narratives. When they had finished, she asked them to practice using sensory details by describing the favorite part of their maps. After everyone contributed, Shannon distributed an excerpt from an essay by Annie Dillard and pointed out the different senses evoked through description. This explanation served as a model for the next exercise: In small groups, the students were to analyze the rest of the passage, find additional examples of sensory images, and report their findings to the class. Working together facilitated the analysis, for it offered the students mutual support within a safe environment and provided the possibility of additional insights from the various members.[58] Because Shannon had given each group the same passage, the students were then able to compare their findings and receive additional input—a process that underscored the value of group work while making the students accountable for their activities.

All of this occurred within a well-organized, fast-paced fifty minutes. Obviously, Shannon was no dilettante—she knew exactly what she was doing, and she had done it well. When I indicated my surprise at her abilities, Shannon did not smile demurely or murmur thanks. Instead, she politely corrected my beliefs about her teaching experience. She had not been "merely" a Sunday school teacher; her experience comprised "much more than that." She had taught classes for adult women, spent one year teaching sixteen-year-olds, one-and-a half years teaching four-year olds, and a number of years "substitut[ing] for various other teachers as needed." These experiences prepared her well for the writing classroom.

Although Shannon began the semester as a strong teacher and writer, she ended it even stronger. She attributed these changes to four interrelated factors: sheer volume of writing, process writing, freewriting, and teaching. Engaging in freewriting made Shannon's writing "freer and more relaxed," which contributed to her confidence as a writer. As a result of simultaneously teaching and reading about writing pedagogy, her "consciousness [had] been raised," she said, and her writing had "improved dramatically."[59] By the end of that semester, Shannon and I had developed a mutual admiration society. When she left St. Louis because her husband had once again been transferred, she gave me the same gift she had given her case-study student—a copy of the *Book of Mormon*.

Carolyn: Composition Pedagogy and Mentoring

By the time Carolyn enrolled in Teaching College Writing, we had reached an uneasy truce. Contrary to our expectations, this relationship and our collaborations continued. The first incident grew out of Carolyn's experiences with collaborative learning. When Teaching College Writing began, I grouped Carolyn with Jimmy and Richard (from chapter 6) because all three were new TAs but relatively experienced writers. Carolyn was a former journalist, Richard was a poet, and Jimmy had won prizes for his academic essays. But once again, my instincts were completely off-base. Although Carolyn was fairly liberal, she was not prepared for Jimmy's revelations about his homosexuality.[60] Because this was the topic of Jimmy's first two essays, peer response became rather awkward. This atmosphere was worsened by the fact that Richard was not only a creative writer but also a perfectionist and thus felt uncomfortable writing academic essays and discussing his drafts.[61] At midterm, Richard's frustrations exploded when Jimmy borrowed and revised one of Richard's lesson plans (which he had freely shared at the beginning of the semester) to teach a segment of Teaching College Writing. Even though Jimmy credited him, Richard was furious. These feelings were then turned on me when I cited Jimmy's lesson during a conference presentation. Richard became convinced that Jimmy and I were trying to steal his ideas, and so he tried to foment a mutiny among his classmates.

I would have known none of this without Carolyn. As Richard's group member and office mate, she was privy to his accusations and witnessed his attempts to incite their classmates. Horrified, she came to my office and described his behavior. Thanks to her warning, I was able to confront Richard about his concerns and, I thought, reassure him. The semester seemingly ended smoothly, and we all went away for Christmas vacation; however, when classes resumed, so did Richard's skullduggery. He continued trying to stir up his fellow TAs and even went so far as to send a letter to the chancellor, accusing me of plagiarizing his teaching materials and undermining his attempts to find a teaching position. Carolyn was torn between loyalty to her fellow TAs and outrage at Richard's behavior, but because of our friendship, she continued confiding in me.

These revelations created a bond between us that strengthened when I observed Carolyn's teaching. Eventually, her supervising instructor agreed that Carolyn could lead discussion groups and prepare the students, many of whom had never taken a writing course, to write their midterm and final essays. She was also responsible for teaching during the week preceding each essay when she led nine, optional, extra-credit peer-response sessions. When I visited one of these sessions, I was struck by Carolyn's voice and sense of authority. Her teaching had to be extremely organized because of the few sessions she had been allowed to work with the students, but she orchestrated it smoothly.

As the students drifted in, Carolyn began writing questions on the board: What do you like about your draft? What do you dislike? What two or three vital questions do you have about your draft? Writing the answers to these questions focused the students' thinking and the day's work. After about five minutes, Carolyn asked the students for their responses, a strategy revealing their common concerns and enabling Carolyn to recognize key issues and reassure the students. She reinforced this by handing out a peer-response sheet and going over the questions so the students could raise any additional questions. Next, Carolyn asked the students to pair off, read each other's papers, and respond to the questions on the peer-response sheet. During this period, she made herself accessible, circulating among the groups, answering questions, and providing positive reinforcement. This was not the frightened young woman I had worried about. Although this represented her first formal teaching experience as well as the first time her teaching had been observed, Carolyn appeared calm and in control.[62]

This demeanor could be attributed to a variety of factors. Throughout her struggles to be accepted, Carolyn's background provided her with the strength and sense of self to believe she would succeed: "I've had to fight for everything I ever wanted. I fought to get into college, I fought to get into grad school, and I fought to be a TA."[63] Carolyn's fighting spirit was re-ignited the semester of Richard's revolt. During this period, I was in the midst of my research for this project and (with the students' permission) tape-recording each group's peer-response sessions. Because Richard so disliked collaboration and eventually so resented me, after midterm, he refused to allow his group members to turn on the tape recorder until he saw me approaching. Because Carolyn was aware of my research, she felt bound to reveal Richard's duplicity. As we discussed how to replicate this aspect of the research, she became increasingly interested in the project; consequently, she asked if she could fulfill an assignment in her research-methods seminar to record field notes by observing the students in Teaching College Writing. When she finished, we used those notes to triangulate the information I collected that semester.

Such experiences helped establish friendship and trust that further strengthened after Carolyn completed her master's degree. She did not have a job, and she didn't want "to lose her brain," as she put it. Because of our friendship, her writing and editing skills, interest in my research, and insider's knowledge, I asked Carolyn if she would like to read and respond to drafts of these chapters. Thus began our collaboration out-side the classroom. After each chapter had been drafted, I sent it to her; when she had read and responded, we met to discuss her comments. These continuing interactions moved our relationship from teacher-stu-dent to mentor-protégé, so it was only natural that when I was asked to recommend someone for a position at a nearby university, I suggested Carolyn. She applied and was hired and then turned to me for advice on selecting texts and organizing her new courses. When I received a call for papers on action research, we moved to the next level of collabora-tion, jointly submitting a proposal, presenting a paper, and going shop-ping afterwards.

In the past few years, we have taken turns encouraging each other to engage in additional projects. We have presented individual papers on the same panel at national conferences; we collaborated on an article about mentoring. This latter project was almost our undoing, for Carolyn and I have opposite schedules and conflicting writing processes. Never-theless, as we agonized over drafts, we recognized the parallels between our relationship and the definitions of mentoring. I had encouraged Carolyn's work, given her criticism and feedback, offered advice about teaching, provided opportunities for her to "showcase" her work, showed her how to establish professional contacts, and discussed her career goals and how to achieve them (Hall and Sandler 3). In return, I received valuable feedback about my teaching and my writing, and I took advantage of professional opportunities to present and publish my work. Male and female scholars disagree on the motives and rewards for mentorship, but Carolyn and I believe our relationship has been nurturing rather than self-aggrandizing. In this, we (not surprisingly) reflect the patterns and purposes of female mentors (Hulbert 251).

These relationships are all too rare in higher education. The high rates of attrition and feelings of alienation at the graduate level suggest that too many faculty are more interested in their own research than in the advising and development of their students (Hulbert 259). Although this failure may be attributed to administrative pressure to produce more with less support and to entrust advisory roles to "student support services," psychologist Kathleen Day Hulbert concludes that "we in higher education are not doing a very good job of guiding and nurturing the next generation" (261). Obviously, mentoring relationships like Carolyn's and mine are rare; in fact, it is the most extensive I've had in twenty years. But providing guidance and support can and should be a part of our pedagogy. Kim, Shannon, and Carolyn possessed the voice and sense of self to establish such a relationship. Their stories, as well as the paucity of these stories among women at the graduate level, underscore the need for change.

IMPLICATIONS FOR TEACHING

In her analysis of the researcher's role in ethnographic research, Elizabeth Chiseri-Strater maintains that "a major goal of the research process is self-reflexivity—what we learn about the self as a result of the study of the 'other'" (119). That goal is more relevant to this chapter than any of the preceding. Rather than welcome my students' strong voices, I doubted and resented them. Although I had grown accustomed to male students' skepticism, when these women questioned the theories or criticized the authors, I felt annoyed and betrayed. Recognizing this attitude was not pleasant; nonetheless, it was (and is) a useful reminder. Like the parents who seem to lavish attention on their needy child and ignore the self-sufficient ones, I discovered a tendency to gravitate toward my female students lacking a strong voice and to avoid those more outspoken. Only when the latter requested advice did my attitude begin to change. I believed I ran a nonhierarchical classroom; however, in my preference for the "needy" and distrust of the independent, I had unconsciously established a reverse hierarchical order.

If I had not been engaged in ethnographic research, I might never have recognized my intolerance; luckily, when I began to analyze and reflect on what I found in my students' essays, drafts, and journals, I realized my mistakes. Comparing my initial reactions to what I learned about these students, it was obvious my first impressions were not always reliable. Rereading Kim's teaching logs, I could see that her comments revealed competence, not complacency. When I observed Shannon in the classroom, I could tell that her prior experiences as mother and Sunday school teacher had served her well: She was nurturing and organized, easily guiding the students through activities that led toward the day's goals. When I reviewed Carolyn's journal entries from her first course, I realized that she, too, had been assertive yet willing to concede doubt and open to different interpretations. What I had perceived as criticisms were actually thoughtful comments tempered with personal experience. This realization became apparent as we talked—which was yet another key factor.

By working together the summer before her assistantship, Carolyn and I changed our relationship from adversarial to cooperative. From those and subsequent conversations, I learned that although I had been mistaken about the strength of Carolyn's voice, I had not mistaken her attitude. When Carolyn applied for her teaching assistantship, she'd been told she would have a difficult time working with me.[64] Thus, when I (mis)placed her in the group with James and Chrissy, when I assigned her to assist in the literature course, and when I again misplaced her with Jimmy and Richard, she thought I disliked her. Neither of us knew the other nor what the other was experiencing at the time.

In a teacher-centered classroom, these misperceptions might have persisted; however, through the writing in our graduate seminars, our conversations prior to her assistantship, and our ongoing discussions, we came to know each other. In sum, the path to awareness can be traced not only to the self-reflection inherent in ethnographic research but also to the strategies inherent in composition and feminist pedagogies. As I observed these TAs' teaching and discussed problems and strategies, my role changed gradually from teacher to coach and confidant. The importance of these roles grew even clearer as I watched Kim, Shannon, and Carolyn coach their students in turn.

The TAs' willingness to take on this role may be traced more to the qualities they brought into the graduate seminar than to the skills I tried to pass on. By their mid-twenties, these young women were relatively self-aware and self-confident. They had achieved this state largely because they had been accorded respect by their parents, whose behavior provided strong, positive role models. This background, combined with their literacy experiences, gave them the confidence to take risks—to find their own way to college and career, to resist society's expectations of a woman's role, to defend themselves, to speak out against sexism—in short, to upset my assumptions about female graduate students. Although their behaviors might not seem extraordinary, they stand in stark contrast to the majority of their female peers. Lacking sufficient self-confidence and self-knowledge, too many of them do as they are told without question. Graduate faculty can perpetuate this behavior by continuing the traditional passive, objectivist pedagogy, or they can challenge the status quo by applying composition pedagogy. Psychologists Mary Ann Gawelek, Maggie Mulqueen, and Jill Mattuck Tarule illustrate both the need and the possibility for such pedagogy:

> Women enter the academic experience with particular learning needs; women, particularly feminist professors, enter the teaching experience with distinctive competencies, attitudes, and feelings; and, an emphasis on the relationship between the teacher and students is fundamentally important to the learning experience of women (and probably men as well). (179–80)

Teachers and professors need to recognize this reality as well as the responsibility of facilitating the development of their students' voices, the value of relationships in enhancing learning, and the pedagogical necessity of using the combined pedagogy of composition, feminism, and constructivism in the classroom to generate discourse communities (181). Gawelek, Mulqueen, and Tarule provide further justification for this approach in discussing the correlation between competence and sex-role identity. Among women, these two areas are usually considered "mutu-

ally exclusive" (183); among female graduate students, the tension between the two is even more extreme as they try to juggle personal construct and performance anxiety with low perceptions of self-efficacy regarding chances of their academic success. Even if women feel competent
outside the academic environment, entering into this context, especially
if they are nontraditional students (as many are), diminishes their sense
of competency. Such feelings are not helped by the traditional expectations within the academy that success is an individual responsibility (185).

Gawelek, Mulqueen, and Tarule have identified specific pedagogical
strategies that help their students to overcome these fears. Not surprisingly, they parallel those suggested throughout this book: The authors
conclude, "The most important factor in supporting women students
to be feminine and competent in their academic endeavors is providing
them the opportunity to increase their self-esteem by creating academic
environments that are welcoming to this important population" (187).

The truth of this statement—as well as the difficulty in enacting it—
can be illustrated by reviewing the women's problems and progress in
the foregoing case studies. Both Barbara (chapter 4) and Missy (chapter
6) stood out because of their strident classroom voices. Gawelek, Mulqueen, and Tarule explain that such a stance often represents women
students' attempts to be autonomous; however, because their voices come
across as "adamant and aggressive," both male and female professors tend
to view these students as "antagonistic and abrasive." Female faculty
members need to understand the reason for this stance—the student's
need for "reassurance that her thinking is valid and that her presentation is appreciated," a need representing the desire for intimacy and
support (190). Barbara was so abrasive that I made no effort to be supportive, and the absence of permanent small groups in Teaching College Writing during her first semester precluded the opportunity for
support from her peers. Conversely, in the Reader Response seminar, the
personal narratives provided Missy the space to reveal her fears and me
with the opportunity to respond to them, while the structure of the
permanent small groups offered her additional feedback and support.

Although Mary Jo and Melva (chapter 4) and Gail and Pattie (chapter 5) were neither loud nor abrasive, their lack of confidence was evident in their various writing blocks. Gawelek, Mulqueen, and Tarule
attribute these feelings to the effects of sociocultural values that reify the

strong objective voice, encourage individualism, and denigrate the personal. To combat these ingrained beliefs and their accompanying feelings, the authors advocate "pedagogical approaches that affirm the use of one's personal experience as a foundation for learning, and validate the broader context of women's lives (not just their identity as students)" (190). Teaching that encourages dialogue and de-centers authority empowers students and contributes to the development of their self-esteem as knowers. For Pattie and Gail, the dialogue and personal relationships established in their small groups provided the necessary support, whereas Mary Jo found it difficult to trust her peers until I offered additional time and understanding. But support from me and her group was not enough for Melva. I fear that the sociocultural values she had internalized as a black woman made it difficult for her to move beyond her long-held beliefs about writing and learning.

Two overarching components of this feminist perspective are the value placed on students' experiences as women and the responsibilities inherent in female professors' roles as authority figures (Gawelek, Mulqueen, and Tarule 192). These elements were evident in the progress of Susan (chapter 5) and Melissa and Jenny (chapter 6). When Susan began graduate school, her experiences as a "tomboy" and subsequent identification with masculine values and pastimes had left her somewhat ambivalent about her femininity and the value of feminist pedagogy, particularly collaborative learning. Sharing these feelings within an all-female seminar, exploring the personal application of *Women's Ways of Knowing* in her reading journal, and collaborating with women in class and on the job combined to help Susan affirm her female experiences.[65] The progress of Melissa and Jenny suggests the empowerment inherent both in small-group work and through teacher-student relationships. In this, Melissa and Jenny reflect Gawelek, Mulqueen, and Tarule's conclusion that "as women teachers, our responsibility is to model an integrated person connected to the student and able to acknowledge our own expertise and our role as evaluator of their learning"—elements integral to the students' conceptions of themselves as professionals (193).

Both Jenny and Melissa have had great success in their chosen fields, Jenny as a high school English teacher and Melissa as a professor and writing program administrator. While their success cannot be wholly attributed to the composition pedagogy they were exposed to during their master's program, the fact that each woman took at least twelve hours of course work employing this pedagogy cannot be overlooked. Indeed, as Gawelek, Mulqueen, and Tarule conclude,

> We began to understand that allowing students to enact the compliant, silent role constitutes lowering standards for them, while supporting them (and ourselves) to be vulnerable and demanding seemed to communicate effectively the dual message of high standards and expectations grounded in trustful explorative dialogue. (194)

In a perfect world, all parents would communicate frequently and empathetically with their daughters and sons, serve as strong role models, demonstrate respect for each other and for their children, and provide an abundance of positive literacy experiences. The schools would build on these strengths by linking writing to learning, practicing constructivist pedagogy, and treating students equally regardless of race, class, gender, or sexual preference. Thus, by the time these students entered graduate school, they might all possess equally strong voices. Of course, it is not a perfect world. Parents and teachers are only human, sexism is still pervasive, and many younger women have grown complacent about the need for a strong voice. But faculty can help to empower their female students by learning from the examples of the young women in this chapter.

8. Changing Our Teaching, Our Students, Our Profession

"Ethnography challenges the dominant positivist view of making knowledge. It demands attention to human subjectivity and allows for author-saturated reconstructions and examinations of a world" (Bishop, *Ethnographic* 153). To be credible, the researcher must demonstrate her reliability. This can be established by carefully constructing research questions and outlining the methodology, fully developing and supporting the narratives using multiple data sources, clearly presenting one's stance and tracing the effects of reflexivity, and moving beyond the local to suggest global applications of the findings (157). That is my goal in this chapter.

When I began this research, my question was simple: How does collaborative learning help female graduate students find their voice in their teaching and their writing? When I discovered that some women resisted group work, the question was revised; because I was aware of the men's resistance, the questions melded the genders. Given a focus on gender meant I had to examine my role in the classroom, but the analysis didn't stop there. Eventually, my research questions encompassed every aspect of composition pedagogy, graduate students' varying degrees of accommodation and resistance, my role in fostering these feelings, and the resulting learning we all experienced. These questions ultimately led me to ask: Why hasn't composition pedagogy been adopted in graduate composition seminars? What does its absence suggest about our understanding and perceptions of teaching? How does its adoption impact graduate students' understanding and perceptions? What role does writing play in generating—and resolving—their resistance?

To answer these questions, this study examined the assumptions and competencies graduate students bring to the composition pedagogy seminar and how these are manifested in their teaching, writing, voice, and behavior. By telling their stories, my aim was to debunk the myths about teaching, especially teaching writing, at the graduate level. The case studies described the many factors impacting graduate students' composing processes and the ways they address or ignore them. To illustrate this complexity, narrative and analysis alternated within the case-study chapters. I allowed the students to speak for themselves by drawing on the writing produced in their response journals, teaching logs, essay drafts, and conversations with me and their peers during collaborative learning. In doing so, I followed one of the most important tenets of feminist research (Sullivan, "Feminist" 47). Equally important, I placed myself on the same level as the participants by examining my own attitudes and assumptions and describing my interactions with them (Harding 8).

These case studies serve as useful reminders of the sociopolitical factors influencing graduate students' views of composition pedagogy. New TAs have to balance their other professors' attitudes about teaching with the ideas and approaches introduced to them; they must weigh the risks of expressive writing with the demands of perfecting the objective voice; they must overcome their need for perfection and their fear of failure. Gender affects all these decisions. Just as the male students have to decide whether to de-center their classrooms, reveal their feelings, and share their writing—at the risk of ridicule from peers and professors—the females fear losing their authority, their newly found or unevenly objective voice, and (what they perceive as) the humiliation of imperfection. Given the general disregard for teaching, reification of the objective voice, and minority status of women in the academy, both genders have valid fears. Why learn to teach if it isn't rewarded? Why waste time in reflective or expressive writing? Why try drafting if the current approach works? Why share an imperfect draft when its problems are obvious?

For a fraction of graduate students, addressing these issues will represent too great a risk. Because composition pedagogy contradicts their conceptions of themselves as teacher and student and damages their feelings of self-efficacy, they may resist working in groups, sharing their writing, writing reflectively, or composing multiple drafts. This resistance affects their teaching. They will refuse to de-center the classroom or allow their students to work independently, believing the teacher needs to maintain authority by lecturing, quizzing, or marking up papers. However, if resisting students can be engaged in composition pedagogy, the majority will overcome their resistance once they regain feelings of self-efficacy.

For most graduate students, writing is problematical, but writing also holds the solution to their problems. Although writing was their entree into graduate school, students rarely enjoy the process. With few exceptions, the students in these case studies agonized over their writing, spending hours perfecting pages, paragraphs, even sentences. Jeff didn't revise because he was afraid to; Susan procrastinated, then ran out of time. Barbara believed each page must be perfect while Pattie and Mary Jo didn't know where to go. Gail and Paul floundered, writing draft upon draft. Having relied on professors to tell them what to say and how to say it, they distrusted their own ideas and those of their peers. The variety and multiplicity of negative feelings about writing suggest these students are not anomalies, nor does this bode well for such students' future careers. How can they teach writing if they dread it? How will they succeed within a university requiring research and publication?

Categorizing their behaviors, however, helps professors (and the students themselves) understand the reasons for and extent of resistance. *Rhetorical* resistance is typical of young graduate students lacking extensive writing experience. Because they learned to "guess" what their professors want and give it to them, they are uncomfortable with process writing and feel it's inappropriate for graduate and undergraduates alike. *Pedagogical* resistance is found among more-experienced writers. Believing that good writing is cosmetically perfect, they tend to agonize over their writing and demand the same of their students. Thus, they may resist drafting and collaborative learning for themselves and their students. *Epistemological* resistance is most common among experienced writers secure in the composing processes. Successful writers, they often dismiss composition theory and pedagogy for themselves although they are somewhat more amenable to adopting it in their classrooms.

Their case studies reveal the possibility of change. By engaging in the very activities they resent and resist, graduate students begin to recognize their composing processes and empathize with their students' struggles. Although male graduate students are more likely than females to resist and will do so longer and more loudly, they generally overcome their resistance before semester's end. This is both a blessing and a curse. Whereas the men's resistance is obvious, the women's is often less so because they may lack the self-confidence to loudly protest.

Women's problems with voice have been documented over the past three decades, but few (if any) studies have focused specifically on female graduate students or studied the role of pedagogy in reclaiming and strengthening voice. Although researchers such as Gesa Kirsch and Mary F. Belenky, Blythe M. Clinchy, Nancy R. Goldberger, and Jill M. Tarule have called for *connected teaching*, a term synonymous with composition and feminist pedagogy, they have not specifically traced the effects. Action research identified three areas of concern: strong writers who feared to speak; voluble speakers but weak writers; and aggressive speakers who quashed their feminine voice to succeed in the academy. Composition pedagogy helped unify and strengthen these voices. Strong writers gradually developed the courage to speak through reflective journaling; weak writers improved their style by keeping response journals and writing multiple drafts; overly aggressive speakers discovered the source (and effect) of this style through reader response. All of these women gained further insights by interacting within strong discourse communities established in their permanent small groups.

Composition pedagogy is no less effective among women possessing strong voices. Such students bring to the graduate seminar the ability to question and critique by linking new information to personal experience. Faculty unaccustomed to these strengths may find themselves skeptical or resentful of such students, but they, too, can profit from the humanism inherent in constructivist teaching. While women like Kim, Shannon, and Carolyn forge their own paths to graduate school, they will need mentors and role models to successfully traverse the shoals of academia. Such interactions benefit both mentor and protégé. Those of us who fought these battles alone realize the comfort of support from like-minded individuals, but we can also learn from these young women as they challenge and present us with new opportunities for professional growth. Rather than view their voices as intrusive, we should help them learn the ropes. Academia needs more strong women.

Traditionally, male students have been mentored and have developed the strong voices expected of them. Consequently, male graduate students are paid little heed, for their typically strong oral and written voices are considered de rigueur by the academy. But this trait often precludes their ability to write reflectively or appreciate the intellectual and pedagogical value of doing so. Composition pedagogy helps ease those strictures. Despite initial resistance, these men eventually gain the courage to write expressively as a result of journaling and the trust established in the ensuing dialogue, by developing personal narratives in which they explore their questions and fears, and through interactions within small groups of like-minded peers. Such experiences similarly influence their teaching.

These issues would not have come to light without action research. Males who loudly resist could be dismissed as unenlightened while females who passively resist might be overlooked. So, too, would the quiet women constituting the majority of female graduate students, sitting silently while their male classmates hold the floor as the few verbal females vie so strongly for attention that they, too, are dismissed as overly aggressive. Without action research, the correlations among these students' attitudes, their writing, and their teaching might be neither considered nor observed. Traditional pedagogy, with its reliance on hierarchical authority, agonistic discussion, assumptions of writing competence, reification of individual learning, and social Darwinism, keeps graduate and undergraduate students and their problems at a distance. This may be traditional, but it is not educational, and it is becoming increasingly untenable.

In interviews with over eight hundred graduate students, Barbara E. Lovitts uncovered a common lament: "There were no support groups, no networks. No one cared about us. We were outcasts" (qtd. in Jacobson, A1). Such feelings led to attrition rates averaging 50 percent—10 percent at law and medical schools, 33 percent at rural state universities, and 68 percent on urban campuses. Attrition rates were highest in the humanities, with rates at the English department of one urban university hovering at 76 percent. Conversely, departments offering a more humanistic, communal environment—like those described by Jennifer G. Haworth and Clifton F. Conrad—maintained a much higher retention rate. In response to Lovitts' findings, university administrators' rationalizations included the size of her study, rejections of its negativity, denial (faculty really do care!), suggestions that fewer TAs be admitted, and blaming the victims. "They [the graduate students] tried something and perceived they failed," asserts Robert E. Thach, dean of the Graduate School of Arts and Sciences at Washington University in St. Louis. "It didn't have to do with the institutions not taking care of them."

Granted, interviewing graduate students at only two universities yields a relatively small sample; nevertheless, among the 816 students Lovitts interviewed, 305 did not complete their studies. The average attrition rate of 50 percent that Lovitts found is supported by other studies.[1] More troubling are the tendencies to deny her claims and blame the graduate students, the majority of whom complained about departments of English.

I should know. I used to feel the same way.

PRACTICING WHAT WE PREACH

When I began drafting this book, I was quite pleased. The first few chapters sounded professional, academic. However, when I showed it to Carolyn (from chapter 7), she noticed a discrepancy between who I was and how I sounded. In the introductory and concluding chapters, my voice sounded formal and distant. In the middle, the case-study chapters, I sounded like myself, but I wasn't in it. I had included only my students and said nothing of my role in the classroom. When Carolyn pointed out these disparities, I discounted her advice. Although I was willing to entertain her suggestions regarding style, clarity, and diction, I could not attend to comments about my voice. When I completed the first draft, I showed it to David Bleich, but to my dismay he agreed with Carolyn. The weight of two consonant opinions was enough to convince me that large-scale revision was necessary; however, it was not until one of my colleagues, Jane Zeni, offered similar advice—followed by the suggestion to freewrite and reflect—that I began considering how to revise. This revelation raised two uncomfortable questions: Why was it so difficult to find my voice, and why was I resisting my readers' feedback?

I found one answer in chapter 4. Just as my resisting students perceived personal voice as inappropriate in the graduate classroom and resisted drafting, sharing drafts in peer groups, and accepting feedback, my personal construct as a feminist professor led me to resist similar incursions on my composing process. Carolyn was a former student so I ignored her advice. Bleich was male so I dismissed his. But Jane was a friend, a feminist, a female. She was my academic equal—the same age, rank, and field, an experienced ethnographer thoroughly versed in the academy's expectations. When she suggested I freewrite and reflect on the factors contributing to my voice, I listened and agreed, for the source of this advice did not conflict with my own personal construct.

I found another answer in chapter 6. Like Jenny, my voice was uniformly strong in the classroom but uneven on paper. Like Missy, I tried to adopt the objective academic voice and leave myself out of the text. Like Auggie, my family background had taught me to suppress the personal. In sum, at every stage of my thinking and writing, I began to perceive parallels between myself and my graduate students. And like them, engaging in the composition pedagogy I espoused helped me overcome my resistance and regain a feeling of self-efficacy.

Reflective writing helped me escape the artificial boundaries I had imposed on myself. As I wrote, I recognized that writing came naturally when I knew my audience. Moreover, because this style was considered appropriate for ethnographic research, my mental editor had granted me "permission" to use my personal voice. But including myself in the case-study narratives was considerably more difficult for I possessed few recent, relevant models. Although I regularly assigned reflective writing to help both undergraduate and graduate students become comfortable with writing, develop their fluency, and recognize or recapture their own voices; although I urged my students to abandon the expected academic style and taught them how to find and develop topics of personal interest; and even though I criticized academics who declared personal writing inappropriate in the university classroom—I had no recent experience in that mode. Personal letters had been abandoned for the shorthand exchanges of e-mail. Reflection had been relegated to the exploration of academic topics. After almost two decades in academia, I could teach my students to find their own voices, but I could not find my own.

When I introduced freewriting and encouraged my students to use that strategy to develop drafts, I assured them it was an integral part of my own composing process. That was not a lie; it was only a partial truth. I did freewrite when I composed, but I composed only academic texts, so delving into my feelings about teaching and trying to write insightfully about my role in the classroom felt not just awkward but incredibly jejune. It was not easy to straddle the line between useful reflection and embarrassing self-disclosure. However, after attempting that balancing act, I gained a renewed respect for my graduate students. As I wrote, I began to reflect on my actions, to remember behaviors, to recall incidents long past, and to comprehend their relevance to my teaching and my writing. To understand my students' actions and reactions, I had to become aware of my own ignorance, prejudice, pride, and practice.

Although I was required to keep a response journal in some of my graduate composition seminars, I don't recall reflecting on my teaching. To a certain extent, that has begun to change. One of the hallmarks of the Preparing Future Faculty (PFF) movement is the requirement that graduate students write reflectively to enhance their teaching and their learning. But how many *faculty* reflect on their teaching? Reflection might occur briefly at the end of each semester as we review our course evaluations, but mine was always pragmatic, extending no further than scribbles in the syllabus margin. Before beginning action research, I do not recall reflecting on my role in the classroom. I was content to continue my pedagogy in the belief that it worked, whether my students realized it or not.

Self-satisfaction also contributed to my stubborn adherence to an overly formal voice. This behavior was out of character, for I had always promoted collaborative learning as the backbone of our writing program. Indeed, my belief in peer response had prompted me to get feedback by giving copies of each case-study chapter to Carolyn and to those student-participants still on campus, yet I resisted Carolyn's most essential (and repeated) advice. Although this recognition was instrumental in focusing my revision, it led to further unsettling realizations. For years, I had been encouraging my graduate students to integrate their personal voices in their writing. When they succeeded, I was pleased, but when they failed, I considered them lazy. I had not regarded the growth of Melissa, Jenny, or Missy with pride or amazement so much as I had doubted the strong voices of Kim, Shannon, and Carolyn. Instead of recognizing the awkwardness Paul, Jeff, or Auggie felt about changing a familiar style of writing, I dismissed their efforts when their voices remained strongly impersonal or emerged only weakly personal. When Ken, Susan, and Mary Jo resisted their peers' feedback, I thought them stubborn because I had not yet undergone a similar experience. Rather than empathizing with Barbara's, Melva's, and Bob's struggles, I had been annoyed at their resistance to change. Even though I was proud of the personal insights achieved by Missy and Jimmy, I had not realized how difficult it might be to dig deep, open up, and reveal painful truths. Believing I had developed my own synthesis of personal and professional voice, I was unaware of how challenging that integration could be.

This process of discovery entailed years of writing and reflecting. It was a long journey, but the results were worth the effort, for it made me realize the incredible progress achieved by my students during a single semester. When I met them, they had completed at least sixteen years of traditional schooling, yet after a month in Teaching College Writing, most of them were integrating their personal voices into their writing and exploring the sources and reasons for their composing processes. They were writing reflectively, risking imperfection, sharing their drafts with virtual strangers, analyzing the effects of their teaching, and experimenting with pedagogical approaches they had seldom experienced and only recently discovered.

These findings convey a mixed message. They reiterate the possibility of change among graduate students while they underscore the difficulties faculty face in changing their teaching. If such changes were difficult for me, imagine how difficult they would be for faculty lacking a background in composition theory and pedagogy. But this account also reveals two keys to change: To understand composition pedagogy and convince students of its value, we must try it ourselves. Like our TAs, unless we become cognizant of our own practices, we will be unable to empathize with our students' struggles, anticipate their resistance, and encourage them to persevere. As this study has painstakingly described, one of the best ways to develop this consciousness is through action research.

ENACTING CHANGE

Changing the way we teach is difficult. For faculty, it requires a reconceptualization, if not a transformation, of their classroom approach. Among graduate students, such changes may initially inspire distrust if not disrespect as well as a degree of resentment, but the majority will overcome their resistance by semester's end.

For change to continue, new teachers need support, collegiality, and continuity. If they experience constructivist pedagogy in only a few of their seminars, TAs will find it easy to revert to more traditional approaches. If they begin teaching in a new environment in which they lack sounding boards or sympathetic comrades, they may begin to lose the confidence to de-center their classrooms or may lack the time to require their students to write and reflect. I have seen this happen more than once with former students, but the opposite can happen, too. Recently, one of my colleagues ran into Bob, the disillusioned student from chapter 4. Still teaching at the same large high school, Bob maintained that Teaching College Writing had made a huge impact on his life: "Tell Sally that I truly enjoy my teaching. In fact, teaching my senior composition course is the high point of my day." Sometimes, resistant students simply need the time and distance to reflect and make changes they could not accept at an earlier point in their lives.

In her conclusion to *Women Writing the Academy*, Kirsch raises the following questions:

> How can we prepare women to gain the authority it takes to speak as professionals as well as the confidence it takes to study new research topics and explore new forms of discourse? How can we broaden our definitions of academic discourse and allow scholars—both men and women—to write in diverse genres for diverse genres? How can we ensure that women who engage in non-mainstream or interdisciplinary work establish their authority in the academy? (134)

Composition pedagogy answers those questions. By making the classroom a site where learning is mutually constructed, faculty can alleviate students' feelings of alienation and help them "advance to higher levels of epistemic development" (Hays 163).

In some quarters, this approach is considered inappropriate. In others, it's considered ethical, for an ethical component of teaching is caring for one's students. These feelings are conveyed through composition pedagogy, classroom interaction, and the resulting relationships. Faculty cannot expect their graduate students, who have been subjected to at least four years of antipedagogical indoctrination, to immediately accept this approach. We can, however, demonstrate ethical teaching through the relationships we establish with them and those we encourage through our classroom practices. Writing-across-the-curriculum pioneer Susan McLeod reinforces this stance:

> The direction of English departments in large part will be determined by the attitudes of the next generation of graduate students. These students also need to understand (and we can help them understand) their affective as well as their cognitive processes—their motivation to become English teachers, their affective responses to teaching composition, their analysis of their own effectiveness in the classroom, their feelings of personal efficacy. ("Pygmalion" 383)

Like her research, McLeod's admonition is applicable across the disciplines.

Clearly, these changes require a major commitment. Indeed, a commitment of this magnitude can proceed only out of a personal belief that good teaching benefits students and in turn improves society. Numerous theoretical studies have noted these benefits and called for pedagogical change, but until now, none of them have actually examined what those changes entail. If change is to be instituted, we will need fewer theoretical studies and more qualitative research. Researchers need to be in the classroom to observe the effects of constructivist teaching. Longitudinal studies are needed across the curriculum to illustrate the impact of this approach on graduate students' teaching, writing, and self-efficacy. Additional demonstrations are necessary to illustrate how collaborative learning helps integrate and address the needs of students who differ not only in their literacy backgrounds but also in race, class, gender, or sexual orientation. Such studies will help develop a better understanding of why some students thrive and others fail.

Action research has the potential to engage both teacher and students, thus making them catalysts for change. That is the first step. The second step involves the results of such studies. If faculty want change to be more than incremental, they must move beyond the individual classroom. In addition to designing graduate courses that apply theory, faculty can effect further change by consulting, providing in-service workshops within the university and at local high schools, and by engaging in collaborative research with faculty at other institutions. Teaching and research should coexist. By linking theory with practice, we help our colleagues and our graduate students reconceptualize both as we simultaneously improve our students' learning. Such agency represents yet another key to change.

Still, changing the way we teach demands more than a receptive mindset. It requires the belief that learning is an active process whose responsibility lies with the professoriate. This will not come easily, but the process may be accelerated if we begin to reflect on our teaching through writing and action research, if we share our findings with colleagues, and if we take the time to experience the activities expected of our students. Most of us learned to teach after years in the classroom, but our graduate students need not wait that long. By changing the way we teach, we can pass on these lessons while demonstrating the interrelationship among research, theory, and practice. If we are willing to take that risk, we will play a significant role in the reconceptualization of teaching and the preparation of the next generation of professors.

Notes
works cited
Index

Notes

1. RESEARCHING TEACHING

1. The concept of resistance is explored more fully in chapters 4 and 5, *Resisting Change* and *Overcoming Resistance.*

2. See Barr Reagan, "Collaborative."

3. See, for example, studies by Gilligan, Aisenberg and Harrington, and Belenky, Clinchy, Goldberger, and Tarule.

4. Ibid.

5. See Barr Reagan, *Double Exposure.*

6. See Mohr and Maclean for detailed definitions and descriptions of teacher research.

2. ESTABLISHING CONTEXT

1. These findings were reported among the results of a 1996 survey of WPAs across the country. For additional findings, see Barr Ebest, "The Next Generation of WPAs: A Study of Graduate Students in Composition/Rhetoric."

2. Several studies have demonstrated that objectivist teaching is both prevalent and ineffective. See for example Langer or Nystrand et al.

3. See Wilson and Gaff.

4. In 1942, Peter Drucker initially captured the spotlight with his insightful predictions regarding the impact of the GI Bill on the American economy. Since then, Drucker has authored over thirty books whose prescience has earned him the title of "foremost business thinker of our age" and "preeminent business philosopher of the twentieth century," "decades in advance of conventional thinking." For more information, refer to any of the eighty Web sites devoted to Drucker and his accomplishments (www.business2.com; accessed Apr. 12, 2001).

5. See Nyquist, Abbott, Wulff, and Sprague, *Preparing.*

3. TEACHING THEORY

1. See Barr Reagan, "Using Reader Response in the Writing Classroom," for further description of how this approach works in a composition course.

2. These findings are supported by Buerkel-Rothfuss and Gray.

3. I offer examples of how to focus these research logs in chapter 5.

4. RESISTING CHANGE

1. In addition to Schon's *Reflective Practitioner*, see also *Educating the Reflective Practitioner* and his edited collection of case studies of reflection, *The Reflective Turn*; Hillocks' *Teaching Writing as Reflective Practice*; and Brunner's *Inquiry and Reflection.*

2. Mary Jo. Response journal. Teaching College Writing (Sept. 7, 1992).

3. ———. Final essay. Reader Response Theory (Aug. 24, 1992).

4. ———. Academic response 5. Reader Response Theory (Feb. 24, 1992).

5. ———. Personal response 1. Reader Response Theory (Jan. 13, 1992).

6. Barbara. Essay 2. Teaching College Writing (Oct. 31, 1994).

7. Carol. Final essay. Reader Response Theory (May 11, 1992). Carol studied Barbara's teaching and learning for her action-research project.

8. Barbara. Essay 2. Teaching College Writing (Oct. 31, 1994).

9. ———. Cover sheet, essay 1. Teaching College Writing (Sept. 14, 1994).

10. See Langer and Applebee.

11. Barbara. Teaching log. Teaching College Writing (Sept. 14, 1994).

12. Melva. Response journal. Teaching College Writing (Aug. 30, 1993).

13. Ibid.

14. Melva. Essay 1. Teaching College Writing (Sept. 27, 1993).

15. ———. Essay 2. Teaching College Writing (Oct. 25, 1993).

16. Bob. Response journal. Teaching College Writing (Aug. 31, 1992).

17. ———. Response journal. Teaching College Writing (Sept. 14, 1992).

18. ———. Response journal. Teaching College Writing (Aug. 31, 1992).

19. Mary Jo. Response journal. Teaching College Writing (Oct. 5, 12, and Nov. 30, 1992).

20. ———. Academic response 2. Reader Response Theory (Feb. 3, 1992).

21. ———. Response journal. Teaching College Writing (Nov. 30, 1992).

22. ———. Midterm essay, Reader Response Theory (Mar. 4, 1992).

23. Barbara. Essay 2. Teaching College Writing (Oct. 31, 1994).

24. Ibid.

25. Ibid.

26. Melva. Response journal. Teaching College Writing (Sept. 20, 1993).

27. ———. Tape recording of peer response. (Sept. 27, 1993).

28. ———. Response journal. Teaching College Writing (Sept. 27, 1993).

29. Ibid.

30. Bob. Response journal. Teaching College Writing (Aug. 31, 1992).

31. ———. Essay 3. Teaching College Writing (Dec. 7, 1992).

32. ———. Response journal. Teaching College Writing (Dec. 7, 1992).

33. ———. Response journal. Teaching College Writing (Oct. 5, 1992).

34. Mary Jo. Academic response 2. Reader Response Theory (Feb. 3, 1992).

35. Karen. Response 4. Reader Response Theory (Feb. 17, 1002).

36. Mary Jo. Personal response 2. Reader Response Theory (Mar. 9, 1992).

37. ———. Academic response 10. Reader Response Theory (Apr. 20, 1992).

38. Mary Jo's beliefs and behavior reflect Tillie Olson's argument that writer's block may stem from a writer's "social milieu" (qtd. in Rose, *Writer's* 101). According to research conducted by Lynn Z. Bloom, this context may include intellectual, artistic, temperamental, biological, and emotional factors (25).

39. Mary Jo. Final essay. Reader Response Theory (Aug. 24, 1992).

40. Barbara. Personal conversation. (Sept. 1994).

41. Melva. Response journal. Teaching College Writing (Nov. 8, 1993).

42. Melva. Tape recording of peer response. Teaching College Writing (Oct. 18, 1993).

43. Ibid.

44. Melva. Essay 2. Teaching College Writing (Oct. 25, 1993).

45. ———. Essay 2, revised. Teaching College Writing (Dec. 13, 1993).

46. ———. Tape recording of peer response. Teaching College Writing (Nov. 29, 1993).

47. Ibid.

48. Bob. Personal response 1. Reader Response Theory (Jan. 13, 1992).

49. ———. Literary response 2. Reader Response Theory (Apr. 6, 1992).

50. ———. Academic response 3. Reader Response Theory (Feb. 10, 1992).

51. Ibid.

52. ———. Literary response 1. Reader Response Theory (Mar. 30, 1992).

53. Kim and Joan. Response to Literary response 2. Reader Response Theory (Apr. 6, 1992).

54. Bob. Literary response 3. Reader Response Theory (Apr. 13, 1992).

55. ———. Literary response 2. Reader Response Theory (Apr. 6, 1992).

56. Kim. Response to Literary response 2. Reader Response Theory (Apr. 6, 1992).

57. Joan. Response to Literary response 2. Reader Response Theory (Apr. 6, 1992).

58. Bob. Final essay. Reader Response Theory (May 11, 1992).

59. See Barr Ebest, "Gender" 54.

5. OVERCOMING RESISTANCE

1. See for example Ashton-Jones, Bauer, or Luke and Gore.

2. See Maher and Tetreault, *The Feminist Classroom*; Ede and Lunsford; or Flynn.

3. Gail. Response journal. Reading-Writing Theory (June 15, 1990).

4. ———. Response journal. Reading-Writing Theory (Aug. 3, 1990).

5. ———. Response journal. Reading-Writing Theory (June 15, 1990).

6. Paul. Response journal. Teaching College Writing (Sept. 16, 1991).

7. ———. Response journal. Teaching College Writing (Sept. 9, 1991).

8. ———. Response journal. Teaching College Writing (Sept. 23, 1991).

9. See Bauer, Flynn, or Ashton-Jones.

10. Paul. Tape recording of peer response. Teaching College Writing (Oct. 21, 1991).

11. Susan. Response journal. Teaching College Writing (Aug. 31, 1992).

12. ———. Response journal. Teaching College Writing (Sept. 14, 1992). These feelings parallel those Bishop found in her case study of Dennis in *Something Old, Something New*.

13. Susan. Response journals. Teaching College Writing (Aug. 31 and Sept. 3, 11, 14, 1992).

14. ———. Response journal. Teaching College Writing (Aug. 31, 1992).

15. ———. Response journal. Teaching College Writing (Sept. 14, 1992).

16. ———. Response journal. Teaching College Writing (Sept. 21, 1992).

17. Jeff. Response journal. Teaching College Writing (Aug. 29, 1994).

18. ———. Response journal. Teaching College Writing (Sept. 12, 1994).

19. ———. Response journal. Teaching College Writing (Oct. 10, 1994).

20. ———. Essay 3. Teaching College Writing (Dec. 5, 1994).

21. Pattie. Response journal. Teaching College Writing (Aug. 29, 1994).

22. Ibid.

23. Ken. Application for Teaching Assistantship (Mar. 15, 1992).

24. ———. Response journal. Teaching College Writing (Sept. 21, 1992).

25. ———. Response journal. Teaching College Writing (Sept. 14, 1992).

26. ———. Response journal. Teaching College Writing (Sept. 21, 1992).

27. ———. Teaching log. Teaching College Writing (Sept. 28, 1992).

28. ———. Teaching log. Teaching College Writing (Oct. 12, 1992).

29. ———. Essay 1. Teaching College Writing (Sept. 28, 1992).

30. Gail. Response journal. Reading-Writing Theory (June 15, 1990).

31. ———. Freewrite. Reading-Writing Theory (June 27, 1990).

32. ———. Response journal. Reading-Writing Theory (June 29, 1990).

33. Paul. Draft 1, essay 1. Teaching College Writing (Sept. 16, 1991).

34. ———. Draft 1, essay 2. Teaching College Writing (Oct. 21, 1991).

35. ———. Draft 2, essay 2. Teaching College Writing (Oct. 28, 1991).

36. Susan. Response journal. Teaching College Writing (Aug. 31, 1992).

37. ———. Response journal. Teaching College Writing (Sept. 21, 1992).

38. ———. Teaching log. Teaching College Writing (Sept. 22, 1992).

39. ———. Response journal. Teaching College Writing (Nov. 23, 1992).

40. ———. Cover sheet, essay 3. Teaching College Writing (Dec. 7, 1992).

41. ———. Introduction, response journal. Teaching College Writing (Dec. 14, 1992).

42. ———. Introduction, final portfolio. Teaching College Writing (Dec. 14, 1992).

43. Jeff. Freewrite. Teaching College Writing (Sept. 13, 1994).

44. ———. Response journal. Teaching College Writing (Sept. 12, 1994).

45. ———. Essay 2. Teaching College Writing (Oct. 31, 1994).

46. ———. Response journal. Teaching College Writing (Aug. 29. 1994).

47. Pattie. Response journal. Teaching College Writing (Sept. 12, 1994).

48. ———. Response journal. Teaching College Writing (Sept. 19, 1994).

49. ———. Essay 2. Teaching College Writing (Oct. 31, 1994).

50. ———. Tape recording of peer response. Teaching College Writing (Oct. 17, 1994).

51. ———. Essay 2. Teaching College Writing (Oct. 31, 1994).
52. Ken. Cover sheet, essay 1. Teaching College Writing (Sept. 26, 1992).
53. ———. Response journal. Teaching College Writing (Oct. 10, 1992).
54. Gail. Response journals. Reading-Writing Theory (June 13–20, 1990).
55. Angie. Response journals. Reading-Writing Theory (June 13–20, 1990).
56. ———. Peer response sheet. Reading-Writing Theory (July 6, 1990).
57. Gail. Freewrite. Reading-Writing Theory (July 6, 1990).
58. Frank Grady. Personal correspondence. (1991).
59. Paul. Cover sheet, essay 1. Teaching College Writing (Sept. 23, 1991).
60. Ibid. Paul's reactions parallel those of Gannett's undergraduate males, for whom personal writing "seemed to function, . . . in a powerful and useful way for focusing, managing, and releasing pressure from academic and social responsibility" (*Gender* 163).
61. Tape recording of peer response, essay 1. Teaching College Writing (Sept. 9, 1991).
62. Tape recording of peer response, essay 2. Teaching College Writing (Oct. 29, 1991).
63. Paul. Response journal. Teaching College Writing (Dec. 2, 1991).
64. Susan. Personal interview. (Dec. 1996).
65. Ibid.
66. Jeff. Teaching log. Teaching College Writing (Aug. 29, 1994).
67. ———. Essay 3. Teaching College Writing (Dec. 5, 1994).
68. Ibid.
69. Ibid.
70. Ibid.
71. Pattie. Research log. Teaching College Writing (Aug. 29, 1994).
72. ———. Essay 3. Teaching College Writing (Dec. 5, 1994).
73. Ibid.
74. Ibid.
75. Studies by Lather; Maher and Tetreault; Tarule; and Gilligan et al. have begun to explore the power of relationships, especially among women, to successful learning.
76. Ken. Teaching log. Teaching College Writing (Oct. 26, 1992).
77. ———. Teaching log. Teaching College Writing (Nov. 2, 1992).
78. ———. Reading log. Teaching College Writing (Nov. 9, 1992).
79. ———. Reading log. Teaching College Writing (Nov. 16, 1992).
80. ———. Draft 2, essay 2. Teaching College Writing (Oct. 24, 1992).
81. ———. Essay 2. Teaching College Writing (Oct. 31, 1992).
82. ———. Cover sheet, essay 2. Teaching College Writing (Nov. 2, 1992).
83. ———. Draft 1, essay 3. Teaching College Writing (Nov. 23, 1992).
84. Tape recording of peer response. Teaching College Writing (Nov. 23, 1992).
85. Ken. Essay 1. Teaching College Writing (Sept. 28, 1992).

6. BUILDING CONFIDENCE

1. See Gannett's review of literature or Gal's for more extensive references.

2. These behaviors are explored in the works of Chodorow, Dinnerstein, and Gilligan.

3. See, for example, Britzman or McLeod.

4. Melissa. Final essay. Reader Response Theory (May 10, 1992).

5. Ibid.

6. Jimmy. Essay 2. Teaching College Writing (Nov. 1, 1993).

7. ———. Essay 1. Teaching College Writing (Sept. 27, 1993).

8. ———. Essay 2. Teaching College Writing (Nov. 1, 1993).

9. ———. Teaching log. (Aug. 30, 1993).

10. Jenny. Personal response 2. Reader Response Theory (Mar. 9, 1992).

11. ———. Personal response 3. Reader Response Theory (Mar. 16, 1992).

12. Ibid.

13. Missy. Personal response 1. Reader Response Theory (Jan. 13, 1992).

14. Gordon Pradl discusses the commonality of this phenomenon (Introduction xv).

15. Auggie. Personal conversation. (Spring 1992).

16. Missy. Personal response 2. Reader Response Theory (Mar. 9, 1992).

17. ———. Personal response 3. Reader Response Theory (Mar. 16, 1992).

18. ———. Personal response 1. Reader Response Theory (Jan. 13, 1992).

19. Auggie. Personal response 1. Reader Response Theory (Jan. 13, 1992).

20. ———. Response journal. Reading-Writing Theory (Apr. 17, 1991).

21. ———. Midterm. Reader Response Theory (Mar. 16, 1992).

22. Melissa. Academic response 1. Reader Response Theory (Jan. 27, 1992).

23. ———. Personal correspondence. (May 1992).

24. ———. Teaching log. Teaching College Writing (Aug. 24, 1992).

25. ———. Reading log. Teaching College Writing (Aug. 31, 1992).

26. ———. Reading log. Teaching College Writing (Sept. 21, 1992).

27. ———. Tape recording of peer response. Teaching College Writing (Sept. 14, 1992).

28. ———. Teaching log. Teaching College Writing (Sept. 28, 1992).

29. ———. Reading log. Teaching College Writing (Sept. 28, 1992).

30. ———. Personal conversation. (Oct. 5, 1992).

31. ———. Reading log. Teaching College Writing (Oct. 16, 1992).

32. ———. Teaching logs. Teaching College Writing (Oct. 16 and 23, 1992).

33. ———. Cover sheet, essay 2. Teaching College Writing (Nov. 2, 1992).

34. ———. Personal conversation. (Nov. 9, 1992).

35. ———. Reading journal. Teaching College Writing (Nov. 16, 1992).

36. Jimmy. Teaching log. Teaching College Writing (Aug. 30, 1993).

37. ———. Essay 2. Teaching College Writing (Nov. 1, 1993).

38. ———. Essay 1. Teaching College Writing (Sept. 27, 1993).

39. ————. Teaching log. Teaching College Writing (Oct. 13, 1993).

40. These feelings were revealed in Carolyn's and Richard's teaching logs following their first peer-response session. The assignment was to "describe your experience of collaborative learning in the development and revision of Essay 1" (Sept. 20, 1993).

41. Jimmy. Essay 2. Teaching College Writing (Nov. 1, 1993).

42. ————. Final portfolio. Teaching College Writing (Dec. 6, 1993).

43. Jenny. Personal conversation. (Jan. 2001).

44. ————. Personal essay 4. Reader Response Theory (Mar. 23, 1992).

45. I observed each group's discussions, as these occurred during class time.

46. Note from Auggie to Jenny. (Mar. 9, 1992).

47. Missy. Personal response 1. Reader Response Theory (Jan. 13, 1992).

48. Bordo refers to this belief as evidencing "personal regression" (148).

49. Missy. Personal response 1. Reader Response Theory (Jan. 13, 1992).

50. ————. Academic response 1. Reader Response Theory (Jan. 27, 1992).

51. Missy's writing reflected what Peter Elbow refers to in *Writing Without Teachers* as playing "the doubting game," an approach to texts he describes as typically "male."

52. At midterm and before the final essay, group members had to synthesize their findings regarding each other's language use.

53. Missy. Final essay. Reader Response Theory (May 11, 1992).

54. Auggie. Response journal. Reading-Writing Theory (Jan. 28, 1991).

55. ————. Teaching log. Teaching College Writing (Aug. 27, 1992).

56. ————. Draft 1, essay 1. Teaching College Writing (Sept. 16, 1991).

57. Tape recording, peer response. Draft 1, essay 1. Teaching College Writing (Sept. 16, 1991).

58. Auggie. Essay 1. Teaching College Writing (Sept. 30, 1991).

59. ————. Teaching log. Teaching College Writing (Sept. 16, 1991).

60. ————. Essay 3. Teaching College Writing (Dec. 16, 1991).

61. Melissa. Draft 1, essay 3. Teaching College Writing (Nov. 23, 1992).

62. Tape recording of peer response, Draft 1, essay 3. Teaching College Writing (Nov. 23, 1992).

63. Tape recording of peer response. Drafts 1 and 2, essay 2. Teaching College Writing (Oct. 18 and 25, 1992). Hays found that silence is typical of women students who "feel invalidated" (165).

64. Tape recording of peer response, Draft 1, essay 3. Teaching College Writing (Nov. 23, 1992).

65. Melissa. Cover sheet, essay 3. Teaching College Writing (Dec. 7, 1992).

66. ————. Essay 3. Teaching College Writing (Dec. 7, 1992).

67. Ibid.

68. Jimmy. Introduction to portfolio. Teaching College Writing (Dec. 6, 1993).

69. ————. Final essay. Reading-Writing Theory (May 9, 1994).

70. ———. Essay 1. Teaching College Writing (Sept. 27, 1993).

71. Jenny. Midterm. Reader-Response Theory (Mar. 16, 1992).

72. Linda. Response journal. Reader-Response Theory (Apr. 27, 1992).

73. Jenny. Midterm. Reader-Response Theory (Mar. 16, 1992).

74. Auggie. Personal response 3. Reader-Response Theory (Mar. 16, 1992).

75. Missy. Personal response 3. Reader-Response Theory (Mar. 16, 1992).

76. Ibid.

77. Ibid.

78. Auggie. Personal response 4. Reader-Response Theory (Mar. 23, 1992).

79. Jenny. Final essay. Reader-Response Theory (May 11, 1992).

80. Missy. Final essay. Reader-Response Theory (May 11, 1992).

81. Ibid.

82. Jenny. Final analyses. Reader-Response Theory (Apr. 27, 1992).

83. Missy. Final essay. Reader-Response Theory (May 11, 1992). Such comments underscore Caplan's conclusions that "the worst mistake [academic women] can make on the job is to remain isolated from other people, especially from other women" (qtd. in Russell, Plotkin, and Bell 144).

84. Ibid.

85. Ibid.

86. Auggie. Personal response 1. Reader-Response Theory (Jan. 13, 1992).

87. ———. Personal response 2. Reader-Response Theory (Mar. 9, 1992).

88. ———. Personal response 3. Reader-Response Theory (Mar. 16, 1992).

89. ———. Personal response 4. Reader-Response Theory (Mar. 23, 1992).

90. ———. Literary responses 1–4. Reader-Response Theory (Mar. 30 to Apr. 27, 1992).

91. ———. Literary response 5. Reader-Response Theory (May 4, 1992). In Auggie's case, as in Jimmy's, these comments seem to answer the concerns raised by various feminists and confirms the responses of Stanger and Bizzell about the value and effects of collaborative learning. This pedagogy did indeed "subvert gender hierarchy and resituate women and men on equal terms" (Ashton-Jones 9), not so much by removing the teacher/authority from the discussion but rather by removing male students and their concerns from center stage.

92. Personal conversation. Auggie is one of my best friends, so I've had many opportunities to talk about old times with him.

93. Auggie. Midterm essay. Reader-Response Theory (Mar. 16, 1992).

94. ———. Final essay. Reader-Response Theory (May 11, 1992).

95. Jenny. Final analyses. Reader-Response Theory (Apr. 27, 1992).

96. Auggie. Final essay. Reader-Response Theory (May 11, 1992).

97. Ibid.

98. Final analyses. Reader-Response Theory (Apr. 27, 1992).

99. Auggie. Final essay. Reader-Response Theory (May 11, 1992).

100. Ibid.

101. Ibid.

7. STRENGTHENING VOICE

1. See Kirsch's discussion in *Women Writing the Academy* (56ff).

2. Maher and Tetreault describe Belenky et al.'s development and discussion of this epistemological position as offering the most important insights in their study ("Women's" 170). Nevertheless, in her analysis of the book's impact, coauthor Goldberger refers to this concept as the least developed and notes that its definition is culturally biased because the examples were drawn from college-educated white women; however, in subsequent studies, Goldberger found that this position can also be attained by women of color with lesser educations in part because of their own "marginality and life struggles" (356).

3. Kim. Essay 1. Teaching College Writing (Sept. 28, 1992); Shannon. Essay 1. Teaching College Writing (Sept. 26, 1994).

4. Carolyn. Response journal. Contemporary American Women Novelists (CAWN) (Jan. 20, 1993).

5. Kim. Essay 2. Teaching College Writing (Nov. 11, 1992).

6. Shannon. Essay 2. Teaching College Writing (Oct. 31, 1994).

7. Carolyn. Essay 2. Teaching College Writing (Nov. 1, 1993).

8. Kim. Essay 1. Teaching College Writing (Sept. 28, 1992).

9. Carolyn. Essay 1. Teaching College Writing (Sept. 27, 1993).

10. Shannon. Essay 1. Teaching College Writing (Sept. 26, 1994).

11. Kim. Personal response 1. Reader Response Theory (Jan. 13, 1992).

12. ———. Midterm essay. Reader Response Theory (Mar. 16, 1992).

13. ———. Final essay. Reader-Response Theory (May 11, 1992).

14. Shannon. Essay 1. Teaching College Writing (Sept. 26, 1994).

15. ———. Personal correspondence. (Summer 1995).

16. ———. Teaching log. Teaching College Writing (Sept. 12, 1994).

17. ———. Response journal. Teaching College Writing (Sept. 19, 1994).

18. Carolyn. Essay 1. Teaching College Writing (Sept. 27, 1993).

19. ———. Personal correspondence. (Summer 1994).

20. ———. Essay 2. Teaching College Writing (Nov. 1, 1993).

21. Kim. Response journal. Reading-Writing Theory (Jan. 21, 1991).

22. ———. Response journal. Reading-Writing Theory (Jan. 28, 1991).

23. ———. Academic response 1. Reader-Response Theory (Jan. 27, 1992).

24. ———. Academic response 3. Reader-Response Theory (Feb. 10, 1992).

25. ———. Final essay. Reader-Response Theory (May 11, 1992).

26. Bob. Final essay. Reader-Response Theory (May 11, 1992).

27. Kim. Final essay. Reader-Response Theory (May 11, 1992).

28. Linda. Discussion leader. Reader-Response Theory (Feb. 24, 1992).

29. Bob. Class discussion. Reader-Response Theory (Feb. 24, 1992).

30. Kim. Final essay. Reader-Response Theory (May 11, 1992).

31. ———. Personal response 2. Reader-Response Theory (Mar. 9, 1992).

32. ———. Personal response 1. Reader-Response Theory (Jan. 27, 1992).

33. ———. Literary response 2. Reader-Response Theory (Apr. 6, 1992).

34. Bob. Final essay. Reader-Response Theory (May 11, 1992).

35. These beliefs were stated in Bob's final essay (May 11, 1992) and exemplified when he announced on the last night of class that he had just sold all his Reader-Response books.

36. Shannon. Essay 1. Teaching College Writing (Sept. 26, 1994).

37. ———. Response journal. Teaching College Writing (Aug. 29, 1994).

38. ———. Teaching log. Teaching College Writing (Sept. 19, 1994).

39. ———. Research log. Teaching College Writing (Sept. 12, 1994).

40. ———. Final essay. Teaching College Writing (Dec. 5, 1994).

41. Ibid.

42. Tim. Personal note to Shannon. (Nov. 28, 1994).

43. Shannon. Final essay. Teaching College Writing (Dec. 5, 1994).

44. Carolyn. Response journal. Contemporary American Women Novelists (CAWN) (Jan. 27, 1993).

45. ———. Response journal. CAWN (Feb. 3, 1993).

46. ———. Response journal. CAWN (Feb. 17, 1993).

47. ———. Response journal. CAWN (Apr. 28, 1993).

48. Because the small groups met during class time, I observed each group.

49. Carolyn. Response journal. CAWN (Apr. 14, 1993).

50. ———. Personal conversations. (Summer 1993).

51. Kim. Response journal. Teaching College Writing (Dec. 7, 1992).

52. ———. Essay 1. Teaching College Writing (Sept. 28, 1992).

53. ———. Teaching logs. Teaching College Writing (Sept. 14 and 21, 1992).

54. ———. Portfolio introduction. Teaching College Writing (Dec. 7, 1992).

55. Shannon. Teaching log. (Oct. 12, 1994).

56. Ibid.

57. Shannon. Teaching log. Teaching College Writing (Oct. 31, 1994).

58. Class observation. (Aug. 29, 1994).

59. Shannon. Response journal. Teaching College Writing (Nov. 28, 1994).

60. Personal conversation. (Fall 1994).

61. Tape recordings of peer-response. Teaching College Writing (Sept. 13 and 27 and Oct. 18 and 25, 1992).

62. Class observation. (Sept. 20, 1993).

63. Carolyn. Essay 1. Teaching College Writing (Sept. 26, 1994).

64. Personal conversation. (Summer 1994).

65. Susan. Final essay. Radical Pedagogy (May 1996).

8. CHANGING OUR TEACHING, OUR STUDENTS, OUR PROFESSION

1. See Re-envisioning the Ph.D. Re-envisioning Project Resources. 2000 Conference & Selected Bibliography. http://www.grad.washington.edu/envision/project_resources/2000_sel_biblio_enrollment.html. Accessed 12/30/04.

works cited

Abbott, Robert, Donald Wulff, and K. Szego. "Review of Research on TA Training." Nyquist, Abbott, and Wulff 111–24.

Academic Program in College Teaching. Graduate School–Teaching Excellence Program. Durham: U of New Hampshire. <http://www.gradschool.unh.edu/pff/pffprogram.html>.

Aisenberg, Nadya, and Mona Harrington. *Women of Academe: Outsiders in the Sacred Grove.* Amherst: U of Massachusetts P, 1988.

Allen, R. R. "Encouraging Reflection in Teaching Assistants." Nyquist, Abbott, Wulff, and Sprague 313–17.

Anderson, Martin. *Impostors in the Temple.* Stanford, CA: Hoover Institution, 1996.

Angelo, Thomas A., and K. Patricia Cross. "Classroom Research for Teaching Assistants." Nyquist, Abbott, and Wulff 99–107.

Aronson, Anne. "Danger Zones: Risk and Resistance in the Writing Histories of Returning Adult Women." *Situated Stories: Valuing Diversity in Composition Research.* Ed. Emily Decker and Kathleen Geissler. Portsmouth: Boynton/Cook, 1998. 56–73.

Ashton, Patricia. "Motivation and the Teacher's Sense of Efficacy." *Research on Motivation in Education.* Ed. Carole Ames and Russell Ames. Vol. 2. Orlando, FL: Harcourt, 1985. 141–74.

Ashton-Jones, Evelyn. "Collaboration, Conversation, and the Politics of Gender." *Feminine Principles and Women's Experiences in American Composition and Rhetoric.* Ed. Louise Wetherbee Phelps and Janet Emig. Pittsburgh: U of Pittsburgh P, 1995. 5–26.

Bandura, Albert. *Social Foundations of Thought and Action: A Social Cognitive Theory.* New York: Prentice, 1986.

Barr Ebest, Sally. "Gender Differences in Writing Program Administration." *Writing Program Administration* 18.3 (1995): 53–73.

———. "Going Against Nature? Women's Resistance to Collaborative Learning." *Common Ground: Feminist Collaboration in the Academy.* Ed. Elizabeth G. Peck and JoAnna Stephens Mink. Albany: State U of New York P, 1997. 227–48.

———. "The Next Generation of WPAs: A Study of Graduate Programs in Composition/Rhetoric." *Writing Program Administration* 22.3 (1999): 65–84.

Barr Reagan, Sally. "Collaborative Learning in the Graduate Classroom." *Writing With: New Directions in Collaborative Teaching, Learning, and Research.* Ed. Barr Reagan, Thomas Fox, and David Bleich. Albany: State U of New York P, 1994. 197–212.

———. "Double Exposure: The Effects of Combined Reading-Writing Instruction on the Composing Processes of Basic Writers." Diss. Indiana U, 1984.

WORKS CITED

──────. "Using Reader Response in the Writing Classroom." *Literary Theory in the Classroom*. Ed. Nancy Williams and Scott Cawelty. Urbana, IL: NCTE, 1989.

Bartlett, F. C. *Remembering*. Cambridge: Cambridge UP, 1932.

Bauer, Dale. "The Other 'F' Word: The Feminist in the Classroom." *College English* 52 (1990): 385–96.

Baxter-Magolda, Marcia B. *Knowing and Reasoning in College: Gender-Related Patterns in Students' Intellectual Development*. San Francisco: Jossey-Bass, 1992.

Bean, John. *Engaging Ideas: The Professor's Guide to Integrating Writing, Critical Thinking, and Active Learning in the Classroom*. San Francisco: Jossey-Bass, 1996.

Belanoff, Pat. "Freewriting: An Aid to Rereading Theorists." *Nothing Begins with N*. Ed. Belanoff, Peter Elbow, and Sheryl I. Fontaine. Carbondale: Southern Illinois UP, 1991. 16–31.

Belenky, Mary F., Blythe M. Clinchy, Nancy R. Goldberger, and Jill Mattuck Tarule. *Women's Ways of Knowing*. New York: Basic, 1986.

Berkenkotter, Carol, Thomas Huckin, and John Ackerman. "Conventions, Conversations, and the Writer: Case Study of a Student in a Rhetoric Ph.D. Program." *Research in the Teaching of English* 22 (1988): 9–41.

Bishop, Wendy. *Ethnographic Writing Research*. Portsmouth, NH: Heinemann, 1999.

──────. *Something Old, Something New: College Writing Teachers and Classroom Change*. Carbondale: Southern Illinois UP, 1990.

──────. *Teaching Lives*. Logan: Utah State UP, 1997.

Bleich, David. *The Double Perspective*. Urbana, IL: NCTE, 1988.

──────. *Know and Tell*. Portsmouth, NH: Boynton-Cook, 1998.

──────. *Readings and Feelings*. Urbana, IL: NCTE, 1973.

──────. *Subjective Criticism*. Baltimore: Johns Hopkins UP, 1978.

Bloom, Harold. *The Closing of the American Mind*. New York: Simon, 1987.

Bloom, Lynn Z. *Composition Studies as a Creative Art*. Logan: Utah State UP, 1998.

Bordo, Susan. "Feminism, Postmodernism, and Gender-Scepticism." *Feminism/Postmodernism*. Ed. Linda J. Nicholson. New York: Routledge, 1990. 137–56.

Bort, Mary, and Nancy L. Buerkel-Rothfuss. "A Content Analysis of TA Training Materials." Nyquist, Abbott, Wulff, and Sprague 243–51.

Boyer, Ernest. "Preparing Tomorrow's Professoriate." Nyquist, Abbott, Wulff, and Sprague 3–11.

Britzman, Deborah. *Practice Makes Perfect: A Critical Study of Learning to Teach*. Albany, NY: State U of New York UP, 1991.

Brodkey, Linda. "Writing Ethnographic Narratives." *Written Communication* 4 (1987): 25–50.

Bruffee, Kenneth. *Collaborative Learning: Higher Education, Interdependence, and the Authority of Knowledge*. Baltimore: Johns Hopkins UP, 1993.

Brunner, Diane D. *Inquiry and Reflection*. Albany: State U of New York P, 1994.

Buerkel-Rothfuss, Nancy L., and Pamela L. Gray. "Teaching Assistant Training: The View from the Top." Nyquist, Abbott, Wulff, and Sprague 29–39.

Cano, Jamie, Christopher N. Jones, and Nancy V. Chism. "TA Teaching of an Increasingly Diverse Undergraduate Population." Nyquist, Abbott, Wulff, and Sprague 87–94.

Caplan, Paula. *Lifting a Ton of Feathers: A Woman's Guide to Surviving in the Academic World.* Toronto: U of Toronto P, 1993.

Carver, Raymond. "What We Talk about When We Talk about Love." *Ways of Reading.* Ed. David Bartholomae and Anthony Petrosky. 4th ed. New York: St. Martin's, 1996.

"Certificate in College Teaching: Department of Kinesiology." 19 Mar. 2001. <http://grad.msu.edu/teaching.htm>.

Chase, Geoffrey. "Accommodation, Resistance, and the Politics of Student Writing." *CCC* 38 (Feb. 1988): 13–22.

Chiseri-Strater, Elizabeth. "Turning In upon Ourselves: Positionality, Subjectivity, and Reflexivity in Case Study and Ethnographic Research." Mortensen and Kirsch 115–33.

Chism, Nancy. "Supervisors and TAs on the Teaching Help They Give and Receive." Nyquist, Abbott, Wulff, and Sprague 318–25.

Chism, Nancy, Jamie Cano, and Anne S. Pruitt. "Teaching in a Diverse Environment: Knowledge and Skills Needed by TAs." Nyquist, Abbott, and Wulff 23–35.

Chodorow, Nancy. *The Reproduction of Mothering.* Berkeley: U of California P, 1978.

Clinchy, Blythe M. "Connected and Separate Knowing: Toward a Marriage of Two Minds." Goldberger, Tarule, Clinchy, and Belenky 205–47.

Comley, Nancy. "Doctoral Studies and the Fine Art of Teaching." *The Future of Doctoral Studies in English.* Ed. Andrea Lunsford, Helene Moglen, and James F. Slevin. New York: MLA, 1989. 43–46.

Connolly, Paul, and Teresa Vilardi, eds. *New Directions in College Writing Programs.* New York: MLA, 1986.

Connors, Robert. *Composition-Rhetoric.* Pittsburgh: U of Pittsburgh P, 1997.

Conrad, Clifton, Jennifer Haworth Grant, and Susan B. Miller. *A Silent Success: Master's Education in the United States.* Baltimore: Johns Hopkins UP, 1993.

Creswell, J. W. *Qualitative Research: Inquiry and Research Design.* Thousand Oaks, CA: Sage, 1998.

Crowley, Sharon. *Composition in the University: Historical and Polemical Essays.* Pittsburgh: U of Pittsburgh P, 1998.

Culler, Jonathan. "Reading as a Woman." *Feminisms.* Ed. Robyn R. Warhol and Diane Price Herndyl. New Brunswick, NJ: Rutgers UP, 1991. 509–24.

Deats, Sara Munson, and Lagretta Tallent Lenker, eds. *Gender and Academe: Feminist Pedagogy and Politics.* Lanham, MD: Rowman, 1994.

Delpit, Lisa. "The Silenced Dialogue: Power and Pedagogy in Educating Other People's Children." *Harvard Educational Review* 58.3 (1988): 280–98.

Diamond, C. T. P. "In-Service Education as Something More: A Personal Construct Approach." Kahaney, Perry, and Janangelo 45–66.

Dinnerstein, Dorothy. *The Mermaid and the Minotaur.* New York: Harper, 1976.

Doheny-Farina, Stephen, and Lee Odell. "Ethnographic Research on Writing: Assumptions and Methodology." *Writing in Nonacademic Settings*. Ed. Lee Odell and Dixie Goswami. New York: Guilford, 1985. 503–35.

Douglas, Geoffrey. *Education Without Impact*. New York: Carol, 1992.

D'Souza, Dinesh. *Illiberal Education*. New York: Vintage, 1991.

Ede, Lisa, and Andrea Lunsford. *Singular Texts/Plural Authors*. Carbondale: Southern Illinois UP, 1990.

Elbow, Peter. *Embracing Contraries: Explorations in Learning and Teaching*. New York: Oxford UP, 1986.

———. Introduction. *Landmark Essays on Voice and Writing*. Davis, CA: Hermagorass, 1994. xi–xlvii.

———. *What Is English?* New York: MLA, 1990.

———. *Writing Without Teachers*. New York: Oxford UP, 1981.

Elbow, Peter, and Pat Belanoff. *A Community of Writers*. 2nd ed. New York: McGraw, 1995.

Emerson, Robert M., Rachel I. Fretz, and Linda L. Shaw. *Writing Ethnographic Field-notes*. Chicago: U of Chicago P, 1995.

Farris, Christine. *Subject to Change: New Composition Instructors' Theory and Practice*. Cresskill, NJ: Hampton, 1996.

———. "Too Cool for School? Composition as Cultural Studies and Reflective Practice." Pytlik and Liggett 97–107.

Flynn, Elizabeth A. "Gender and Reading." Flynn and Schweikert 267–88.

Flynn, Elizabeth A., and Patrocinio Schweikert, eds. *Gender and Reading*. Baltimore: Johns Hopkins UP, 1986.

Freire, Paulo. *Pedagogy of the Oppressed*. New York: Continuum, 1970.

Fulkerson, Richard. "The English Doctoral Metacurriculum: An Issue of Ethics." *Foregrounding Ethical Awareness in Composition and English Studies*. Ed. Sheryl I. Fontaine and Susan M. Hunter. Portsmouth, NY: Boynton/Cook, 1998. 121–43.

Fulwiler, Toby. "The Quiet and Insistent Revolution: Writing-Across-the-Curriculum." *The Politics of Writing Instruction: Postsecondary*. Ed. Richard Bullock, John Trimbur, and Charles Schuster. Portsmouth, NH: Heinemann, 1991. 179–88.

Gal, Susan. "Between Speech and Silence: The Problematics of Research on Language and Gender." Roman, Juhasz, and Miller 407–31.

Galvin, Kathleen M. "Building an Interactive Learning Community: The TA Challenge." Nyquist, Abbott, Wulff, and Sprague 263–74.

Gannett, Cinthia. *Gender and the Journal*. Albany: State U of New York P, 1992.

Gardiner, Lion F. *Redesigning Higher Education*. Report 7. Washington, DC: Graduate School of Educ. and Human Dev., George Washington U, 1994.

Garland, Martha McMackin. "Newman in His Own Day." *The Idea of a University*. Ed. Frank M. Turner. New Haven, CT: Yale UP, 1996. 265–83.

Gawelek, Mary Ann, Maggie Mulqueen, and Jill Mattuck Tarule. "Woman to Woman: Understanding the Needs of Our Female Students." Deats and Lenker 179–200.

Gebhardt, Richard. "Scholarship, Teaching, and the Future of Composition Studies." *Writing Program Administration* 20 (Spring 1997): 7–16.

George, Diana. "Working with Peer Groups in the Composition Classroom." *CCC* 35 (1984): 320–26.

Gere, Anne Ruggles. *Writing Groups.* Carbondale: Southern Illinois UP, 1987.

Gilligan, Carol. *In a Different Voice.* Cambridge: Harvard UP, 1982.

Gilligan, Carol, and Lyn Mikel Brown. *Meeting at the Crossroads.* New York: Ballantine, 1993.

Giroux, Henry. *Theory and Resistance in Education.* South Hadley, MA: Bergin, 1983.

Gleason, Jean Berko. "Sex Differences in Parent-Child Interaction." Roman, Juhasz, and Miller 254–64.

Glickman, Rose L. *Daughters of Feminists.* New York: St. Martin's, 1993.

Goldberger, Nancy R., Jill Mattuck Tarule, Blythe M. Clinchy, and Mary F. Belenky, eds. *Knowledge, Difference, and Power.* New York: Basic, 1996.

Graduate Minor in College Teaching. Columbia: U of Missouri. 2003. <http:// web.missouri.edu/~gradschl/mict/>.

Gray, Pamela L., and Nancy L. Buerkel-Rothfuss. "Teaching Assistant Training: The View from the Trenches." Nyquist, Abbott, Wulff, and Sprague 40–52.

Grumet, Madeleine R. *Bitter Milk.* Amherst: U of Massachusetts P, 1988.

Hall, Roberta M., and Bernice R. Sandler. *Academic Mentoring for Women Students and Faculty: A New Look at an Old Way to Get Ahead.* Washington, DC: Project on the Status and Educ. of Women, Assn. of Amer. Colleges, 1983.

Harding, Sandra. *Feminism and Methodology: Social Science Issues.* Bloomington: Indiana UP, 1987.

Harste, Gerald, Virginia Woodward, and Caroline Burke. *Language Stories and Literacy Lessons.* Portsmouth, NH: Heinemann, 1984.

Hatch, Deborah, and Christine Farris. "Helping TAs to Use Active Learning Strategies." Nyquist, Abbott, and Wulff 89–97.

Hawkins, Thomas. *Group Inquiry Techniques for Teaching Writing.* Urbana, IL: ERIC Clearinghouse on Reading and Communications Skills, 1976.

Haworth, Jennifer G., and Clifton F. Conrad. *Emblems of Quality in Higher Education.* Boston: Allyn, 1997.

Hays, Janice. "Intellectual Parenting and a Developmental Feminist Pedagogy of Writing." Phelps and Emig 153–90.

Helmers, Marguerite H. *Writing Students: Composition, Testimonials, and Representations of Students.* Albany: State U of New York P, 1994.

Henley, Nancy M., and Cheris Kramarae. "Gender, Power, and Miscommunication." Roman, Juhasz, and Miller 383–406.

Hillocks, George. *Teaching Writing as Reflective Practice.* New York: Teachers College P, 1995.

———. *Ways of Thinking, Ways of Teaching.* New York: Teachers College P, 1999.

Holmes Group. *Tomorrow's Teachers.* East Lansing, MI: Holmes, 1986.

WORKS CITED

Hulbert, Kathleen Day. "Gender Patterns in Faculty-Student Mentoring Relationships." Deats and Lenker 247–64.

Hurtado, Aida. "Strategic Suspensions: Feminists of Color Theorize the Production of Knowledge." Goldberger, Tarule, Clinchy, and Belenky 372–92.

Irigaray, Luce. "This Sex Which Is Not One." Warhol and Herndyl 350–56.

Iser, Wolfgang. "The Reading Process: A Phenomenological Approach." Reader-Response Criticism. Ed. Jane P. Tompkins. Baltimore: Johns Hopkins UP, 1980. 50–69.

Jacobson, Jennifer. "Why Do So Many People Leave Graduate School Without a Ph.D.?" Chronicle of Higher Education 2 June 2001: A1.

John-Steiner, Vera, Robert J. Weber, and Michele Minnis. "The Challenge of Studying Collaboration." American Educational Research Journal 35:4 (1998): 773–83.

Jordan, Judith V. "Empathy and Self Boundaries." Roman, Juhasz, and Miller 153–64.

Kahaney, Phyllis. Afterword. "Knowledge, Learning and Change." Kahaney, Perry, and Janangelo 191–200.

Kahaney, Phyllis, Linda Perry, and Joseph Janangelo. Theoretical and Critical Perspectives on Teacher Change. Norwood, NJ: Ablex, 1993.

Kearney, Patricia, and Timothy G. Plax. "Student Resistance to Control." Power in the Classroom. Hillsdale, NJ: Erlbaum, 1992. 85–100.

Kirsch, Gesa E. "Methodological Pluralism." Kirsch and Sullivan 247–69.

———. Women Writing the Academy. Carbondale: Southern Illinois UP, 1993.

Kirsch, Gesa E., and Patricia A. Sullivan. Methods and Methodology in Composition Research. Carbondale: Southern Illinois UP, 1992.

Kolodny, Annette. Failing the Future. Durham, NC: Duke UP, 1998.

Ladson-Billings, Gloria. The Dreamkeepers. San Francisco: Jossey-Bass, 1994.

Lambert, Leo M., and Stacey L. Tice, eds. Preparing Graduate Students to Teach. Washington, DC: American Assn. of Higher Educ., 1993.

Langer, Judith. Effective Literacy Instruction: Building Successful Reading and Writing Programs. Urbana, IL: NCTE, 2002.

Langer, Judith, and Arthur Applebee. How Writing Shapes Thinking. Urbana, IL: NCTE, 1987.

Lather, Pattie. Getting Smart. New York: Routledge, 1991.

Latterell, Catherine. "Training the Workforce: An Overview of GTA Education Curricula." Writing Program Administration 19.3 (Spring 1996): 7–23.

Lenzner, Robert, and Stephen Johnson. "Seeing Things as They Really Are." Forbes (10 Mar. 1997): 122–27.

Lovitts, Barbara E. Leaving the Ivory Tower: The Causes and Consequences of Departure from Doctoral Study. Lanham, MD: Rowman, 2001.

Luke, Carmen, and Jennifer Gore. Feminisms and Critical Pedagogy. New York: Routledge, 1992.

Maher, Frances A., and Mary Kay Tetreault. The Feminist Classroom. New York: Basic, 1994.

————. "Women's Ways of Knowing in Women's Studies, Feminist Pedagogies, and Feminist Theory." Goldberger, Tarule, Clinchy, and Belenky 148–74.

Martin, Laura M. W. "Understanding Teacher Change from a Vygotskian Perspective." Kahaney, Perry, and Janangelo 71–86.

McKeachie, Wilbert J. "Learning, Teaching, and Learning from Teaching." Nyquist, Abbott, Wulff, and Sprague 223–31.

McLeod, Susan H. "Pygmalion or Golem? Teacher Affect and Efficacy." *CCC* 46.3 (1995): 369–85.

————, ed. *Strengthening Programs for Writing Across the Curriculum.* No. 36. San Francisco: Jossey-Bass. Winter, 1988.

Miller, Richard E. *As if Learning Mattered.* Ithaca: Cornell UP, 1998.

Miraglia, Eric, and Susan McLeod. "Whither WAC? Interpreting the Stories/Histories of Enduring WAC Programs." *Writing Program Administration* (Spring 1997): 46–65.

Mohr, Marian, and Marion Maclean. *Working Together: A Guide for Teacher-Researchers.* Urbana, IL: NCTE, 1987.

Mortensen, Peter, and Gesa E. Kirsch, eds. *Ethics and Representation in Qualitative Research.* Urbana, IL: NCTE, 1996.

Moss, Beverly. "Ethnography and Composition." Kirsch and Sullivan 153–71.

Mountford, Roxanne D. "Engendering Ethnography: Insights from the Feminist Critique of Postmodern Anthropology." Mortensen and Kirsch 205–227.

Murray, Donald. *Learning by Teaching.* Portsmouth, NH: Heinemann, 1982.

Neisser, Ulric. *Cognition and Reality.* San Francisco: Freeman, 1976.

Newkirk, Thomas. "The Narrative Roots of Case Study." Kirsch and Sullivan 130–52.

Newman, John Henry. *The Idea of a University: Re-Thinking the Western Tradition.* Ed. Frank M. Turner. New Haven, CT: Yale UP, 1996.

Noddings, Nel. *Philosophy of Education.* Boulder, CO: Westview, 1995.

Nyquist, Jody D., Robert Abbott, and Donald Wulff. *Teaching Assistant Training in the 1990s.* San Francisco: Jossey Bass, 1989.

————. "The Challenge of TA Training in the 1990s." Nyquist, Abbott, and Wulff 7–13.

Nyquist, Jody D., Robert Abbott, Donald W. Wulff, and Jody Sprague, eds. *Preparing the Professoriate of Tomorrow to Teach.* Dubuque, IA: Kendall-Hunt, 1991.

Nyquist, Jody D., and Donald H. Wulff. *Working Effectively with Graduate Assistants.* Thousand Oaks, CA: Sage, 1996.

Nystrand, Mark, Adam Gamoran, Robert Kachur, and Catherine Pendergast. *Opening Dialogue: Understanding the Dynamics of Language and Learning in the English Classroom.* New York: Teachers College P, 1997.

Ormrod, Jeanne Ellis. *Educational Psychology.* 2nd ed. Upper Saddle River, NJ: Merrill, 1998.

Payne, Darin, and Theresa Enos. "TA Education as Dialogic Response: Furthering the Intellectual Work of the Profession Through WPA." *Preparing College*

Teachers of Writing. Ed. Betty P. Pytlik and Sarah Liggett. New York: Oxford UP, 2002. 50–62.

Pelzcar, Michael J., Jr., and Lewis C. Solomon, eds. *Keeping Graduate Programs Responsive to Student Needs.* San Francisco: Jossey-Bass, 1984.

Perry, William. *Forms of Ethical and Intellectual Development in the College Years.* San Francisco: Jossey-Bass, 1999.

Phelps, Louise Wetherbee, and Janet Emig, eds. *Feminine Principles and Women's Experience in American Composition and Rhetoric.* Pittsburgh: U of Pittsburgh P, 1995.

Pradl, Gordon. Introduction. Kahaney, Perry, and Janangelo xi–xxii.

"Preparing Future Faculty: History." 19 Mar. 2001. Council of Graduate Schools. <http://www.preparing-faculty.org/PFFWeb.History.htm>.

"Preparing Future Faculty: Useful Resources. 19 Mar. 2001. <http://preparing-faculty.org/PFFWeb.Resources.htm>.

"Preparing Future Faculty Web: Contents Page." 19 Mar. 2001. Council of Graduate Schools. <http://www.preparing-faculty.org/PFFWeb.Contents.htm>.

Pytlik, Betty, and Sarah Liggett. *Preparing College Teachers of Writing.* New York: Oxford UP, 2002.

Qualley, Donna J. "Being Two Places at Once: Feminism and the Development of 'Both/And' Perspectives." *Pedagogy in the Age of Politics.* Ed. Patricia A. Sullivan and Qualley. Urbana, IL: NCTE, 1994. 25–42.

Rankin, Elizabeth. *Seeing Yourself as a Teacher.* Urbana, IL: NCTE, 1994.

Ray, Ruth. Afterword. "Ethics and Representation in Teacher Research." Mortensen and Kirsch 287–300.

———. "Composition from the Teacher-Research Point of View." Kirsch and Sullivan 172–89.

———. *The Practice of Theory.* Urbana, IL: NCTE, 1993.

Rickly, Rebecca J., and Susanmarie Harrington. "Feminist Approaches to Mentoring Teaching Assistants: Conflict, Power, and Collaboration." Pytlik and Liggett 108–20.

Roman, Camille, Suzanne Juhasz, and Cristanne Miller, eds. *The Women and Language Debate.* New Brunswick, NJ: Rutgers UP, 1994.

Rose, Mike. *Lives on the Boundary.* New York: Penguin, 1989.

———. *Writer's Block: The Cognitive Dimension.* Carbondale: Southern Illinois UP, 1984.

Rosenblatt, Louise. *The Reader, the Text, the Poem.* Carbondale: Southern Illinois UP, 1978.

Russell, Constance L., Rachel Plotkin, and Anne C. Bell. "Merge/Emerge: Collaboration in Graduate School." *Common Ground: Feminist Collaboration in the Academy.* Eds. Elizabeth G. Peck and Joanna Stephens Mink. Albany, NY: State University of New York P, 1998. 141–54.

Russell, David R. *Writing in the Academic Disciplines, 1870–1990.* Carbondale: Southern Illinois UP, 1991.

Sadker, Myra, and David Sadker. *Failing at Fairness*. New York: Scribner's, 1994.

Scherer, Pamela D. "A Framework for TA Training: Methods, Behaviors, Skills, and Student Involvement." Nyquist, Abbott, Wulff, and Sprague 257–64.

Scholes, Robert. *The Rise and Fall of English*. New Haven: Yale UP, 1998.

Schon, Donald. *Educating the Reflective Practitioner*. San Francisco: Jossey-Bass, 1987.

———. *The Reflective Practitioner*. New York: Basic, 1987.

———. *The Reflective Turn*. New York: Teachers College P, 1991.

Schweikert, Patrocinio P. "Reading Ourselves: Toward a Feminist Theory of Reading." Flynn and Schweikert 31–62.

Seidel, Lee, and Jerry Gaff. "Preparing Future Faculty (PFF): Optional or Required? You Be the Judge." *Journal on Excellence on College Teaching* (Aug. 02): 1–7.

Shor, Ira. *Empowering Education*. Chicago: U of Chicago P, 1992.

Showalter, Elaine. "Regeneration." *PMLA* 114 (May 1999): 318–28.

"Similar Versions of PFF." 19 Mar. 2001. <http:www.preparing-faculty.org/PFFWeb.like.htm>.

Slevin, James. "Disciplining Students: Whom Should Composition Teach and What Should They Know?" *Composition in the Twenty-first Century*. Ed. Lynn Z. Bloom, Donald Daiker, and Edward White. Carbondale: Southern Illinois UP, 1996. 153–65.

———. *The Next Generation*. Washington, DC: American Assn. of Colleges, 1992.

Smith, Frank. *Understanding Reading*. 5th ed. Hillsdale, NJ: Erlbaum, 1988.

———. *Writing and the Writer*. New York: Holt, 1982.

Smith, Page. *Killing the Spirit*. New York: Penguin, 1991.

Sprague, Jo, and Jody Nyquist. "A Developmental Perspective on the TA Role." Nyquist, Abbott, Wulff, and Sprague 295–312.

Stake, Jane, and Francis Hoffman. "Putting Feminist Pedagogy to the Test: The Experience of Women's Studies from Student and Teacher Perspectives." *Psychology of Women Quarterly* 24 (2000): 30–38.

Stanton, Ann. "Reconfiguring Teaching and Knowing in the College Classroom." Goldberger, Tarule, Clinchy, and Belenky 25–56.

Steinem, Gloria. "Ruth's Song: Because She Could Not Sing It." *Ways of Reading*. Ed. David Bartholomae and Anthony Petrosky. 4th ed. New York: St. Martin's, 1993.

Sternglass, Marilyn. *The Presence of Thought: Introspective Accounts of Reading and Writing*. Norwood, NJ: Ablex, 1988.

Sullivan, Patricia A. "Ethnography and the Problem of the 'Other.'" Mortensen and Kirsch 97–114.

———. "Feminism and Methodology in Composition Studies." Kirsch and Sullivan 37–61.

———. "Writing in the Graduate Curriculum: Literary Criticism as Composition." *Journal of Advanced Composition* (fall 1991): 283–99.

Sykes, Donald. *Profscam*. New York: St. Martin's, 1988.

Tappan, Mark. "Relational Voices and Moral Development: Reflections on Change." Kahaney, Perry, and Janangelo 1–18.

Tarule, Jill Mattuck. "Voices in Dialogue: Collaborative Ways of Knowing." Goldberger, Tarule, and Clinchy 274–304.

Taylor, Jill McLean, Carol Gilligan, and Amy M. Sullivan. *Between Voice and Silence.* Cambridge, MA: Harvard UP, 1995.

Treichler, Paula. "A Room of Whose Own? Lessons from Feminist Classroom Narratives." *Changing Classroom Practices.* Ed. David B. Downing. Urbana, IL: NCTE 1994. 75–103.

Trimbur, John. "Collaborative Learning and Teaching Writing." *Perspectives on Research and Scholarship in Composition.* Ed. Ben McClelland and Timothy Donovan. New York: MLA, 1990. 87–109.

Turner, Frank, ed. *The Idea of a University.* New Haven, CT: Yale UP, 1996.

Unger-Gallagher, Victoria J. "The Role of the TA in the Interactive Classroom." Nyquist, Abbott, Wulff, and Sprague 275–83.

Von Blum, Paul. *Stillborn Education: A Critique of the American Research University.* Landham, MD: UP of America, 1986.

Wall, Susan. "Rereading the Discourses of Gender." *Pedagogy in the Age of Politics.* Ed. Patricia A. Sullivan and Donna J. Qualley. Urbana, IL: NCTE, 1994. 166–82.

Walvoord, Barbara E., Linda L. Hunt, H. Fil Dowling Jr., and Joan D. McMahon. *In the Long Run.* Urbana, IL: NCTE, 1997.

Warhol, Robyn R., and Diane P. Herndyl. *Feminisms: An Anthology of Literary Theory and Criticism.* New Brunswick, NJ: Rutgers UP, 1997.

Weiler, Kathleen. *Women Teaching for Change.* New York: Bergin and Garvey, 1988.

Wilson, Robert C., and Jerry G. Gaff *College Professors and Their Impact on Students.* New York: Wiley, 1975.

Zeni, Jane. *Writinglands.* Urbana, IL: NCTE, 1990.

Index

237

37; pedagogical context, 57–58; skill-based, 38–39; writing and, 58–59. *See also* graduate students

Teaching College Writing course, 65, 68

teaching logs, 57, 68–69, 129, 144, 149–52, 158

teaching strategies, 31–32, 54–55, 73, 115, 120, 123–25, 152–53; action research as, 124–25; detachment, 169–70; for drafts, 196; for sensory details, 194

Teaching Writing as Reflective Practice (Hillocks), 86

Tetreault, Mary Kay, 20, 225n2

Thach, Robert E., 208

Theory and Resistance in Education (Giroux), 66

theory of the world, 44–45

Tice, Stacey L., 26

traditional attitudes toward teaching, 11, 18, 52, 118; Germanic vs. colonial model of education, 23–26, 34; struggle against, 25–26; writing, views of, 58–60

traditional pedagogy, 19, 158, 161, 208; effects on self-efficacy, 149–52

triarchic theory, 44, 45, 62

Trimbur, John, 109

Turner, Frank M., 23, 24–25

undergraduates, 4–5, 18, 27, 43, 187–88, 194

Understanding Reading (Smith), 44, 134

UNH Teaching Excellence Program, 40

unified-discourse communities, 24

university departments, 45

University of California–Berkeley Classroom Research Project, 35–36, 60

University of Missouri–Columbia, 39–40

University of Missouri–St. Louis, 16

University of New Hampshire (UNH), 40

utilitarian education, 23, 25

Veysey, Laurence, 24

voice, 19, 60, 206–7; authority and, 138, 178; collaborative learning and, 156–57; development of, 164–65; gender and, 137–39, 140–47; knowledge and, 84, 138, 175–77; literacy and, 183–91; male students and, 167–70; muted feminine, 145–46; self-

efficacy and, 152–54, 183–91; unification of, 161–62; women's, 83–85, 100. *See also* confidence; voice, strengthening

voice, strengthening, 174–75, 207; applying theory, 191–98; constructed knowing and, 174, 175–77, 187, 191; context of research, 177–79; familial expectations and, 175–76, 178, 179–83; feminist perspective and, 184–86; implications for teaching, 198–99; nonfamilial relationships and, 181–82; nurturing perspective and, 186–88. *See also* voice

Von Blum, Paul, 25

Vygotsky, Lev S., 132

Wall, Susan, 90

Walvoord, Barbara E., 34

Ways of Thinking, Ways of Teaching (Hillocks), 65

Weber, Robert J., 97–98

Weiler, Kathleen, 20

"What We Talk about When We Talk about Love" (Carver), 94–95

women's studies programs, 191

Women's Ways of Knowing (Belenky et al.), 84, 87–88, 100, 127, 138, 202

Women Teaching for Change (Weiler), 20

Women Writing the Academy (Kirsch), 137, 138, 160, 165, 213

Woodward, Virginia, 82

workshops, 18, 36–37

writer's block, 6, 83–85, 122, 218n38

writing: devaluation of, 58–60; freewriting, 4, 68–69, 105–6, 111, 113; rationale for, 61; as solitary act, 109–10; types of, 53, 59–60, 89, 115. *See also* writing experience

writing across the curriculum (WAC), 32–34

Writing and the Writer (Smith), 51–52

writing-as-process, 3, 10, 31–32, 62, 140

Writing Ethnographic Fieldnotes (Fretz, Emerson, and Shaw), 14

writing experience: cynical, experienced writers, 116–17; inexperienced writers, 111–13; personal construct and, 103–10; self-efficacy and, 118–22. *See also* writing

Writing Groups (Gere), 109

Sally Barr Ebest, an associate professor of English, has coordinated the campuswide teaching-assistantship workshops at the University of Missouri–St. Louis since 2000 and was the director of composition there from 1987 to 2004. Ebest is the coauthor or coeditor of several books, including *Writing from A to Z*. Her work has appeared in *College English*, *WPA: The Journal of Writing Program Administrators*, *The Journal of Basic Writing*, and *Teaching College Writing;* she has also contributed chapters to numerous books about writing pedagogy and TA training.